Reducing Poverty on a
Global Scale

Reducing Poverty on a Global Scale

Learning and Innovating for Development

Findings from the Shanghai Global Learning Initiative

Edited by
Blanca Moreno-Dodson

A publication of the World Bank
Washington, DC

©2005 The International Bank for Reconstruction and Development / The World Bank
1818 H Street NW
Washington DC 20433
Telephone: 202-473-1000
Internet: www.worldbank.org
E-mail: feedback@worldbank.org

1   2   3   4   08   07   06   05

This volume is a product of the staff of the International Bank for Reconstruction and Development / The World Bank. The findings, interpretations, and conclusions expressed in this volume do not necessarily reflect the views of the Executive Directors of The World Bank or the governments they represent.

The World Bank does not guarantee the accuracy of the data included in this work. The boundaries, colors, denominations, and other information shown on any map in this work do not imply any judgment on the part of The World Bank concerning the legal status of any territory or the endorsement or acceptance of such boundaries.

Rights and Permissions
The material in this publication is copyrighted. Copying and/or transmitting portions or all of this work without permission may be a violation of applicable law. The International Bank for Reconstruction and Development / The World Bank encourages dissemination of its work and will normally grant permission to reproduce portions of the work promptly.

For permission to photocopy or reprint any part of this work, please send a request with complete information to the Copyright Clearance Center Inc., 222 Rosewood Drive, Danvers, MA 01923, USA; telephone: 978-750-8400; fax: 978-750-4470; Internet: www.copyright.com.

All other queries on rights and licenses, including subsidiary rights, should be addressed to the Office of the Publisher, The World Bank, 1818 H Street NW, Washington, DC 20433, USA; fax: 202-522-2422; e-mail: pubrights@worldbank.org.

ISBN-10: 0-8213-6362-x
ISBN-13: 978-0-8213-6362-1
eISBN-10: 0-8213-6363-8
DOI: 10.1596/978-0-8213-6362-1

Library of Congress cataloging-in-publication data has been applied for.

Contents

Foreword

Our world is out of balance. Of the six billion people now on earth, one billion hold 80 percent of the income; the other five billion share less than 20 percent of it. In the next 20 years, two billion people will be born—all but 50 million of them in developing countries. By 2025, seven billion out of eight billion people will live in developing countries; in 2050, the split will be eight billion out of nine billion. And poverty, inadequately addressed, will grow along the same lines.

But relieving poverty is not central on the global agenda. Terrorism, Iraq, Afghanistan, strains in the transatlantic alliance, budget deficits, parochial problems that are more visible and seem more immediate garner active attention. Military expenditures top $1,000 billion, whereas farmers in wealthy areas receive $300 billion from tariff protection and agricultural subsidies, and $50-$60 billion is dispatched in overseas development assistance. Mere lip service is paid to the equally dangerous and inevitable problems that accompany poverty. It is now time to acknowledge that *peace and stability are not possible until poverty is alleviated.*

Poor people, no matter what country and no matter what conditions they live in, have spoken their desires. We want a life that is secure; we want a voice and a chance to be heard; we want our children to be educated; we want to be safe. Rather than charity, we want an opportunity, a chance. And we want to contribute to our better life.

In those words we find our task. And the task has challenges: the challenge of management, the challenge of leverage, the challenge of resources.

In 2002 the World Bank commissioned a body of research, more than 100 case studies of poverty-relieving projects and programs. The cases offer evidence of ideas (both good and not so good) that can be adapted, mined for lessons, and applied in our development efforts.

For about a year, we conducted a number of field visits, global discussions, and analytical work, which culminated in Shanghai in 2004, where we convened a conference of representatives of the North and the South, ministers, and members of civil society and of the private sector to address the question, What can we do collectively to bequeath to younger people a world that is safe and secure, one on which life will be vibrant and stable? At the conference the focus was on the case studies, and the goal was to broaden our approach to alleviating poverty. The conference was not a place to put together doctrines or impose best practices. Rather, it offered a forum for the exchange of ideas; an environment in which to share experiences, peer to peer; and the opportunity to learn from one another.

But our aim in commissioning the cases and convening the conference was greater than all of that. Our aim was then and is now to go beyond what we've done in the past—to expand, to extend, and to scale up poverty reduction. We cannot continue to be content with successfully completing a project here or a project there. The development world is full of what I call feel-good projects. When asked, what have you done for saving water, or what have you done for the environment, we can offer a long list of successful projects we've done: 200 kilometers of highway in this country, ten bridges in that country, assistance to a hundred schools somewhere else. But we've learned that feeling good about individual projects is not enough. The challenges we face are just too big. It's not a hundred schools; it's 10,000 schools. It's not ten bridges; it's 5,000 bridges. It's not a thousand people, but millions and billions of people.

We have to discover how to move from our feel-good successes, how to scale up these initiatives to a depth and breadth where we can really have an impact on poverty, where we can achieve the Millennium Development Goals.

This we know: Scale requires time. Scale requires management. Scale requires continuous adaptation of our programs, policies, and practices. It demands attention to continuity, to a consistent strategy that remembers the past and makes allowances for political and social changes.

The case studies commissioned by the World Bank, presented at the conference, and discussed in this volume reveal some common themes on scaling up poverty reduction. First, we have to set strategic targets. We have often fallen into the trap of setting targets based on the available money. That kind of means-driven action is not adequate. Instead, we must look at the challenges presented by each situation, identify the stretch target we want to achieve, and then find ways to reach that target over time. We have to understand that success is *not* spending the $50 billion satisfactorily. Success is reaching the overall strategic target that we are trying to achieve.

Absolutely critical to successful scaling up is our changing our view of development and of the people in developing circumstances.

Development is not something that we professionals dream up and deliver to poor people, and we must not define and confine poor people as objects of our charity or our development practices. These people are the asset, and we must help them become active participants in moving out of poverty.

In scaling up we must engage the community of people who are poor and who are searching for a better life in the quest for solutions to their problems. They know more about poverty than we do. They know more about what they need than we do. We can help them in terms of structure and approach. We can provide infrastructure and resources. But we have to learn to value and incorporate the existing assets of people in poverty, of youth, of women—people rich in capacity and rich in desire to improve their own lives.

Again, there is imbalance in our world—imbalance brought about by conditions of profound poverty for the immense majority of humans. The challenges of such poverty have been identified by the Millennium Development Goals. And people have put together projects and programs to try to address the challenges of poverty. Now each of us must work politically to ensure that alleviating poverty is the central focus of the global agenda.

James D. Wolfensohn
Former President
The World Bank

Millennium Development Goals

Goal 1: Eradicate extreme poverty and hunger

Between 1990 and 2015, halve the proportion of people whose income is less than one dollar a day

Between 1990 and 2015, halve the proportion of people who suffer from hunger

Goal 2: Achieve universal primary education

Ensure that, by 2015, children everywhere—boys and girls alike—will be able to complete a full course of primary schooling

Goal 3: Promote gender equality and empower women

Eliminate gender disparity in primary and secondary education, preferably by 2005, and at all levels of education no later than 2015

Goal 4: Reduce child mortality

Between 1990 and 2015, reduce by two-thirds the under-five mortality rate

Goal 5: Improve maternal health

Between 1990 and 2015, reduce by three-quarters the maternal mortality ratio

Goal 6: Combat HIV/AIDS, malaria, and other diseases

By 2015, have halted and begun to reverse the spread of HIV/AIDS

By 2015, have halted and begun to reverse the incidence of malaria and other major diseases

Goal 7: Ensure environmental sustainability

Integrate the principles of sustainable development into country policies and programs and reverse the losses of environmental resources

By 2015, halve the proportion of people without sustainable access to safe drinking water

By 2020, have achieved a significant improvement in the lives of at least 100 million slum dwellers

Goal 8: Develop a global partnership for development

Develop further an open, rule-based, predictable, nondiscriminatory trading and financial system

Address the special needs of the least developed countries

Address the special needs of landlocked countries and small island developing states

Deal comprehensively with the debt problems of developing countries through national and international measures in order to make debt sustainable in the long term

In cooperation with developing countries, develop and implement strategies for decent and productive work for youth

In cooperation with pharmaceutical companies, provide access to affordable essential drugs in developing countries

In cooperation with the private sector, make available the benefits of new technologies, especially information and communications

Acknowledgments

This volume was prepared by a team led by Blanca Moreno-Dodson under the general direction of Frannie A. Léautier, Vice President of the World Bank Institute. The book would not have been possible without her rich insights, overall guidance on knowledge dissemination following the Shanghai Conference, and substantial contributions to the contents.

The team contributing to the book consisted of M. Ziad Alahdad (chapter 7), Kim Cuenco (chapter 4, Infrastructure section), Roberto Dañino (chapter 4, Judicial Reform section), Ariel Fiszbein (chapter 6), Coralie Gevers (chapter 6), Ronald Kim (chapter 7), Karen Lashman (chapter 4, Education section), Frannie Léautier (introduction, chapter 1, and chapter 8), Mohini Malhotra (chapter 5), Waleed Malik (chapter 4, Judicial Reform section), Gift Manase (chapter 4, Health section), Blanca Moreno-Dodson (introduction, chapter 2, and chapter 8), Michele de Nevers (chapter 1), Egbe Osifo-Dawodu (chapter 4, Health section), Anne Ritchie (chapter 4, Microfinance section), Mark Sundberg (chapter 1), Lisa Taber (chapter 4, Microfinance section), and Yan Wang (chapter 3).

The team wishes to thank the many people who were instrumental in bringing this initiative to fruition. First and foremost, James D. Wolfensohn for his inspiration and leadership to launch the Scaling Up Poverty Reduction Global Initiative, which culminated with the Shanghai Conference and brings us now to this volume.

Peer reviewers were Alejandro Foxley, Ian Goldin, Frannie Léautier, Marlaine Lockheed, Martin Ravallion, and Dani Rodrik. Roberto Zagha provided very inspirational thoughts, as well as strong support throughout the process. Chapter 6 benefited from the guidance of François Bourguignon. Chapter 7 received input from Bruno Laporte and from the Operations, Policy, and Country Services Network, notably Jim Adams, John Underwood, and their team. Comments were also received from Ruben Lamdany and Ajay Chhibber.

The draft manuscript was reviewed by the World Bank Board of Directors Committee of Effectiveness on July 20, 2005. Comments from the Executive Directors were also incorporated.

The conceptual framework presented in chapter 1 was designed by a World Bank working group comprising David Dollar, Tamar Manuelyan Atinc, Blanca Moreno-Dodson, Deepa Narayan, Michele de Nevers, Akihiko Nishio, Sudhir Shetty, and Yan Wang. The group worked under the leadership of the World Bank Steering Committee for the Shanghai Conference, which comprised Ian Goldin, Jemal-uddin Kassum, Frannie Léautier, Gobind Nankani, and Nick Stern. The Steering Committee also benefited from guidance from François Bourguignon when he became the World Bank Chief Economist in 2003. Michele de Nevers was the Director responsible for the Shanghai Global Learning effort and provided oversight for the case studies that formed input into this guide, as well as for the field trips and the conference itself, which were rich opportunities for reviewing the case materials.

Excellent research assistance was provided by Kelly Jones who worked on the annex and chapter 6. Ashok Dhareshwar contributed to the boxes and tables presented in chapter 3. Alfred Friendly contributed background material based on summaries of some selected case studies. Keri Morisch handled logistical arrangements efficiently. Christine Cotting and Nancy Berg, from UpperCase Publication Services, Ltd., served as copyeditors and advised the authors on preparation of their manuscripts.

Finally, the production of this volume was made possible by the World Bank Office of the Publisher.

Acronyms

ACEs	Asociaciones Comunales para la Educación (Community Associations for Education)
ADB	Asian Development Bank
APJR	Action Program for Judicial Reform (Philippines)
ARC	Agrarian Reform Community
ARISP	Agrarian Reform Infrastructure Support Project (Philippines)
ASA	Association for Social Advancement
ASEM	Asia-Europe Meeting
BANSEFI	National Savings and Financial Services Bank (Mexico)
BRAC	Bangladesh Rural Advancement Committee
BRI	Bank Rakyat Indonesia
CARTAC	Caribbean Regional Technical Assistance Centre
CAS	Country Assistance Strategy
CBD/CDD	community-based development/community-driven development
CDD	community-driven development
COFOPRI	Committee for the Formalization of Private Property
CSD	Centre for Social Development (India)
DIME	Development Impact Evaluation
DOTS	Directly Observed Treatment Short-Course (Nepal)
DPEP	District Primary Education Project (India)
DPIP	District Poverty Initiatives Project (India)
ECD	Early Childhood Development Program (Philippines)
EDUCO	Educación con Participación de la Comunidad (Education with Community Participation; El Salvador)
EFA	Education for All
EGS	Education Guarantee Scheme

EPU	Economic Planning Unit (Malaysia)
EU	European Union
FDI	foreign direct investment
FPE	free primary education
GDP	gross domestic product
GMS	Greater Mekong Subregion
HIPC	Heavily Indebted Poor Countries
IDA	International Development Association
IDU	injecting drug user
IFC	International Finance Corporation
IFPRI	International Food Policy Research Institute
IMF	International Monetary Fund
IMG	Independent Monitoring Group
ISE	Istanbul Stock Exchange
JICA	Japan International Cooperation Agency
Kalahi-CIDSS	Kapitbisig Laban Sa Kahirapan–Comprehensive and Integrated Delivery of Social Services
KDP	Kecamatan Development Project
K-Rep	Kenya Rural Enterprise Program
KSBP	Kazakhstan Small Business Program
LGOPAD	Leading Group Office on Poverty Alleviation and Development (China)
LGPR	Leading Group for Poverty Reduction (China)
LPWRP	Loess Plateau Watershed Rehabilitation Project (China)
MDG	Millennium Development Goal
MFI	microfinance institution
MSE	micro and small enterprise
NBS	National Bureau of Statistics (China)
NGO	nongovernmental organization
NRM	National Resistance Movement (Uganda)
NRSP	National Rural Support Programme (Pakistan)
ODI	Overseas Development Institute
OECD/DAC	Organisation for Economic Co-operation and Development/Development Action Committee
OED	Operations Evaluation Department
PHC	Primary Health Care (Islamic Republic of Iran)
PKSF	Palli Karma Sahayak Foundation (Bangladesh)
PMO	Project Management Office
PRS	Poverty Reduction Strategy
RCCE	Rapid Coverage for Compulsory Education (Turkey)
RHC	Rural Health Center

RHH	Rural Health House
RMB	renminbi
RTC	Record of Rights, Tenancy and Cultivation
SAGARPA	Secretariat of Agriculture, Livestock, Rural Development, Fisheries, and Nutrition (Mexico)
SAPAP	South Asia Poverty Alleviation Program
SEZ	Special Economic Zone
SFD	Social Fund for Development (Yemen)
SOE	state-owned enterprise
SWPRP	Southwest Poverty Reduction Project (China)
TFP	total factor productivity
TVE	Township and Village Enterprise
UNDP	United Nations Development Programme
UPP	Urban Poverty Project
USAID	U.S. Agency for International Development
WHO	World Health Organization
WTO	World Trade Organization
ZAMSIE	Zambia Social Investment Fund

Introduction

Frannie A. Léautier and Blanca Moreno-Dodson

The Challenge of Poverty

Development practitioners have worked for half a century to pull millions of people out of poverty, disease, and fear—to offer them hope and to support peace—but the challenge of poverty remains enormous. More than half of the people in developing countries— 2.8 billion people—live on less than $2 a day, and 1.2 billion of those people earn less than $1 a day. These statistics represent real people who do not have the means to satisfy their basic needs. They are hungry, isolated, and vulnerable to weather, war, and sudden fluctuations in international markets. The disparity in levels of income, health, and education between developed and developing economies grows greater, even as levels of absolute poverty decline.

In the past 20 years, many regions with large concentrations of extremely poor people have made little progress in reducing their poverty. Even in cases where there have been country-level or regional achievements, gaps in skills, knowledge, and capacity to collect and learn from these experiences, coupled with little knowledge on how to extract these ideas for results at a scale, have often kept these stories unreported. The good work and positive experiences that might have been adopted and adapted to make remarkable differences in people's lives have not always been appropriately shared with the rest of the world.

The Goals That Have Been Set

The first of the Millennium Development Goals (MDGs; see p. xi), created by the international community in a series of United Nations conferences during the 1990s, calls for halving, by 2015, the proportion of the world's population living in extreme poverty (on less than $1 a day, measured at international prices or purchasing power parity). That's an ambitious goal. Can we possibly reach it? At this point, there is no way to predict success with any conviction.

We take some hope from the experiences of developing countries in Asia, especially China and India: With half the world's population, the region's economies collectively reduced extreme poverty by more than half between 1978 and 2003. And there are other bright spots of experience that offer ideas to be picked and turned into tools that would fit the needs of other regions, suggesting ways of entering the fray through different doors. Initiatives in Chile and Uganda, for example, offer suggestions that may be useful for people battling poverty half a world away.

In general, there are many lessons to be gleaned from policy reforms worldwide that have contributed to improved living standards for poor men, women, and children, by providing them with better income opportunities and social protection while empowering them to have a voice in society.

What Needs to Shift

But business as usual in the practice of development will not win the day, and will not accomplish the MDGs. What is needed is a substantive shift in the level of urgency and commitment that local and international leaders put on the issue of poverty reduction. Also needed are methods to enable ideas to flow within and across countries, and by which countries can create real opportunities to experiment and discover policies and practices that offer useful implementation lessons. Building institutions, particularly those that generate good governance, is also critical, as it enables poverty reduction results to be maintained and sustained. Furthermore, countries need policies that enable people to expand effective initiatives, scaling them up in a manner that reduces poverty.

Reducing poverty on a global scale would require the sharing and analyzing of experiences that have led to positive outcomes in the developing world, to define and explore the reasons for their achievements. And this sharing and analysis must be informed by practitioners, policy makers, and development partners worldwide. As countries try to extend approaches conducive to results to new places, or sustain them over time, they need to learn from others' experiences, including the mistakes and missteps.

Why a Learning Process?

The urgency to meet the MDGs and recognition of the critical need for more comprehensive information about what is happening in the realm of development around the world prompted the World Bank to launch a *global learning process* about "Reducing Poverty on a Global Scale." The time was right. A climate characterized by strong political will to invest in development, the recent evolution of communication tools and technologies making it possible to connect people from around the world as they practice in their workplaces, and an appreciation of the importance of sharing ideas and practices to build capacity for development led the World Bank, with the government of China as a partner, to create a platform for a global exchange of experiences in poverty reduction.

The year-long global learning process, sponsored by the World Bank in cooperation with other multilateral and bilateral donors, comprised a series of learning events and activities that drew on leading-edge information and brought together participants in the development community who might otherwise have had no direct access to one another.

The Practitioner's Perspective

Independent experts and practitioners from around the world developed 106 case studies, elaborating on the factors that contributed to the achievements of particular antipoverty initiatives. The case studies were aimed at answering a number of critical questions: How have countries implemented reforms that are conducive to poverty reduction? How did they go about it? What can be learned from the achievements and failures in the countries, programs, and projects presented for study? What are the key enabling factors, and what seem to be the main constraints holding countries back?

The global learning process used the case study approach to examine how a wide range of countries undertook poverty reduction initiatives. The cases looked at development examples that offer learning potential about implementation factors and challenges encountered along the way. The learning process was meant to be a pedagogical exercise for sharing and extracting lessons from country experience.

Case Identification

The cases were identified through a process of consultation with World Bank operational teams, network staff, and other development partners. In each case, World Bank staff in the regional vice presidencies, and representatives from other development partner institutions, were asked to nominate development experiences that were considered to have been significant in terms of geographic and participant coverage, and/or sustainability over time. A formal, quantitative impact evaluation was not required. The cases cover a range of countries, regions, sectors, themes, and approaches to reducing poverty. The cases were chosen so that they would illustrate, as a package, a wide array of development stories, and that is where their main value lies.

Choice of Authors—Voices of Practitioners

Case study authors were identified by the nominating agencies. They were generally not staff of international development institutions but, in the majority, practitioners in the developing world. The objective was to find authors who had participated in the case and were from the country to tell the story from the perspective of a practitioner, rather than academics or outside "experts."

Pedagogical Purpose

The cases were seen as pedagogical instruments, intended to promote a better understanding of development practices. To be able to share and compare lessons across cases, those who chose the cases were given guidance on the range of initiatives desired, and the authors of the cases were given pedagogical advice on preparing the case that was meant to ensure some standardization in presentation and consistency in coverage.

Analysis through Experiential
Interviews and Visits

The studies were analyzed against the World Bank's conceptual framework for poverty reduction, and peer-reviewed by a mix of practitioners, policy makers, and executives during multicountry, interactive videoconferences, and then were subjected to further analysis. There were 28 global dialogues involving approximately 850 people (through videoconferences and online discussions) among authors, practitioners, policy makers, and representatives from academia and civil society; 21 of these dialogues were recorded, watched, and debated using online discussions and in follow-up face-to-face meetings. The dialogues produced valuable feedback for the authors, who could benefit from an instant review of their work.

In parallel, field visits put practitioners and policy makers on the ground to witness the selected initiatives firsthand. These visits to 11 sites in 8 countries enabled 150 people to get much deeper into projects and programs developed in the case studies. Interviews and conversations with experts, stakeholders, and other central actors onsite added the vital human dimension and made possible the exchange of real, practical, and experiential knowledge.

A Global Classroom

The global learning process culminated May 25–27, 2004, at a working conference convened in Shanghai. Summaries of all case studies were compiled, published, and distributed to attendees. Key actors involved in the selected developing-country initiatives shared their insights with peers from other developing and developed countries. There were 1,200 participants who discussed and debated some selected cases over two days. Because of the mix of heads of state, heads of international development agencies, ministers and directors responsible for implementation, business leaders, nongovernmental organizations, academics, and young people, the conference was enriched by diverse perspectives and interests, and further enhanced the extraction of key lessons. An important feature of the learning environment was the role of the media. The year-long learning process resulted in the production of seven video documentaries that featured country and program/project examples in ways that were easy for everyone to follow. The presence of more than 400 journalists at the Shanghai Conference, as well as the presence of the journalists during the field visits, enabled the rapid flow of ideas and kept global interest in the issue alive for a whole year.

The World Bank has placed a great deal of emphasis on this global learning process because sharing experiences, and fostering peer-peer learning and solutions, are deemed necessary to accelerate results to achieve the MDGs.

The Book: A Singular Objective for a Varied Audience

It is the World Bank's commitment to exchanging experiences and sharing lessons and discoveries that now brings us to this book. The different chapters capture the findings of a subset of case studies prepared along different poverty dimensions for the Shanghai Conference.

The authors of the chapters are World Bank staff members who were somehow involved in the Shanghai initiative, coaching and guiding the production of the case studies, leading thematic discussions in Shanghai, and participating in the peer-review process.

The book attempts to contribute to the broader existing knowledge on poverty reduction and the effectiveness of aid by placing a special emphasis on lessons in implementation, as well as operational implications for policy makers and development practitioners.

A Learning Guide

The book is intended to be a learning guide to various implementation aspects of multidimensional poverty reduction initiatives. Its objective is to enlighten development practitioners about implementation achievements. It doesn't recommend particular solutions or claims that the selected cases represent best practices, and it doesn't pretend to cover all potentially valuable development lessons worldwide. Instead, it targets key findings from the broad range of selected examples and weaves them into a topical narrative.

Who Should Read This Book?

The audience for this volume includes international, regional, and local practitioners and policy makers, members of nongovernmental organizations, civil society, and the private sector, donors and development partners, as well as researchers and scholars. Certain to find value here are the hundreds of people who participated in the global learning process and attended the Shanghai Conference, as well as the thousands of men and women who daily visit the Website dedicated to this peer-to-peer learning experience (www.reducingpoverty.org), searching for ideas, innovations, and news of interesting approaches to poverty reduction programs. To help readers draw the maximum benefit from the learning process, at that site and on the CD that accompanies this book readers will find, respectively, full versions and summaries of all the case studies, a subset of which is further analyzed in detail in this volume.

What Is Unique Here?

What makes this book different from other publications that are motivated by the urge to reach the MDGs and are focused on the overall challenges of alleviating poverty and increasing the effectiveness of aid? In addition to the global and interactive process described above, centered on the experience of practitioners and enlightened by the tacit knowledge embedded in the expertise of the large number of people who participated, all of which has led to the content of this book, the focus on "scaling up" poverty reduction offers a new dimension, and a new way of looking at poverty. Given that the selection process was not done through scientific sampling, we want to emphasize, however, that the studies represent a broad range of worldwide experiences rather than prescriptions for best practices.

Scaling Up: An Operational Definition Scaling up poverty reduction is presented here as a concept that draws on different elements of sustainability through time and space for a given development intervention (see the various definitions of scaling up in chapter 1). The macroeconomic dimension refers to sustained and shared growth as the solid foundation for poverty reduction in a particular country. At a microeconomic level, scaling up is related to continued and increased effects resulting from projects, programs, and/or practices, associated with reaching more beneficiaries locally, nationally, and internationally. Scaling up poverty reduction does not imply, however, mere "replication." Country and context specificity appear to be intrinsic in all experiences analyzed in the book.

The Conceptual Framework Starting with this concept in mind, under the overarching umbrella of poverty reduction, the conceptual framework for this global initiative was built around four implementation factors (commitment and political economy for change, institutional innovation, learning and experimentation, and external catalysts) and two main pillars (investment climate and social inclusion).[1] These were the two main pillars of the World Bank's framework for poverty reduction, and were consistent with the *World Development Report 2000,* which highlighted three dimensions of poverty reduction: opportunities, protection, and empowerment.

The Importance of Implementation Factors The variety of examples analyzed in this book illustrates how different implementation factors, grouped under those broad four categories, have somehow contributed to the process of scaling up at the country, program, practice, and project levels. In some instances, they have triggered better investment climates by promoting good governance, solid infrastructures, and openness to trade. In some others, they have fostered better social inclusion by facilitating poor people's access to markets, assets, and services.

A Process for Identifying Critical Insights The insights that these cases offer into the practical challenges of reducing poverty are a key distinguishing feature of this book. The chapters focus more on *how* policies and programs were defined and implemented, thus differentiating them from other studies that assess the ultimate impact on the number of people living in poverty. The emphasis is placed on implementation factors and intermediary indicators, rather than on final impact, except for the few cases subjected to rigorous impact evaluation, where a counterfactual has been established[2] (see chapter 6). The main reason for this focus on *how* things get done is based on the general weakness of implementation capacity relative to policy capacity at the country level.

Emphasis on the Implementation Process There is also a strong emphasis on "contribution," as opposed to "attribution," in the following sense: The initiatives being considered are not the only ones that could have determined the observed achievements. The book makes this specific trade-off because the main intention of the cases is pedagogical: to understand better the variety of approaches toward reducing poverty and to extract lessons that are transportable to other situations.

Validity of the Lessons Learned Finally, because the case studies analyzed do not cover exactly the same time horizon (5–20 years), given their different natures (country program, single-sector project, multisector approach) and types of policies, the validity of the lessons extracted needs to be tested by time.

Structure of the Book

Country-Specific Lessons

The country stories presented in chapter 2 provide a compact guide to the diversity and, in particular, to the fluid mix of implementation options that have been attempted to reduce poverty at the country level. Different country types are represented, including middle-income countries (China, Korea, and Poland), low-income countries (Tanzania and Uganda), and countries that have come out of conflict (El Salvador) or crisis (Indonesia).

The chapter tries to extract what Chile, China, Costa Rica, El Salvador, India, Indonesia, the Republic of Korea, Malaysia, Poland, the Russian Federation, Tanzania, Tunisia, and Uganda have in common. Although they implemented different courses of action, at different times, under very different circumstances, their continuous engagement in poverty reduction efforts, sometimes shaped by different types of governments in power, appears to have been critical to their achievements. In particular, none of these countries managed to reduce poverty without addressing their macroeconomic imbalances and creating solid foundations for growth. In addition, they all implemented parallel, although distinct, social measures oriented toward their poor people.

They also were able to develop and sustain institutions that produced good governance. And they created an environment in which learning and adaptation took place.

Responsiveness—whether to crisis, to the stimulus of technology, or to an external shock—seems to have been another key ingredient in those countries' experiences. It was often associated with their ability to innovate, to adapt institutional capacity, to learn from experience, and to turn external factors into catalysts for change so as to benefit their populations. The importance of an environment for learning and adaptation was further emphasized in countries that had to manage crisis or choose among a suite of ideas from outside.

The case of China deserves special attention because of its track record in achieving sustained economic growth and the most rapid large-scale poverty reduction in human history over the last 25 years.[3] Chapter 3 first reviews the evidence on development and poverty reduction in China, focusing on the sources and patterns of growth, and on the distribution of opportunities. Furthermore, the chapter analyzes China's incentives and approaches used to learn fast from their own experiences and those of other countries.

Sectoral and Thematic Lessons

Following the country analyses, chapter 4 presents a variety of sectoral and thematic examples in infrastructure, judicial system reform, microfinance, health, and education—all intended to illustrate how initiatives at the sector level can scale up and trigger tangible outputs that may affect the living standards of poor people.

Each of the thematic sections pulls out lessons that are generic and those that are specific to that theme or sector. Among the generic lessons (and it holds true in the country cases) are the issues of commitment and leadership, particularly around how leaders emerge, how they form coalitions for change, how they define where to start and how to sequence reforms and implementation steps, and how they guarantee continuity of reforms and implementation. Capability to define goals and deliver short-term outputs is also emphasized. In the thematic sections there are detailed descriptions of the processes that were tried, as well as how project and program teams put in place and used monitoring and evaluation systems. Issues of external and domestic financing are covered, as is the role that external catalysts have played, whether through knowledge, ideas, and technical support, or partnerships and cooperation agreements.

The infrastructure section focuses on how to overcome the daunting challenge of making infrastructure investments accessible to the poor. Although the effort requires comprehensive investment planning, including the geographical areas where the poor populations live and work, as well as long-term resource mobilization and increased private sector participation, the achievements often spread across sectors, facilitating access to schools, hospitals, and markets and producing better income-earning opportunities. This section draws lessons from interesting experiences in Brazil, China, Ghana, Morocco, and Vietnam, among others.

The section on judicial systems refers to institutions, enforcement of decisions, legal framework, and societal commitment as the four critical dimensions of the judiciary for promoting good governance and empowering poor people, which we also expected to attract domestic and foreign investment. Valuable insights are reaped from the examination of cross-cutting strategies, priorities, and local ideas in the cases of Guatemala, Rwanda, the Philippines, and Russia. Because institutions that generate good governance are considered important vehicles for poverty reduction, this section is of particular merit to those interested in examples of implementation in formal and informal settings.

The microfinance section presents a broad range of organizations that can deliver financial services to segments of the population previously excluded from the formal financial system. The stories presented illustrate how financial cooperatives, nongovernmental organization microfinance institutions, and commercial banks can all expand their coverage and include those segments in their clientele, through improvement of government regulation and oversight, and the development of organizational and technological networks, among others. Evidence from Bangladesh, India, Kazakhstan, Kenya, Mexico, Mongolia, Tanzania, and Zimbabwe illustrates how microcredits can help poor people build their income-generating capacity, which in turn gives them the opportunity to improve family nutrition, health care, and schooling, and to avoid or ameliorate deprivation when income suddenly declines.

The health section indicates that progress toward improving the health standards of the poor has been made in some countries and regions. The examples provided are from the Islamic Republic of Iran, extending access in rural areas; Nepal, combating tuberculosis; West Africa, defeating riverblindness; and Manipur, India, Thailand, and Uganda, fighting the war on HIV/AIDS.

The authors suggest that, given the tremendous health challenges faced globally, further engagement of political leaders worldwide in discussion on health issues, and long-term donor commitment and aid predictability are still required. The section also emphasizes the need to strengthen evaluation of the impacts of innovative health initiatives before bringing them to scale. This section provides the strongest reasoning as to why it is critical to have an approach to experimentation and learning embedded in implementation practices so that countries can discover quickly what works. The HIV/AIDS case from Manipur illustrates how ad hoc trials led to the discovery of the best way to provide treatment and prevention. Such discovery would be difficult if there was no environment for trial and experimentation.

The education section attempts to explain how extending access to education to the poor can be achieved, with a special emphasis on girls' education. Understanding and exploiting close interrelationships and synergies between education supply and demand, carefully prioritizing and targeting investments, and widening stakeholder participation appear to be crucial elements, as illustrated in the examples from Egypt, India, Kenya, Malawi, Tanzania, and Uganda, among others.

Community-driven Development and Social Funds

Chapter 5 extracts lessons from a portfolio of 13 community-driven development (CDD) and social funds, in countries such as Brazil, Indonesia, Malawi, Pakistan, Yemen, and Zambia. It illustrates how this type of initiatives, usually deeply embedded in local grassroots, can scale up across sectors; can constitute an alternative, although often temporary, source of public services, particularly in postconflict or crisis contexts; and are prone to cross-country learning and fertilization. The chapter challenges the notion of the long-term sustainability of such programs unless they are better integrated into government structures.

Evaluating the Impact on Poverty

Chapter 6 reviews the use of impact evaluations among the Shanghai case studies and discusses key challenges to expand the use of this type of evaluation as a learning tool and as a necessary step to scale up development initiatives. The chapter identifies the challenges that need to be met in order to promote effective development interventions based on rigorous impact evaluations, and discusses current World Bank efforts to help address those challenges. A key issue in impact evaluation is balancing the need to know with statistical certainty that a process or policy is having a positive effect on the lives of the poor against political pressure to accelerate implementation when early results seem to indicate that there is success. This calls for development of impact measures that are easy to define and collect, and simple to communicate, but trackable and amenable to analysis.

This chapter includes a detailed annex with the results of the impact evaluations undertaken for the Shanghai case study sample.

Operational Implications

Chapter 7 attempts to extract some of the operational implications from previous chapters, using specific cases; identifies ways in which the development community can incorporate some of these lessons into its efforts to scale-up poverty reduction; and elaborates on how the World Bank is positioning itself to accommodate, support, and promote programs, projects, and practices that offer such learning potential.

The chapter examines several dimensions emerging from the Shanghai case studies, such as country ownership, capacity development, knowledge, learning and innovation, sequencing and timing, result-based management systems, and donor alignment and harmonization. It also discusses operational implications for donors that arise from the findings of the case studies, and offers a brief update of what the World Bank is doing within each dimension.

Looking to the Future

Finally, chapter 8 presents the way forward by identifying issues for future research, based on the findings of the different chapters. Some of the important lessons for future research relate to leadership. The cases point to different approaches to forming coalitions for sustained change. There are cases where a single leader is in place for a long time (Korea, Malaysia, and Uganda) or where leaders have been able to embed implementation in centralized bodies or agencies (China and Malaysia). Other leaders have been consistent in implementing their approaches because they have been using smart communication with technocratic support (Uganda). Which style of leadership best fits which situation is an important question. The critical issues for research are whether to have political or policy continuity and the kind of compromises needed in a democratic setting (Chile), and the challenges and approaches for guaranteeing a smooth transition between political regimes (Korea and Malaysia).

In this concluding chapter, the book also interrogates the readers about how to create an environment for learning and innovation. A number of factors appear in the cases, such as the need to have some competition, perhaps between local governments (Chinese provinces) or service providers (Costa Rican health providers), as a way of creating opportunities for learning and discovery. Also apparent is a need to involve enough people to get a broad range of ideas shared (Chile). The role of explicit experimentation, as done in China, seems to be significant. How one balances these approaches is a critical research issue.

Finally, this chapter discusses unresolved issues specifically related to the three initial dimensions of scaling up outlined in chapter 1 and illustrated throughout the book. Fiscal space and external financing refer to the macroeconomic foundations of scaling up. Sustainability over time involves the intertemporal dimension, and the interdependency between rural and urban areas is a reflection of the obstacles encountered when scaling up geographically.

Notes

1. This conceptual framework was designed by a World Bank working group under the leadership of Nick Stern, World Bank chief economist, in 2002.

2. Although most case studies in the sample have been subject to some kind of quantitative and/or qualitative evaluation, only 16 of them have undergone impact evaluation, using a counterfactual.

3. In addition, China's role in facilitating the "Poverty Reduction on a Global Scale" initiative and hosting the Shanghai Conference in May 2004 must be acknowledged.

1

The Framework for Analysis

Michele de Nevers and Mark Sundberg

The Millennium Development Goals (MDGs; see p. xi) are ambitious in scope and time horizon. Achieving them will require accelerating the process of reducing poverty while sustaining growth and development. How can this be done? Can these ambitious goals be met? What is known about the countries that have made progress so far? What can be learned from the lessons of these examples? Examining these questions was the main goal of the global learning process and the Shanghai Conference, which attempted to learn from development achievements—in different dimensions.[1] The global learning process aimed to uncover the factors that were critical for countries to achieve development outcomes on a scale, and to share these lessons with other countries and regions.

Hope and lessons come from around the world—Chile in South America, Tunis and Uganda in Africa, and Poland in Eastern Europe. The experiences of Asian developing countries—with half the world's population—are notable because they basically met the MDG for poverty reduction in the 25 years ending in 2003. They collectively reduced extreme poverty by more than 50 percent over the period from 1978 to 2003. What is important about the Asian experience is that, up to 1978, the developing countries in the region in general were not doing well. So, clearly, there was some shift in institutions and policies that enabled many—though not all—locations to reduce poverty at historically unprecedented rates. Whereas some Asian countries have been successful in

achieving the income poverty goal, in other regions many countries
have realized the kinds of gains in health and education outcomes
envisaged by the MDGs as well.

However, there are some regions with large concentrations of extremely poor people—such as Sub-Saharan Africa and South Asia—
where there has been little progress with poverty reduction over the
past one to two decades. Meeting the MDGs will depend critically on
accelerating achievements in these regions. There are isolated projects
and localized programs in these areas that have helped improve people's lives. But how can countries and communities expand those interventions to levels that really make a dent in poverty numbers?

Despite their progress, Asian developing countries are still home
to about half of the extreme poor in the world. India has the
largest absolute number of extreme poor. Although it is heartening
that India has cut its poverty rate in half, it still has a huge poverty
problem. Bangladesh, Pakistan, and Vietnam all have high propor-
tions of extreme poor as well. And although China's poverty using
the $1/day line—is down to about 15 percent, that still represents
about 200 million people.

In many of these countries improvements on the health and education aspects of the MDGs is lagging as well. Thus, an important
agenda of poverty reduction remains, and it was thought that the
insights from the Shanghai cases about what has led to achievements in other locations could be helpful to countries, and to the
regions and communities within them.

There are a number of different dimensions to expanding and
accelerating development. This chapter first develops and defines
the concept of scaling up, and then defines and addresses its various dimensions, their role in choosing and preparing the cases, and
their relevance to learning from international experience.

What Does Scaling Up Mean?

There is widespread recognition that achieving the objectives of the
MDGs will require much greater effort by developing and developed countries. It will require expanding development assistance
within new and more ambitious strategies for poverty reduction—
it will require scaling up programs, projects, and practices.

Implicit in the concept of scaling up is the need to go beyond
business as usual, to embrace new technologies, new institutional
arrangements, and new approaches that will enable countries and

communities to overcome capacity constraints and improve development effectiveness.

On one side of the development equation, four dimensions can be distinguished:

- *"Macroeconomic framework" scaling up* refers to measures at the national level to improve the economic, social, and institutional environments for growth and poverty reduction. These are efforts that aim to change the terms on which markets and communities interact to streamline and strengthen the growth response in the economy, to ensure that growth benefits the poor. Reforming financial markets, rationalizing the tax system, reshaping the public sector to reduce direct economic intervention and promote private competition, retargeting social expenditures, and so forth, all represent reform initiatives that are national in scope. They refer to efforts to promote the consistency and poverty-reducing effects of economic policy reforms at the country level.

- *Intertemporal scaling up* means expanding the duration, continuity, and sustainability of individual project or program interventions to deepen their impact. This is particularly important for initiatives that have a long gestation period to reap their full benefits or may have intergenerational effects, such as expanding compulsory education and education service delivery to enhance productive employment opportunities and future income generation for children.

- *Spatial scaling up* refers to enlarging projects, practices, or programs geographically to reproduce the benefits from one locality in another. Reproducing a project that has worked in one district should bring similar benefits to the next district. However, there may also be important externalities that will not be achieved in full unless there is national or widespread ownership. One example is the struggle to eradicate a communicable disease. Failure to scale up an effective immunization delivery program across localities can undermine efforts even in the original pilot district.

- *International and cross-border scaling up* refers in particular to creating a better international environment for poverty reduction and exploiting critical cross-border externalities. This may include international cooperation and commitments on trade liberalization to expand market access for developing country exports, debt relief initiatives, and cooperation on making aid flows larger and more effective in financing devel-

opment, as well as transfer of knowledge about useful development practices across countries and regions (spatial scaling up
across borders). It also refers to cross-border coordination on
such issues as transport, trade facilitation, or tax enforcement.
International collaboration and harmonization efforts, be they
as simple as agreement on common standards for railway
track gauge or for sharing information on taxpayers, can contribute significantly to development effectiveness if there is sufficient cross-border fertilization.

Across each of these dimensions there are both constraints and enabling (catalytic) factors critical to reducing poverty effectively. Constraints may arise across implementation levels—at the national level,
local service delivery level, or through allocative mechanisms governing resource flows between levels of government. Many types of constraints can prevent results from happening: macroeconomic, financial, institutional, limited physical and human capital, sociocultural
barriers, or problems related to governance and administration.[2]

Examining the enabling factors was the central exercise in initiating the Shanghai case studies and the global learning process.

The Analytical Framework

The case studies were selected under the overarching objective of
growth and poverty reduction. For the first dimension (the x axis,
so to speak), the question of *what to do* to create a promising environment for poverty reduction was outlined. The framework used
for this dimension was the *two-pillar strategy*[3] for poverty reduction favored by the World Bank: investment climate and empowerment (or social inclusion). These two pillars of poverty reduction
derive from the principles outlined in the *World Development Report 2001*, and presuppose a model of poverty reduction in which
committed policy makers undertake policy reforms that elicit actions by the private sector and civil society that lead to pro-poor
(poverty-reducing) growth. The selection of cases demonstrating actions consistent with this model leaves out the possibility that other
models may better explain how poverty reduction actually happens.

- **Pillar 1.** *Creating an investment climate* requires creating the
  conditions for markets to exist and function effectively. Improving governance, promoting openness to trade and investment, and creating the appropriate infrastructure are the
  main factors thought to facilitate investments that can lead to
  growth and reduce poverty.

- **Pillar 2.** *Empowerment (or social inclusion)* refers to the conditions that enable poor people to participate in political processes and local decisions; make state initiatives more accountable and responsive to poor people; and remove social barriers that result from distinctions of gender, ethnicity, race, religion, and social status. Facilitating access of the poorest populations to assets, services, and markets is necessary to ensure inclusive and sustainable poverty reduction.

For the second dimension (the y axis), those who chose the studies and the study authors were asked to consider *how* the approaches described on the x axis were scaled up. To achieve some degree of comparability across the wide range of cases, the studies considered four *implementation factors,* the hypothesis being that these factors are commonly among the drivers of any implementation process. These four factors are commitment and political economy for change, institutional innovation, learning and experimentation, and external catalysts.

- *Factor A. Commitment and political economy for change* refers to the commitment of decision makers to implement policies that facilitate poverty reduction, and to promote change and consensus building in support of poverty reduction goals.
- *Factor B. Institutional innovation* relates to building the institutional capacity to find innovative solutions to emerging problems, to eliminate institutional obstacles to implementation, and to adapt to changing economic and political circumstances.
- *Factor C. Learning and experimentation* take place when new solutions are tested in an experimental manner and evaluation is incorporated in the process of deciding whether to continue and expand a particular approach. Positive experiences are usually emulated widely and can trigger knowledge spillovers that are used in new locations. Learning can include scanning international and local policies, programs, and projects; selectively adopting new approaches; and adapting them to local conditions. Impact evaluation is a crucial component of learning and experimentation. When applicable, it is the one sure way to tell if a project is achieving its goals (see chapter 6).
- *Factor D. External catalysts* are factors and agents that trigger change in support for the reforms led by the country's decision makers.

Analyzing interactions between these *strategic pillars* and the *implementation factors* enabled us to understand better how successfully scaling up programs, polices, and projects so as to lead to

significant development outcomes. Here are some examples (identified by pillar [1 or 2] and factor [A, B, C, or D]):

1.A: Commitment to reforms and the politics of change have
      led to openness to foreign investment and agricultural land
      reform policies, which have accelerated growth in China.

2.A: Commitment to social inclusion has been the main factor
      behind education and health programs that have raised so-
      cial standards in Chile and Costa Rica.

1.B: Institutional innovation and effective implementation mech-
      anisms have been responsible for large-scale investments in
      roads and electricity in China, Thailand, and Vietnam.

2.B: Looking for innovative solutions to facilitate poor people's
      access to social services has translated into cost-sharing
      schemes in education and health in a variety of countries
      such as Egypt, El Salvador, and India, which have translat-
      ed into expanded access to schools and medicines.

1.C: Experimentation and the embedded learning process have
      played a very important role in rural poverty initiatives in
      China, such as the Loess Plateau project.

2.C: An incorporated evaluation system has translated into bet-
      ter education services to the poor in India and Mexico.

1.D: External catalytic factors, such as a better-coordinated
      donor intervention, have improved transparency in the use
      of resources in Uganda.

Using the above framework, the Shanghai cases can be grouped
into a matrix structure, depicted in Figure 1.1. On the x axis of the
matrix are the pillars, investment climate and social inclusion On the
y axis are the four implementation factors. The concern of the learning process was to learn across both dimensions of the matrix, but to
emphasize learning *how to do (implementation)* rather than learning
what to do.

Creating the Environment for Poverty Reduction

Let us now look at the elements of the framework in greater detail.

Investment Climate Recent work in economic history and development emphasizes the importance of property rights and the ability of the government to regulate in a fair way with a minimum of
corruption and interest-group capture, and to create the conditions

Figure 1.1 Analysis Framework Matrix for the Global Learning Process

Poverty Reduction

Implementation factors	Pillar 1. Investment climate				Pillar 2. Social inclusion		
	Rule of law/ governance	*Openness to trade and investment*	*Quality of infrastructure*	*Access to markets*	*Access to assets*	*Access to basic services*	
A. Political commitment							
B. Institutional innovation							
C. Learning and experimentation							
D. External catalysts							

for markets to function effectively. The key issue seems to be whether people investing for the future—be it starting a small firm or sending their children to school—are confident that they will reap the benefits of what they sow. In an environment with poor property rights, any surplus accumulated by individuals is more likely to fund capital flight or out-migration than to be reinvested in the local economy.

Under the broad heading of *investment climate,* cases were selected to illustrate important lessons in the areas of *rule of law and governance, openness to trade and investment,* and *quality of infrastructure.*

Investment climate studies point to the importance of local governance. Developing the highway system or telecommunications is a national issue, but many of the key factors that affect firms on a day-to-day basis involve local government. How bureaucratic and corrupt is the local government? Moreover, when local government is corrupt, it is unlikely that local water, power, and other infrastructure will work well. Although China or India in general may be doing well, the variation across locations within each country is huge. One critical issue is how the poor locations can learn from the good ones.

Openness to trade and development can do much to help poor countries grow faster and reduce poverty. Several of the Shanghai cases examine the benefits of trade and transport facilitation, using information technology to link farmers to markets, reducing administrative barriers to entrepreneurship, and implementing various export promotion strategies.

The quality of infrastructure can help improve the environment to conduct business, and a rise in economic activity can increase demand for improved infrastructure. China's flagship production locations have quite good infrastructure, compared with other parts of the country and with other countries at similar levels of development 10 years ago. Power, telecommunications, and ports all work relatively well. It takes an average of 8 days to clear customs in China, 12 days in Bangladesh, and 17 days in Pakistan. This provides a critical market access advantage to Chinese firms and helps explain their rapid growth in recent years. The development of the highway system has helped create a better-connected internal market.

Empowerment/Social Inclusion As seen in the cases of China, India, and others, many poor people have benefited from their greater prosperity. But the ability of the poor to benefit from and contribute to growth depends critically on whether they have *access to mar-*

kets, access to assets, and *access to basic services.* The Shanghai case sample was constructed to illustrate achievements in each of these important areas.

From worldwide experience it is clear that money alone, or merely increasing public expenditures, does not necessarily lead to improved social inclusion for the poor. If the funds meant for poor people do not reach them, people cannot benefit. If teachers do not show up in schools, if doctors and nurses do not show up in health clinics, or if they charge for free drugs, or treat people so rudely that they do not return, poor people will not gain. Similarly, if the road leading to the market where farmers can sell their products is in very bad condition and makes transportation difficult, it will reduce the income-earning opportunities for them. Making effective use of existing or new resources requires policies and institutional relationships of mutual accountability between policy makers/politicians and service providers and citizens, particularly poor people.

Enabling poor men and women to play their roles effectively requires an empowering approach to development, which sees poor people as key resources and partners, and taps into their knowledge, skills, vigilance, and deep motivation to move out of poverty. Nobody has more at stake in poverty reduction than poor people themselves. The challenge is to remove obstacles from their way, invest in their assets and capabilities, and increase their access to opportunity.

Regarding access to assets, some land reform case studies of countries like India and Peru illustrate how providing access to land as an important asset for the poor leads to income-generating activities and overall better social inclusion. Similarly, the microfinance case studies (see chapter 4) examine how access to credit can help the poorest populations make a living for their families and have a voice in the society.

In addition, access to basic public services also helps the poor find a place in the society. Most of the countries in which extremely poor people are concentrated—Bangladesh, China, India, and Vietnam, for example—have high population density on their arable land, and some significant shift of the labor force out of agriculture into services and manufacturing has to be part of a comprehensive poverty reduction program in these locations. Hence the importance of primary education, which is crucial if people are to move easily into the modern manufacturing and service sectors.

Aside from being a means to poverty reduction, universal education is an important end in its own right—one of the key MDGs. One of the major objectives of the Shanghai cases was to understand how programs have promoted mass education, even in low-growth environments. In China's case, there was massive improvement in literacy in the 20 years before economic reform began. Bangladesh and parts of India have had impressive achievements in recent decades, especially with female literacy. And Bangladesh has made major improvements in reducing fertility and child mortality rates through targeted interventions. In India, the national primary education campaign is working well in some locations, and not at all in others. How do we understand these differences and can the lagging locations learn from the more advanced ones?

The general issue here is how to provide effective services to the poor, when typically the local government in poor locations is more part of the problem than part of the solution. A common feature is the importance of participation of the poor in the design and implementation of programs.

Implementation Factors

What are the characteristics of initiatives that have resulted in genuine change and sustained poverty reduction outcomes? Once identified, what lessons can be taken away about how to manage the implementation of poverty reduction programs, projects, and practices?

The first characteristic to be explored is the importance of stakeholders' commitment to poverty reduction and political economy for change. In the clearest case of national-level reform—China—there was a visible change in the national strategy for poverty reduction around 1977–1978 and on emergence of a group of leaders firmly committed to reform and to ensuring that the mass of people benefited from reform. In several other cases of country-level reform, this issue of leadership and commitment also was important (see chapter 2 on Indonesia and chapter 3 on China).

For microreforms—improving schools or health campaigns—leadership is often important as well. The general issue here is how new leaders and political coalitions break through policy logjams that were holding back progress, and how reforms are sequenced to achieve sustainability and maximum potential (chapter 4 covers examples such as El Salvador on education).

Although there is broad agreement that certain types of institutions are critical for development, it is also clear that there is no single blueprint for institutional reform. For this reason, the better reformers have often been quite flexible and have allowed institutions to emerge in a bottom-up fashion. We need to understand better this willingness to be flexible about institutional arrangements and how institutions develop from the bottom up. The cases cover a wide range of institutional arrangements, from community organizations such as the Kecamatan Development Project in Indonesia to international programs such as riverblindness eradication in Africa.

Another characteristic that we observe in some programs is explicit experimentation and an active process of learning. China has been a leader in this area. On a number of important issues, reforms have been tried at a province or local level; positive interventions have been deliberately scaled up and failed ones abandoned. One of the most important challenges for the Shanghai cases was to illustrate how this process of experimentation works and what can be done to promote it.

India has also increasingly moved to a model of encouraging local experimentation and even competition. What has happened in India is that a number of states—mostly in the south—seem to be actively learning from each other and from the outside world, with the result that there is dynamic change. On the other hand, states such as Uttar Pradesh, Bihar, and West Bengal seem captive to their poor institutions. A key question for geographically expansive countries, such as China and India, is whether decentralized reform will eventually bring lagging regions into the dynamic processes, or alternatively will lock in permanent regional inequalities. That is why it is so important to understand what promotes learning and change, and to discover how and when decentralization is an effective tool to spur change in lagging regions.

Experimentation and learning are really about a willingness to look around and be open to new options. This openness includes cross-country learning. Vietnam, for example, borrowed from China in developing its agricultural reforms. Mexico's PROGRESA system of cash transfers for education was borrowed from Brazil and, in turn, has been borrowed and adapted by nearby Central American countries. Cost-sharing health schemes have spread across West Africa. What promotes this cross-country learning? What determines whether programs can be emulated from one country to another?

A final issue to explore is the role of external catalysts, including development agencies. An interesting point about all of the reform episodes is that development agencies and foreign donors played virtually no role in the early stages of reform. The Chilean, Chinese, Indian, and Vietnamese reforms can be seen as basically homegrown affairs in which determined political groups first decided to improve their countries' performance, and then turned to various outside agencies for advice and funding.

Aside from the big, national reform movements, there are numerous examples of local reforms in governance, infrastructure, education, health, and other sectors. Donors have been catalytic in several cases, such as the eradication of riverblindness in Africa. But in other cases donor attempts to reform policies and institutions have been heavy-handed—in general, imposing conditions from the outside has not been an effective vehicle for lasting change. These experiences have led to a growing awareness of the importance of ownership on the part of reformers at both the national and the local levels. Among the key questions asked of case study authors was what helped countries harness their internal capacity to develop a home-grown development change process? Are the approaches transferable across countries? The intent of the global learning process was to identify some answers to the questions posed in this chapter.

Notes

1. The full name of the World Bank initiative is "Reducing Poverty on a Global Scale," which culminated with the Shanghai Conference on May 25–27, 2004.
2. Constraints to absorptive capacity are discussed in detail in World Bank (2004).
3. The two-pillar strategy for development is articulated in Stern (2001) and more recently in Stern, Dethier, and Rogers (2005).

References

Stern, Nicholas. 2001. *A Strategy for Development*. Washington, DC: World Bank.

Stern, Nicholas, Jean-Jacques Dethier, and F. Halsey Rogers. 2005. *Growth and Empowerment: Making Development Happen*. Cambridge: MIT Press.

World Bank. 2004. "Aid Effectiveness and Financing Modalities." Development Committee, World Bank, Washington, DC.

———. 2001. *World Development Report, 2000/2001, Attacking Poverty*. Washington, DC.

2

Observations at the Country Level

Blanca Moreno-Dodson

The 13 country stories presented in this chapter are as varied as the countries they concern—Chile, China, Costa Rica, El Salvador, India, Indonesia, the Republic of Korea, Malaysia, Poland, the Russian Federation, Tanzania, Tunisia, and Uganda—and the policy approaches they describe.[1]

Although similar factors are at work in many of the accounts, the combinations of priorities and programs adopted in different countries never follow exactly the same pattern. The studies tell of different courses, followed by different countries, at different times, under different circumstances. Examined together, they provide a compact guide to the diversity and, in particular, to the fluid mix of implementation options that have been and can be tried to increase the scope and effectiveness of poverty reduction efforts.

The emphasis is placed, although not exclusively, on the four implementation factors of the original framework presented in chapter 1—leadership, institutional innovation, learning and experimentation, and external catalysts—because they are expected to contribute to poverty reduction achievements. The country examples illustrate the complexity of finding an appropriate implementation package for a particular country, which includes elements of all of them. With a few exceptions, there is not enough evidence to draw conclusions on final impact on the poor. Even in the Republic of Korea and Tunisia where poverty has diminished steadily over several decades, the analysis is as valuable for the discussion of measures taken to deal with setbacks as for the description of the policies behind the long-term achievements.

The variety of the experiences recounted argues persuasively that no single model of development is or can be universally applicable. As mentioned in the case of Uganda, a portrait of notable achievements simply offering technical assistance to reproduce Uganda's innovations would not be adequate for reducing poverty somewhere else.

Similarly, Malaysia's economic planners declare that the first lesson of 30 years of work is that each country must formulate its core development philosophy, policies and plans suited to its particular circumstances and needs. Attempts to replicate the Malaysian model fully in any other developing country would not produce the same results.

Some stories underline the positive role of private investment; others make the case for effective government intervention. Some innovative strategies come in the wake of crisis; others respond to stagnation or progress judged steady but too slow or unbalanced.

This range of perspectives on the challenge of reducing poverty is not surprising. Recent studies of economic growth performance during the 1990s have also found that different models produced different outcomes—positive and negative—in different countries and settings (World Bank 2005a). The central realization of the 1990s, maintains one such analysis, is that there are no "best practice" policies that will always yield the same positive result—*there is no unique way to foster development*. Sustained growth depends less on whether policies conform to some ideal best practice than on whether they add up to an effective growth strategy.

Growth strategies are country specific, time specific, and institutions specific, and they take into account initial conditions. In any given context, one set of measures is more important than others, and the art of formulating the strategies relies on the ability to discover what is most appropriate to a particular context, and to abandon policy approaches when it is evident that they will not yield the results being pursued.

In East Asia, as a case in point, the growth that was called for some time a "miracle" rested on no one common policy foundation or sequence of implementing actions. Korea discouraged foreign direct investment (FDI). Malaysia and Singapore sought it. Indonesia maintained high levels of protection well into the early 1990s. Thailand opted for liberalized trade much earlier than that.

In the course of the 1990s, moreover, no single pattern of economic policy set priorities for action. As India reduced its very high trade barriers, for example, it encountered new problems of trade logistics, such as port infrastructure and customs procedures. Malaysia's determination in the 1990s to achieve equitable development, despite some negative effect on the pace of growth, reflected a political determination that economic progress had to serve national unity. China's concern for greater equity arose later in the decade and from a realization that achievements in reducing poverty on a national scale was still leaving millions of rural residents behind.[2]

According to our basic conceptual framework, one premise of this book's analysis is that sustained growth and poverty reduction strategies expand their potential impact and reach when they rest on policies that upgrade a country's *investment climate* while giving *social inclusion* a high priority. The ex post analysis has revealed that macroeconomic stability is absolutely necessary, although not sufficient, in promoting growth and reducing poverty and inequality.

Improvements in *investment climate* traditionally require reforming policies and practices to give both domestic and foreign investors a reasonable assurance of

- a market-driven regime that facilitates trade, infrastructure, and financial flows
- a stable, transparent, and efficient system of law and regulation along with impartial, timely judicial recourse.

Market failures related to coordination leakages and information spillovers need to be overcome in order to promote an investment climate conducive to business. In addition, prominent space must be given to the need for good governance and effective sociopolitical institutions to underpin development.

The idea that development is about getting good governance and institutions "right" is now widely accepted and there is nothing particularly new in the fact that development and solid institutions are closely linked (Besley 2005). However, reforms in this area often take longer periods of time to crystallize, and even when they do come together, it is more difficult to assess performance improvements quantitatively. The explicit discussion of governance in Tunisia suggests that the country could have achieved stronger economic and social performance if the overall governance quality had been improved and a more transparent and participatory style of policy making had been put in place.

In the realm of *social inclusion,* several countries have developed strenuous efforts to promote shared growth that benefits the poorest strata of society by facilitating their access to markets, assets,

and services. The central priority of Malaysia's development planning and implementation over several decades was to ensure that
government interventions at all levels went first to improving the
lot—from health and education to credit access and jobs—of the
Malay majority among whom the incidence of poverty was high.

In Uganda, the fight against poverty became the government's
major priority area in the mid-1990s after President Yoweri Museveni mobilized members of parliament, donors, and his own ministers, and took them to Luwero District to bring donors and politicians face to face with the state of roads, schools, and dispensaries,
and the extent of poverty in the countryside.

Chile's approach to social inclusion was also sharply revised
when the results of strong economic growth were shown to have
bypassed significant urban clusters of poor people.

In Tunisia, where explicitly pro-poor policies were rather traditional, the high cost and low efficiency of long-standing subsidies
for food staples produced an innovative shift in the early 1990s to
a self-selecting system of subsidies only for products most likely to
be bought by low-income consumers. According to the country
story, the key feature of Tunisian development can be traced to the
development of education, social security, health care, and aid to
the poorest people, population control through enhancement of
women's status, and investments in basic infrastructure.

Concomitant with the explicit or implicit prominence given to
investment climate and social inclusion policies, the country stories
discuss a variety of implementation factors that shape the growth
and poverty reduction efforts.

In this context, alongside the diversity of experiences, a measure
of continuity is also apparent. Different countries, as discussed below, adopted similar strategies and priorities. However, the continuous engagement of a country's top officials in poverty reduction
efforts—as in the Uganda intervention noted above—is one widely
cited test.

Responsiveness—whether to crisis or the stimulus of technology
or to an external shock—is another factor frequently noticed. It is
often associated with the ability to innovate, adapt institutional capacity, learn from experience, and make external factors become
catalysts of change in order to benefit the country's population.

Consistent with the framework outlined in chapter 1, the first
section of this chapter starts discussing the role that the country
stories attribute to growth as the solid foundation for reducing
poverty and inequality. The remainder of the chapter examines
how the four categories of implementation factors have con-

tributed to achieving those ultimate goals in the selected countries. The second section looks at the role played by different types of determined, engaged *leadership* in developing and sustaining antipoverty policy and programs. The third section attempts to measure a key element—*innovation*—in different countries' governing agencies or implementing institutions. Under that heading, it relates policy shifts occasioned by crises, by the independent discovery of flaws in existing approaches, and by the need to respond to such outside influences as trade competition. The fourth section gives a brief account of different countries' efforts to *monitor* the outcomes of antipoverty initiatives and to *learn* from both positive and negative findings. The final section discusses the role of *external catalysts*, especially the role of donors, in shaping, redirecting, and reinforcing antipoverty strategies.

Reducing Poverty and Inequality: Economic Growth as the Solid Foundation

Although countries may have achieved similar results implementing different strategies and different sequences to fit their own circumstances, all countries in our analysis have made steps toward reducing poverty and inequality by creating solid foundations for growth, which in turn has required that macroeconomic imbalances be addressed.

Economic Growth

All of the country stories analyzed indicate that growth cannot be sustained without macroeconomic stability, which also appears to be crucial in enabling governments to finance poverty reduction strategies, particularly in times of adversity.

In Chile, where growth with equity was the announced goal during the 1990s, budget surpluses earned before the 1998 recession could be used to protect the poor in bad years.[3] This is "where conservative fiscal policies and progressive social policies meet."

Indonesia's 30 years of uneven economic advance—until the 1997 Asian crisis—began with and derived in some measure from macroeconomic stabilization, the first phase of economic liberalization. Surging oil revenues in the 1970s pushed austerity measures to one side, but when that income stream shrank in the next decade, a return to balanced budgets helped revive growth. In the two decades before the 1997 crisis, the poverty rate (by head count) dropped from 40 percent to 11 percent, thanks to a combination of policies that set the macroeconomic and structural conditions for rapid growth, while linking the poor rural population with that rapid growth by investing in infrastructure, agriculture, education, and health.

For Tanzania, where macroeconomic stability was only attained in the late 1990s after more than a decade of effort, the achievement (along with other related reforms) opened the way for debt reduction under the Heavily Indebted Poor Countries (HIPC) Initiative and for increased donor support for poverty alleviation efforts.

In all country stories, economic growth seems to have helped the poor population, not only society in general. Where *economic growth* was strong, numerous case studies assert that both the numbers of poor people and their share in the population diminished. The evidence is persuasive, even though the claimed poverty-reducing effect tended to be stronger in urban than in rural settings. Furthermore, when growth was sustained, not just episodic, it led to more durable poverty reduction effects.

Chile pursued economic growth as key to shrinking both poverty and inequality. Chile sustained economic growth from 1960 to 2003 at an annual average of 4.3 percent and reduced poverty from 24.0 percent in 1987 to 9.6 percent at present (World Bank 2005d).

For China, the correlation is strong. China's large-scale poverty reduction has been achieved mainly through economic growth, and when rural economic growth slowed, so did the pace of poverty reduction. (See chapter 3 of this volume for further detail on the China country story.)

In Tunisia, where gross domestic product (GDP) grew at an average annual rate of 5 percent between 1961 and 2001, the incidence of poverty fell fivefold from 1975 onward (from 21.9 percent of the population to 4.2 percent, according to Tunisian data). Equally, Costa Rica was able to halve the incidence of poverty nationally from more than 18.0 percent to 9.5 percent between 1986 and 2000, thanks in part to sustained growth averaging 4.7 percent over the past 30 years.

The opposite effect is also true. The studies of Poland and the Russian Federation document the reverse linkage. In Poland, economic slowdown significantly undercut the 1994–1998 gains in poverty reduction. Even though the Russian Federation's efforts at macroeconomic stabilization and liberalization were slow and inconsistent for most of the 1990s, eventual progress in lowering inflation became a key factor in subsequent recovery of output. In

Russia, when economic recovery started in 1999 it brought a noticeable reduction of the poverty that had actually spread and intensified during the preceding years of drastic output decline.

From 1992 to 2003, Poland averaged annual GDP growth of 4.2 percent, compared with a negative average growth in Russia of –1.2 percentage points. This reflects a general decline in the Russian economy from 1991 onward, until consistent growth began in 1999. From 1999 to 2003 Russian GDP grew an average of 6.7 percent per year.

In terms of poverty, the number of Russians living on less than $2 a day increased from 23 percent to 36 percent of the population between 1994 and 1998, before falling to 8 percent by 2002. During the same period, extreme poverty in Russia more than doubled from 6 percent to 13 percent, and then fell to 2 percent by 2002. In comparison, poverty statistics for Poland remained consistently around 2 percent or 3 percent of the population from 1985 to 2002 (World Bank 2005d).

Reducing Poverty and Inequality

Regarding the correlation between growth and poverty reduction, there is certainly variation both across and within countries. Although many countries exhibiting sustained growth have managed to reduce the prevalence of poverty within their population, others have achieved overall growth but continue to struggle with the challenge of raising the incomes of the poor. Even within countries noted here as exemplary stories for poverty reduction, such as China and Chile, achievements were not always due to growth alone.

The country stories in our sample clearly connect growth to decreases in poverty. However, some point to (1) the limits of growth's impact on poverty reduction unless parallel social measures are implemented, and (2) the inequalities that growth may maintain or even exacerbate, at least initially.

Figure 2.1 depicts poverty reduction in the past 20 years for several countries that have exhibited sustained economic growth. It also shows reversals during periods or years when growth was not great enough to lift people out of poverty, as in China at the end of the 1990s or Chile in 1993.

Chile experienced consistent growth from 1988 to 2000 and yet saw poverty prevalence actually increase in the early and mid-1990s. This is likely the result of the gradual learning process of implementing social programs. Initiated in the early 1990s, they

Figure 2.1 Percentage of the Poulation of Selected Countries
Living on Less Than $2 per Day

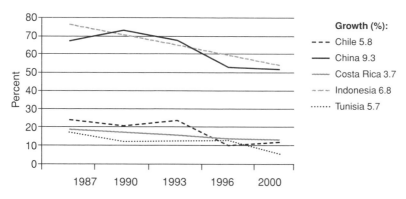

Source: World Bank Developent Indicators 2005.

proved ineffective at first, but improved as Chile began to address
implementation imbalances and institutional constraints.

China's poverty reduction program, always oriented to the rural
areas where poverty was far greater than in urban settings, under-
went consecutive improvements to push for faster progress against
poverty and widening inequalities, particularly in the late 1990s.[4]
When originally introduced, the so-called 8-7 Plan mainly targeted
the lagging rural areas and involved, among other things, increasing annual funding for poverty reduction by 50 percent, thus re-
versing a decade of decline in such outlays. Subsidized loan programs accounted for the greatest increase in funding, but the rapid
reduction in poverty under the 8-7 Plan was a joint effect of economic growth, other social measures specifically oriented toward
the poor, agricultural price increases, and rural-urban migration.
Stimulated by booming opportunities elsewhere, significant numbers of the rural poor moved from the countryside to the areas
where strong economic growth was occurring.

In Uganda from 1992 to 1996, economic growth left the poor
behind. This could be attributed to the lapse between Museveni's
focus on growth-promoting economic reforms, beginning in 1992,
and the focus on social programs and human development that did
not fully emerge until 1995. Beyond that point we see continued
economic growth correlated with declining poverty.

Clearly, overall growth does not inevitably raise the incomes of the poor, but with a focus on making growth pro-poor, via effective social programs, economic growth can lift many out of poverty. Hand-in-hand with economic growth, a country must implement social programs to help break the cycle of poverty.

Regarding the relationship between growth and inequalities, in the short term, rapid growth may lead to higher inequalities because not all segments of society can experience improvements at the same time. In the long run, however, disparities seem to threaten countries by preventing them from sustaining growth. These lessons have led some policy makers to conclude that unless inequalities are addressed, their growth strategies will not produce durable results. Some of our country studies point indeed to an implicit double causality between growth and inequality.[5]

For Malaysia, the goal of economic policy from 1970 onward was mainly national unity, with development policy tilted to benefit the majority (but economically disadvantaged) Malay population. The pursuit of that priority might have led to the diversion of scarce resources from activities that would have generated more rapid economic growth. If the policy crowded out privately owned firms, however, it produced a more desired outcome: the virtual absence of racial strife.

The Russian Federation recorded steep increases in inequality (Gini coefficient) as a previously nonexistent private sector became a growth engine. According to empirical research cited in the study, the polarization of the Russian society grew steadily through the 1990s, accelerating after the 1998 crisis and continuing, rather than diminishing, in more recent years of economic growth. In the years 2000–2002, as an example, research found that 45 percent of the total growth of wages was concentrated in the top 10 percent of the highest-paid employees, whereas the lowest-paid workers benefited from less than 3 percent of the total growth in wages.

Although Poland has not seen such sharp inequality as has Russia, the "new" (posttransition) poor people in both countries are noticeably alike. In both countries, a considerable proportion of the rural population lives in poverty, and the trend toward feminization of poverty is apparent.

Unlike their Polish counterparts, however, a large proportion of Russian pensioners fall into the new poor category, where many job-holders are also found. Employed people account for approximately 40 percent of the total number of poor people.

At the Top: Taking Responsibility

Where leaders lead, results follow. Such is one distinct lesson of country stories on the implementation of poverty reduction strategies in Uganda, China, Chile, Korea, and Malaysia. With the above-noted instances of the significance of high-level political engagement, the cases of Poland and the Russian Federation offer indirect but reinforcing evidence for the same conclusion.

Uganda

The Ugandan case credits strong and single-minded political leadership not only with backing needed reforms that underpinned steady growth but also with developing targeted social projects when growth alone produced an insufficient reduction in poverty.

Coming to power in 1986 as the victor in a civil war, Uganda's National Resistance Movement (NRM) had a populist character. Power was concentrated in the president, enabling clear decision making, especially in the early years. Between 1987 and 1992, however, that prerogative was exercised only reluctantly in support of the free-market reforms that later boosted growth and diminished poverty. Ideologically attracted to the state-led model that Uganda had followed in the 1960s, the NRM and President Museveni only chose to cooperate with the International Monetary Fund (IMF) and the World Bank in May 1987, and they embraced liberal reforms out of economic desperation.

The adoption of extensive reforms in 1992 was due partly to the technocratic advocates of reform, especially Emmanuel Tumusiime-Mutebile, the permanent secretary in the Ministry of Planning and Economic Development, and a core team of other bureaucrats. Pressed by donors[6] who also played a key role in compelling government to undertake reforms, President Museveni took decisive action in 1992. He merged the ministries of finance and planning and development, and named Tumusiime-Mutebile both the new body's permanent secretary and the secretary to the treasury. Giving such authority to the leading supporter of liberal reform within the bureaucracy, the president also depoliticized hiring in the new ministry, raised salaries, and backed the use of foreign advisers in technical support roles.[7]

The Uganda story also pays tribute to the president's role in pushing economic reform and reformers to confront rural poverty. A trip to the countryside that he organized in September 1995 brought donors and politicians face to face with the state of roads, schools, and dispensaries and the extent of poverty. That eye-opening expedition laid the political groundwork for the 1997 adoption of the Poverty Eradication Action Plan and for the fight against poverty becoming government's major priority area.

As a consequence of the overall development program implemented since 1992, total exports in Uganda have more than tripled (from $150 million a year to nearly $500 million a year in 2005), export prices have increased, and import prices have dropped. Annual foreign direct investment has increased from $4 million to $220 million (World Bank 2005c). Furthermore, since 1997, GDP per capita has grown an average of 2.93 percent annually (World Bank 2005d) and the population living below the national poverty line has decreased from 44 percent to 35 percent (Appleton 2001).

It becomes clear that able civil servants and strong outside pressure played major roles in moving Uganda to liberal reforms and, when those alone did not significantly raise rural well-being, to a comprehensive campaign of poverty relief. To set change in motion and overcome opposition to reform, a clear and uncontested center of power was a significant asset. Through the pursuit of good policies, strong leadership (both individual and institutional) can bring about progress.

China

To formulate and oversee implementation of its poverty reduction policies and programs, China's government in 1986 created a new, high-level body—the Leading Group for Poverty Reduction (LGPR) under the State Council and usually headed by a vice premier—and entrusted it with the responsibility to design China's poverty reduction policies and programs; allocate poverty reduction funds; and coordinate the relationship among the different ministries, departments, and agencies participating in poverty reduction.

In itself, the LGPR's establishment indicated the importance the Chinese Communist Party and the country's government gave to poverty reduction. Incorporating that concern as a priority within the structure of central economic and political decision making reflected a major commitment to address the social and economic gap between backward, rural China and its rapidly developing metropolises.

Although it was not the only determining factor, this type of leadership helped the government of China achieve remarkable poverty reduction rates. Sixty-seven percent of the population lived on less than $2 a day in 1987. By 2001 that figure was reduced to 47 percent. Over the same period, extreme poverty (less than $1 per day) was nearly halved, from 29 percent to 17 percent (World Bank 2005d).

Government resources were mobilized at all levels to pursue the strategies developed centrally. Not only were mini-LGPRs established at the provincial, prefectural, and county levels to mirror those of the central government, but also most government ministries, departments, and agencies were involved in activities to alleviate rural poverty, and thus became part of the national poverty reduction system. For instance, the Ministry of Education has been responsible for managing compulsory primary education projects and the Ministry of Health for improving health and hygiene in poor regions. Party and government organizations, large state-owned enterprises, and agencies attached to and financed by the government have shared the responsibility for poverty reduction in their assigned poor counties.

As in Malaysia (see that country story below), the use of a powerful central agency to direct antipoverty programs ensured both strong central control and the continuing political commitment of the most senior Chinese policy makers. The LGPR was a useful coordinating instrument to achieve multidepartmental cooperation in poverty alleviation until the strategy shifted toward greater grassroots involvement.

Chile

The three presidential administrations that have governed Chile since 1990 reflected not only political continuity (a center-left opposition to the preceding regime of Augusto Pinochet) but also a commitment, made and kept, to keep the fight against poverty at the top of the agenda. The consequence of steady pursuit of a new "growth with equity" development strategy, the case study asserts, was to halve the incidence of poverty between 1990 and 2000, reducing it from 40 percent to 20 percent of the population.

The country's story illustrating leadership should not be seen, however, as a self-congratulatory chronicle of political virtue rewarded. Its message is more cautionary. The compromises judged necessary to retain power by political parties can slow down the fight against poverty and weaken the outcomes of sound social programs. Specifically, a determined effort to achieve educational reform—a key antipoverty strategy for improving the quality of and equity in education—was undercut by its reluctant partners in the National Teachers Union.

Although spending on education grew during the 1990s at an average annual rate of 10.6 percent (higher even than the pace of outlays on health [9.4 percent] and above the 8 percent increase in social expenditures overall), that effort did not translate into higher scores in math and language skills. After a 10 percent increase in learning scores in the 1990–1996 period, scores stagnated. Similar diminishing returns characterized the spread of health services relative to inputs, and were reflected as well in the slowing pace of poverty reduction after 1996.

Public health workers, doctors employed in public hospitals, and teachers acted as entrenched conservative forces who managed to resist efficiency-oriented changes designed to improve performance and combat poverty. It took three governments and 12 years for teachers to accept an external evaluation of teacher performance and agree on very timid and slow procedures for removing the worst performers.

Assessing the decreasing returns to social expenditures, we learn that the opponents of reform were based in labor unions that had been important members of the center-left coalition that took power in 1990. At that time it was politically obvious that confronting those who had fought against Pinochet was not a wise course to pursue at the very beginning of a new democratic government. With hindsight, though, courageous leadership from the top would have earned significant returns in reducing poverty. It probably would have paid to confront the vested interests of teachers and health workers upfront. The number of days lost in strikes, even the political costs to the government, would have been rapidly compensated for by immense welfare gains because more flexible, decentralized, incentive- and user-oriented social services would have been provided.

Malaysia and Korea

The stories of Malaysia and the Republic of Korea affirm that the steady determination of policy makers is a vital factor in the pursuit of economic development and a concomitant reduction in poverty. Perhaps the key factors in Korea's story were the commitment to economic development by authorities at the highest level and the strong perception that policies that had been announced would, in fact, be implemented.

Malaysia's economic planners listed political stability as one
noneconomic pro-growth factor. The same coalition of parties
ruled the country from 1970 into the 21st century, thus lessening
the uncertainties normally associated with frequent shifts in governments propagating different ideologies. Prime Minister Ma-
hathir bin Mohamad ruled the country for more than two decades
beginning in 1981. During those two decades, Malaysia's GDP
tripled (from $30 billion to $103 billion), and the current account
balance improved from a deficit of $3.5 billion to a surplus of
more than $13 billion (World Bank 2005b). Malaysia reduced the
population living on less than $2 a day from 15 percent to 9 per-
cent in the decade from 1987 to 1997 (World Bank 2005d).

A lesson from Malaysia's experience is that for economic growth
to be sustained, there have to be strong governments in power on a
sustained basis. Strength comes from representing all major groups
in the society, and clean leaders must be genuinely committed to and
capable of leading the nation rather than to serving their own personal goals.

The comprehensive institutional framework to manage critical
components in national development emerges from the Malaysia
case study as a bulwark of economic policy making. Significantly,
the description makes clear that the Economic Planning Unit (EPU)
of the Prime Minister's Department (actually a ministry) was the
lead agency in national development formulation and evaluation.
The Ministry of Finance, however, remained all along the main
agency in charge of implementation. The EPU produced two long-
term industrial master plans as well as six five-year plans and an
equal number of midterm reviews between 1970 and 2000.

The EPU-supervised planning process placed the prime minister in
a central position to oversee policy choices. That power and responsibility were further confirmed when new agencies—the National Economic Action Council and its executive committee and working
group—were formed in 1997 when recession struck the Malaysian
economy. The prime minister chaired both the 24-member council
and the six-member executive committee in swiftly preparing the National Economic Recovery Plan, which became the basis for overcoming the crisis.

In Korea, which has always had many development plans, the
importance of high-level political commitment lay in convincing
the public that the government meant what it said. Acceptance of
the actions of President Park Chung Hee, who came to power in a
1961 military coup, was critical. In addition to strengthening the
planning process, President Park placed great emphasis on carrying

out announced policies. Their implementation was accomplished through a rigorous structure of rewards and punishments, including compulsion and administrative discretion.

One positive outcome of the regime's putting economic development unambiguously at the top of its priorities and of the decidedly firm power wielded in that cause was a remarkable shift in business confidence. Where only one in five Korean entrepreneurs felt that decisions were always or almost always implemented under the rule of President Syngman Rhee, 78 percent of entrepreneurs polled said of the Park period that decisions were always implemented and that it was "impossible" to avoid complying.

Such confidence clearly helped Korea shift from an agricultural to a manufacturing economy, and to rapid growth driven by exports. During Park's tenure, GDP per capita in Korea rose from $1,133 to $3,323. Improvements in exports were even more dramatic, growing nearly 500 times over, from $32 million to $15 billion annually, an increase in exports' share of GDP from 5 percent to 26 percent (World Bank 2005d).

Until his assassination in 1979, President Park maintained active, personal oversight on policy, attending monthly economic briefings with his full cabinet and the heads of big business and financial organizations, quarterly meetings of the Trade Promotion Conference, and an annual gathering with senior officials of individual ministries. Commenting, suggesting solutions to problems, and issuing orders at the latter two sessions, the president imparted valuable clarity on the direction of policy and on the unequivocal nature of his involvement in economic management.

Poland and Russia

Both countries had to weather the collapse of totalitarian regimes, but Poland managed its transition strategy more speedily and consistently, achieving stronger growth and attendant reduction in poverty. It must be mentioned that Poland's candidacy for the European Union (EU) acted as a positive external catalyst and helped stimulate the type of leadership required for a faster pursuit of macroeconomic stability, growth, and poverty reduction goals.

There is evidence that the countries that proceeded with reforms in the fast manner, as did Poland, suffered a smaller decline than did countries implementing gradual reform, such as Russia.

It can be noted that the pace and certainty of reform policy in both countries reflected in some measure the cohesion and strength of political leadership, or the lack of it. At least for the first four post-communist years, the Solidarity movement and its leader Lech Walesa held power in Poland with a firm, democratically elected majority. In Russia, Boris Yeltsin ruled for two years without an electoral mandate and, even though his economic reform program won a resounding endorsement by referendum in April 1993, his authority was undermined that fall during a violent confrontation with the legislature and, starting the next year, by civil conflict in Chechnya.

In many Central and Eastern European countries, the early achievements of economic stabilization helped strengthen the constituency in favor of further reform, both political and economic. Russia's leadership was unable to score any such early accomplishments, a failure that arguably conditioned its very uneven antipoverty performance throughout the 1990s.

Responsive Innovation and Adaptation

Many of the country stories record examples of profound policy and institutional innovations. Poland and Russia both attempted dramatic shifts from centrally planned to market-driven economies, a process China accomplished not just through sweeping reforms but through continuing innovation in the implementation of antipoverty programs and the institutions that manage such programs.

Such nuts-and-bolts adaptation to changing conditions (or even failure) is the subject of this section. Here we look at the case studies of Costa Rica and El Salvador, where unmet needs in health and education called forth a reshaped policy response; of Chile, where antipoverty strategies evolved from income support to targeted efforts to reach the most vulnerable populations; of Indonesia, where crises actually afforded reformers the opportunity to alter economic and political courses; and of Tunisia, where trade liberalization and, particularly, an agreement with the EU spurred a move to help microenterprises. The innovation on which this section focuses concerns governing institutions and their response to challenge.

Costa Rica and El Salvador

Early in the 1990s two Central American countries, dissimilar in many respects, faced comparable antipoverty challenges: how to gain efficiency in health services in Costa Rica and how to improve educational outcomes in El Salvador. The countries chose parallel paths: decentralizing responsibility and accountability for service delivery, while strengthening the policy and regulatory responsibilities of the public sector.

In both settings, the crucial policy innovation involved a new reliance on private resources and energies in areas where the state had long dominated. The shift was perhaps more remarkable in Costa Rica where the state had been central in financing and providing public health services. Despite outlays as a share of GDP that were among the highest in Latin America and the Caribbean, and despite impressive results in raising life expectancy and lowering infant mortality, Costa Rica's public health system was facing serious challenges. Costs were rising faster than funding. Patients were waiting long periods for tests, specialists, and surgery. Doctors neglected their public duties for their private practices, and were not penalized for their actions. Hospitals were rundown, equipment was obsolete, and staff morale and productivity were low.

Acknowledging the problem and its roots in a health structure dominated by public spending (accounting for 80 percent of all expenditures, compared with the Latin American and Caribbean regional average of 43 percent), Costa Rica's government undertook a systemic reform early in the 1990s. Intensively debated before its adoption, the reform constituted a significant innovation in the space it opened for private health providers. Aside from major organizational changes that eliminated inefficient duplication of effort in the public sector, the reform created new financial incentives in the form of performance contracts for hospitals and established private health cooperatives with the responsibility to provide integrated services in specific metropolitan areas.

Giving more responsibility and accountability to local and private actors while strengthening the public sector's policy and regulatory responsibilities, Costa Rica continued to improve its health outcomes. From 1990 to 2002, overall life expectancy increased from 77 to 79 years, and infant mortality decreased from 15 to 9 deaths per 1,000 live births. Costa Rica also cut public health sector spending from 6.7 percent of GDP in 1990 to about 5.3 percent in 1999. Out-of-pocket health expenditures remained constant, as did the number of doctors and hospital beds per 1,000 people. Equally, the reforms ensured such equitable delivery of services that the lowest income decile received 19.7 times more in health services than their contributions by quotas.

In El Salvador at the end of the 1980s, a dozen years of civil war had left the education system—like most of the country's social services—so weak that it reached only four out of five primary-school-age children (even fewer in rural areas). Additionally, more than a quarter of the population was illiterate. Highly bureaucratized and inefficient, the system provided parents and teachers with little involvement in administration. Even before the January 1992 peace accords, Salvadoran authorities were seeking ways to overhaul the system and strengthen its performance.

The reform that evolved from their efforts represented a major social innovation in the way it engaged private forces in rebuilding and managing primary and secondary education. A Ministry of Education campaign began encouraging schools to seek and welcome support from the community, the private sector, nongovernmental organizations (NGOs), and private agencies or foundations. The country's foremost teachers union initially opposed the decentralization as a move to privatize education and mounted strikes and work stoppages against the program and its provision that gave communities, rather than the cronyism-plagued ministry, the power to hire teachers and determine their benefits.[8]

One outcome has been a significant increase in school enrollments, with net primary enrollments rising from 73 percent to 90 percent (1990–2002). Much of the increase was in rural areas, indicating a pro-poor performance of El Salvador's educational spending. Additionally, students are staying in school longer. Primary-school completion rates rose from 62 percent to 86 percent over the same period. Behind a reform that transferred resources and decision-making capacity to schools and empowered communities and parents lay effective government leadership, strong stakeholder participation in service delivery, and firm private support. Incorporating that last element was an innovation that makes El Salvador's poverty reduction efforts noteworthy.

Chile

As in El Salvador, Chile's previously discussed efforts at reform in education and public health ran into opposition from labor unions that delayed the presumed beneficial effects of the contemplated changes. A broader and more effective innovation in antipoverty strategy, however, came from recognizing that, although robust economic growth was a solid foundation, it had to be reinforced by aggressive social policies designed to further improve the lot of the poor. Because Chile was committed to fiscal stability, the decision to increase spending on public health, low-income housing, and education required raising taxes (by 3 percent of GDP in the years after 1990) that had been cut drastically under the Pinochet regime.

A more recent innovation in implementing the poverty reduction strategy is scaling up experiments from the 1990s to focus intensively on the country's 220,000 extremely poor families as units, rather than as residents of a particular area or clients of one or more social service providers. In place of the more typical approach—fitting the poor population into uniform, national, or local programs—the Chile Solidario program began in 2002 to involve the head of the family in a mutual commitment with public agencies to jointly identify the sources of vulnerability and risks for the family and then design an integral, coordinated action to cover the main deficits, such as minimum income, access to basic social services and to schooling and training, and empowerment for adults.

This participatory approach has still to prove its effectiveness. Early evaluations indicate a strong motivational effect on the women involved but also suggest a tendency to create a paternalistic, clientilistic relationship and unsatisfactory outcomes in terms of empowering families and motivating them to network with community organizations. The program has been at work too short a time to judge its success in moving the extremely poor people from dependency to self-reliance. Although it is innovative and takes into account the right variables, the program will probably need close monitoring and just-in-time corrections and improvements.

Indonesia

With an eye to the history of Indonesia's antipoverty policies, it is fair to say that crisis has been the mother of invention more than once. During two crises—a political upheaval in 1966/67 and a financial near-collapse in 1997—technocrats gained the authority to design policy for the recovery of the country and its economy. Their innovative approaches in pursuing macroeconomic stability, notably through regular, rapid depreciations to adjust absorption and restore competitiveness, and in matching rural education efforts to the adoption of Green Revolution technology to raise rice production, paid off on both counts, even as the technocrats lost policy-making influence.

Although it has its risks, using bad economic times as a window of opportunity to get good policies in place is likely to increase a country's chances of moving forward. Moreover, using pragmatic approaches to pressing issues—such as food security in the 1970s —may be preferable to more ideological policy stances. In Indonesia, it could be argued, a penchant for improvisation—an aversion to ideological diktat—begets innovations, of which one strikingly successful instance arose in the field of rural microfinance.

Rooted in a system of credit subsidies for rice farmers, but completely unsubsidized since 1989, the Unit Desa (or village bank) outlets of the Bank Rakyat Indonesia (BRI) in 2002 held a portfolio of 2.7 million loans. They served 16 million savers; posted a consistent 95 percent repayment rate; and, making profits even in crisis years, have been a profitable venture highly beneficial to rural development.

The system grew, in effect, from a policy error and a decision to correct course. When heavy losses from the original farm credit subsidy program forced its termination in 1983, BRI was also forced to revamp its subdistrict-level banking activities. Organizationally, it made each Unit Desa a profit center staffed by employees who gained equal status with all BRI workers. It also developed a new commercial loan targeted at low-income borrowers and began to experiment with three types of savings instruments, each with positive real interest rates. Ninety-eight percent of the branches were profitable by 1996, compared with none in 1983. Over the same period, the savings mobilized under these changes rose from $18 million to $3 billion; the number of loans outstanding rose by 641,000, to 2,488,000; the value of loans outstanding rose from $103 million to $1.7 billion; and the total arrears as a percentage of the outstanding loans decreased from 33.3 percent to 3.6 percent (World Bank 2004).

At a higher level of policy, the deregulation of interest rates gave BRI new leeway. At the implementation level, the decision to treat poor farmers as valued clients turned an innovation into an institution. The story of BRI, built on the rubble of an unsustainable subsidized credit scheme, is further evidence of the remarkable inventiveness of Indonesia's authorities. Rather than abandoning the 3,000 BRI branches in the early 1980s, the authorities saw the value of this network and put it to work for a better purpose, giving the rural poor access to sustainable finance.

Tunisia

Since 1981 Tunisia has had a limited (22,000 projects) credit program for small business, especially handicrafts, in its array of antipoverty initiatives. In 1997 it widened the concept for government-backed financing of small-scale projects by creating a bank specifically to reach borrowers who lacked the collateral needed for commercial loans. Two years later, it launched a program of microcredit disbursed through NGOs to small-scale development projects.

All these programs aim directly or indirectly at job creation and are considered to be positive experiences to some degree. A different, innovative approach to small business—and 94 percent of Tunisia's 87,000 officially registered firms employ fewer than 250 people—began operating in the 1990s as a "microstructural adjustment" effort aimed at enabling participants to compete with EU enterprises. This capacity-building effort, backed by the EU and the World Bank, has supplied assistance to more than half of 2,000 firms considered eligible for investment credits.

As an innovation, it is an example of building on previous experience to enhance poverty reduction through economic growth, the mainstay of Tunisia's approach to poverty for many decades. It is also, however, a reflection of an implementation program adapting to a policy departure—in this case, Tunisia's strategy of gradual trade liberalization adopted in the 1990s.

In that context, the mid-1995 conclusion of a free trade association agreement with the EU changed the competitive environment for Tunisian firms. Following this agreement, trade between Tunisia and the EU has increased dramatically. From 1994 to 2002, imports from the EU rose by more than 40 percent and exports to the EU increased by more than 70 percent.[9] The microstructural adjustment program is one response to that catalytic shift.

Tunisia's effort to adapt to increased commerce with the EU is just one example of trade liberalization's spurring not only economic change but, in consequence, some redirection of antipoverty strategies.[10]

Watching the Steps:
The Monitoring and Evaluation Process

Accurate information and analysis do not guarantee timely corrective action. However, without solid evaluation of the impact of various programs—farm subsidies in Indonesia, consumption subsidies in Tunisia, underfunded reliance on municipal governments in Chile—national leaders and their international partners cannot know what approach needs to be fine-tuned, scrapped, or scaled up to continue the fight against poverty.

Chile, as noted earlier, not only shifted its antipoverty strategy when data showed progress was inadequate, but also assigned public officials to accompany and monitor each extremely poor family engaged in the Chile Solidario program, which was designed to overcome the deficiencies of earlier efforts. Moreover, using a variety of consistent tools based exclusively on performance, Chile has pioneered systematic monitoring and evaluation of government programs at the national level that is considered a model for Latin America and even for developed countries. Indicators cover efficiency, effectiveness, and quality, among others. All indicators are reported to the Chilean congress, and are firmly integrated into decision making, program design, and program management.

China offers another example of course correction based on monitoring and evaluation. As noted above, at the start of the 21st century China narrowed the focus of its antipoverty strategy—the 8-7 Plan launched in 1994—by making villages rather than counties the basic targeting unit. The decision grew in part from the findings of rural poverty studies conducted in the 592 designated poor counties, where improved monitoring followed from a high-level conference convened in September 1996 to evaluate the performance of the 8-7 Plan.

Among the key factors, the emphasis on learning and experimentation is very predominant in the case of China. Poverty reduction is a process of constant learning and exploration. Over the past quarter of a century, and under the 8-7 Plan specifically, China's poverty reduction management methods have been tested and improved through experiments with the objective of increasing their efficiency. Learning from experience has been harnessed through the administrative system, conducting analysis, collecting feedback from government agencies involved in poverty reduction programs at the central and local levels, and drawing lessons. To promote the sharing and dissemination of knowledge, agencies involved in poverty reduction organize annual workshops to learn lessons from ongoing poverty reduction activities and to benefit from outside expertise. Top-level government officials participate in regular policy workshops, discussing issues of policy implementation and exploring policy implications of the lessons learned.

Named for its leader, University of Toronto professor Gerry Helleiner, the continuing evaluation process in Tanzania (the Helleiner process) enabled all parties to speak candidly and prompted them to self-examination. Producing its own reports in 1997, 1999, and 2000, the process led to the 2002 creation of a joint institution, the Independent Monitoring Group (IMG). Comprising six independent members—three Europeans, two Tanzanians, and a senior Ugandan official—the group has institutionalized periodic evaluation of government as well as donor performance. It has become an embodiment of an accountability framework.

One outcome of this exercise in cooperative monitoring has been an increased flow of aid that the case study credits with helping improve public service delivery, reintroduce universal primary-school education, abolish school fees, increase the availability of drugs and medical supplies in primary health service units, and expand and rehabilitate the road network. Increases in assistance also helped banking reform and gave impetus to trade liberalization. "The Helleiner process helped build trust between government and donors and fostered transparency on both sides," the case study concludes. "More importantly, it launched the partnership approach to development."

Tanzania's IMG constitutes another variation of a common practice: measuring the positive (or negative) outputs of antipoverty strategies to guide policy makers on the next steps to take. Although other countries may tend to view data gathering and analysis as domestic duties, Tanzania's policy makers believe that the absence of standardized methodology or independent scrutiny can interfere with the utility of monitoring work.

By contrast, monitoring and evaluation of export performance, at least, were conducted at the highest level during the Park regime in Korea. Within a year of President Park's seizing power, the Ministry of Commerce and Industry began setting export targets classified by commodity and destination. Exporters who reached their stipulated targets would receive favorable access to credit and other inducements; exporters who failed could swiftly suffer from economic and other sanctions. The president himself also chaired a monthly meeting of exporters during which export targets were discussed and impediments to achieving them were removed.

In Malaysia, monitoring development policies and plans was regarded as valuable for producing an important set of inputs to the coordination function that aligned various ministries and state and local officials to carry out the national development strategies formed under the prime minister's guidance. Not surprisingly, an agency in the Prime Minister's Department—the Implementation Coordination Unit—managed the multilevel monitoring work. It was well known for introducing a system or technique of monitoring development projects called the Rural Economic Development (RED) Book. On a weekly and monthly basis, the system monitored the progress achieved in constructing each physical project (for example, a school or hospital) and in spending the budget allocated for it, compared with the progress they should achieve during the same period.

External Catalysts

A number of country stories illustrate the productive role of international assistance in helping countries reform broad economic policy when the intervention supports homegrown reforms and promotes ownership in the country.

In Tunisia, a loan by the World Bank supported a program that included a particularly innovative reliance on a self-selection mechanism to improve the targeting of food subsidies to poor people. The reform has cut the cost of the subsidies and transformed the program from one that transferred more absolute benefits to the rich than to the poor into one that mainly benefits the poor.

The relationship between international donors and national policy makers, however, is not always a smooth collaboration. After the near-collapse of its currency and economy, Indonesia called on the IMF in early October 1997 for program support. It was the first such call the country had made since 1973. Initially it accepted a modest tightening of fiscal and monetary policy but did not abide by conditions relating to the closing of a number of insolvent banks. A more specific implementation timetable for bank closures agreed to in January 1998 did not restore the system's credibility, and a further IMF agreement in April 1998, envisioning the gradual abolition of fuel subsidies, backfired. After three days of violent protests following the announcement of immediate high increases in fuel and bus fare prices, President Soeharto was forced to leave the office he had held for nearly 20 years.

Conducting a slow and uncertain political transition, Indonesia at the end of 2003 became the last country affected by the Asian crisis to graduate from the IMF program and, with much-changed policies, resume some of the growth that had served in preceding decades as a major force to reduce poverty.

When a developing country accepts the need for reform and the potential of policy change to aid in reducing poverty, the relationship with donors can be highly productive. In Uganda, as noted earlier, action by the IMF and the World Bank to suspend aid in 1992 broke a pattern of high-level indecision about reform that had marked the Museveni regime since it had come to power. One consequence of this defining moment was Uganda's becoming the first country to qualify for HIPC debt relief, an achievement that opened the way for increased foreign aid in such areas as road building, primary education, and HIV/AIDS control.

The collaboration in poverty reduction went beyond infrastructure and social services investments to a multifaceted engagement with reform and reformers. Donors, particularly the IMF and World Bank, cultivated a bureaucratic elite committed to reform. They helped create specially funded units within key ministries, helped establish a research center and a master's degree program at Makerere University, and trained government workers. Technical assistance programs from the World Bank and other donors strengthened capacity and expertise in the institutions handling economic reform.

In Tanzania, the direct dialogue with development partners has been an important catalyst in the economic reform process, informing the early debates on economic issues and indirectly contributing to homegrown programs. It also has facilitated greater government ownership of the process and helped government-donor relations evolve from confrontation to partnership approaches. Furthermore, it has triggered the need to focus on aid effectiveness and to reexamine and improve aid delivery mechanisms.

In the late 1970s, during the long rule of President Julius Nyerere, the IMF suspended its support program, occasioning not only a shrinking of other donor contributions but also an internal debate on the need for economic reforms. When Nyerere's successor, although an energetic supporter of liberalization in his first term, failed thereafter to curb massive tax exemptions or the flow of credit to public enterprises, the World Bank and other donors suspended their adjustment disbursements. The impasse was only broken by a Danish-Tanzanian agreement in 1994 to evaluate—in fact, to mediate—the country's relationships with donors. The process, which focused on aid effectiveness, government credibility, and the government's ownership of the reform program, played a catalytic role in helping Tanzanians see that reform was indeed off track and in building a more balanced framework for government-donor cooperation.

In China, international organizations contributed knowledge as well as significant funds to poverty reduction. In total, international development agencies, international financial institutions, bilateral agencies, and international NGOs contributed some RMB10 billion during 1994–2000, when the 8-7 Plan was implemented. Even more importantly, their poverty reduction activities in China have influenced and changed government's perception of poverty and have enhanced understanding of approaches to addressing poverty. The introduction of participatory poverty reduction practices and integrated poverty reduction planning in China can be credited partly to the support of international organizations (see chapter 3 of this volume for further detail).

Learning from Experience

This chapter began by stressing the differences among case studies, countries, and approaches to the challenge of enlarging the scope and intensifying the impact of effective poverty reduction strategies. The fact that no formula is repeated from country to country might suggest that there is no useful, practical knowledge in these pages. That conclusion would be mistaken.

Each study tells of policy makers trying to adjust to achievements or failures, or to partial accomplishments. All tell of major or minor changes in original plans. Each in its own way draws lessons to be studied and perhaps tested in different forms in another region, culture, or economic environment. The messages do not spell out a single course to be followed; rather, they signal the value of innovating and of learning from the experiences and examples of others.

Notes

1. The following cases are analyzed in this chapter: A. Foxley, Successes and Failures in Poverty Eradication: Chile; W. Sangui, L. Zhou, and R. Yanshun, The 8-7 National Poverty Reduction Program in China—The National Strategy and Its Impact; J. Marquez, Costa Rica and El Salvador: Finding the Appropriate Role for the Public and Private Sectors in Poverty Reduction; India: Local Democracy and Empowerment of the Underprivileged—An Analysis of Democratic Decentralization; B. Hofman, E. Rodrick-Jones, and K. W. Thee, Indonesia: Rapid Growth, Weak Institutions; Republic of Korea: Four Decades of Equitable Growth; Economic Planning Unit, Prime Minister's Department, Malaysia: 30 Years of Poverty Reduction, Growth and Racial Harmony; M. Dabrowski, O. Rohozynsky, and I. Sinitsina, Poland and the Russian Federation—A Comparative Study of Growth and Poverty; A. Muganda, Tanzania's Economic Reforms and Lessons Learned; S. Ghali and P. Mohnen, The Tunisian Path to Development: 1961–2001; Uganda: From Conflict to Sustained Growth and Deep Reductions in Poverty. Unless otherwise noted, statistics and quoted portions of this chapter are taken from the relevant country stories.

2. These observations do not necessarily mean that either country has achieved perfect social inclusion because there are still socially marginalized groups in both countries.

3. Because the poverty figures change in response to economic cycles, policy makers should differentiate between hardcore and cyclically induced poverty, and use fiscal policy to protect the poor countercyclically in times of adversity.

4. Incidentally, the period of widening inequalities in China coincides with the period of most aggressive openness and promotion of foreign direct investment.

5. These observations are also supported by the empirical literature. Efficiency (production factors being remunerated according to their productivity) and equity (income and human capital being shared equally by all segments of the population) are often the subject of compromise. See, for example, Schwartz and Ter-Minassian (2000) for a review of the literature. On the one hand, with the rich having a higher savings rate than the poor, an increase in inequalities may translate into faster growth because of the induced increase in the overall savings. On the other hand, three arguments in favor of reducing inequalities are put forward: (1) high income inequality ensures political instability that impedes growth (Barro 1991); (2) positive effects of health and education are likely to create an incentive effect to improve labor productivity and savings, thus growth; and (3) higher levels of equity contribute to increased growth by promoting the accumulation of production factors.

6. The IMF and the World Bank stopped providing balance of payments support.

7. As a homegrown politician, he purchased expertise from outside but also undertook civil service reform to keep and attract skilled staff.

8. See the education section of chapter 4 for a discussion of EDUCO in El Salvador.

9. Data are from UN Comtrade, the UN Commodity Trade Statistics Database, hosted by the United Nations Statistical Division and available online at http://unstats.un.org/unsd/comtrade.

10. Similarly, in Korea the Park regime's decision to give exports priority as a base for growth required the development of a literate, technically prepared workforce. That prompted investment in education, with consequent reductions in poverty. For Chileans, although a more open trade regime fueled strong economic growth and underwrote extensive social programs, growth alone did not reach "outsiders" in the workforce, the unemployed, and those whose jobs were only temporary and poorly paid. The authorities' response has been to complement the stimulus of trade-fueled growth with innovative social outreach programs.

References

Appleton, Simon. 2001. "Poverty in Uganda, 1999/2000: Preliminary Estimates from the Uganda National Household Survey." Photocopy. University of Nottingham, UK.

Barro, Robert J. 1991. "Economic Growth in a Cross Section of Countries." *Quarterly Journal of Economics* 106 (May): 407–501.

Besley, Timothy. 2005. "Introduction." In *Development Challenges in the 1990s: Leading Policymakers Speak from Experience,* ed. T. Besley and N. R. Zagha, 1–13. Washington, DC: World Bank.

Schwartz, G., and T. Ter-Minassian. 2000. "The Distributional Effects of Public Expenditure." *Journal of Economic Surveys* 14 (July).

World Bank. 2005a. *Economic Growth in the 1990s: Learning from a Decade of Reform.* Washington, DC: World Bank.

———. 2005b. Malaysia-at-a-Glance. Available at www.worldbank.org/data/countrydata/aag/mys_aag.pdf.

———. 2005c. Uganda-at-a-Glance. Available at www.worldbank.org/data/countrydata/aag/uga_aag.pdf.

———. 2005d. World Development Indicators Online. Available at www.worldbank/data/wdi2005.

———. 2004. "Financial Sector Policy Issues Note: Vietnam Bank for Social Policies." Annex 5: Bank Rakyat Indonesia as a Possible Model for Transformation. Financial Sector Group, East Asia and Pacific Region, Hanoi, Vietnam.

3

Development as a Process of Learning and Innovation: Lessons from China

Yan Wang

In the last quarter of a century, China has achieved sustained economic growth and the most rapid, large-scale poverty reduction in human history. Using the government of China's official absolute poverty (destitution)[1] measure, the number of people in rural poverty fell from 300 million to 26 million between 1978 and 2004 (NBS 2005). Using the World Bank's $1-per-day income measure, nearly 400 million people were lifted out of poverty from 1981 to 2001 (World Bank 2005b), representing a decline of poverty incidence from 53 percent in 1981 to 8 percent in 2001 (Ravallion and Chen 2004).

A considerable body of literature has attempted to identify the secrets of the China story. Several debates have taken place on the sources of growth and poverty reduction in China. Suggested driving factors have ranged from rapid capital accumulation, with high saving and investment rates, to productivity growth attributable to institutional reforms (*gai ge*) and openness to trade and foreign direct investment (*kai fang*); from a strong government and interventionist approach to fiscal decentralization and local initiative; and, more recently, from rapid growth to pro-poor growth.

China is a fascinating but extremely complex story that has attracted and continues to attract much research and analysis. The eight case studies on China written by Chinese practitioners and researchers for the Shanghai Conference reflect various parts of the story, focusing on events that happened later in the 1990s.[2] The studies can be classified as follows:

- The 8-7 National Poverty Reduction Program, focused on the period 1994 to 2000—a targeted program (case 1; also box 3.1)
- Two studies on rural poverty–oriented projects that have been scaled up across provinces: the Southwest Poverty Reduction Project (SWPRP) and the Loess Plateau Watershed Rehabilitation Project (LPWRP) (cases 2 and 3; also boxes 3.2 and 3.4)
- Three studies on sectoral programs—education, rural roads, and water supply and sanitation (cases 4, 5, and 6)
- One study on China's institutional innovation and private sector development—the Sunan and Wenzhou models (case 7; also box 3.3)
- A paper on a unique model of regional cooperation—the East helping the West to reduce poverty: Shanghai helping Yunnan (case 8).

This chapter attempts to synthesize this diverse set of initiatives into a cohesive whole and link them with other recent relevant studies on poverty reduction, for the story is not complete without drawing from the large body of literature on China's reforms since 1978. The main added value of the chapter is going to be on hitherto-less-stressed aspects of the China story: the role of learning, experimentation, homegrown versus modern institutions, and self-discovery.[3]

Clearly, China did not do everything right in the past 25 years and there are both positive and negative lessons to be learned. With the benefit of hindsight, some policies can be identified now as clearly not so pro-poor, such as taxing farmers for industrialization, restricting rural-urban migration until recently, and prolonging an urban bias in public service provision and other policies. The government has started to address these issues and, therefore, this chapter only summarizes them briefly.

The framework of this chapter is based on the following premises:

- Development is a process that is full of uncertainties, and each country has its own particular political, cultural, and historical background (World Bank 2005a). Because of this uncertainty and country specificity, development must be a process of learning and innovation.
- Differing from *knowledge*, which is a stock concept, *learning* is a series of actions to acquire knowledge, to gain capacity, and to adapt to new institutions. Just as growth is a *flow* con-

cept, learning is a flow concept: It is the accumulation of knowledge that empowers actors, learners, firms, local governments, or other entities to take action. Highlighting as it does the actors—the individuals or entities who take action—this concept of learning captures aspects not usually covered in the knowledge-economy literature.

This chapter will first review the evidence on "what worked" to allow rapid development and poverty reduction in China, including the sources of growth, the patterns of growth, and the distribution of opportunities. Later the "how" aspect of the China story will be discussed—the incentives and approaches that enabled China to learn fast from its own experience and that of others. The taxonomy table provided in the annex to this chapter (table A3.1) functions as a key linking the case studies to specific learning and innovations involved. The last section summarizes the lessons from unsuccessful policies and concludes with new challenges that China faces.

"What Worked"—The Driving Factors

China's large-scale poverty reduction has been achieved mainly through rapid economic growth and institutional transformation, but the progress of poverty reduction has been highly uneven across time and space (figure 3.1). Some have argued, correctly, that the pattern of growth was crucial in reducing poverty, and that the sectoral composition of the growth made a difference: Nearly half of the poverty reduction was attributable to the implementation of rural reforms that involved the initiation, experimentation, and scaling up of the Household Responsibility System from 1979 to 1984 (Ravallion and Chen 2004; Lin 1992; Qiu 2005).

It is further argued, also correctly, that both income growth and poverty reduction are outcomes of policies. The questions, then, are how to achieve rapid growth, how to maintain stable growth for more than 25 years and avoid significant interruptions, and what kind of growth most benefits the poor?

Sources of Rapid Growth

Policy reforms that established homegrown and indigenous institutions (through learning and experimentation) seem to be key to success in productivity growth on a national scale. China lagged behind many neighboring countries after more than 10 years of turmoil during the period of the so-called Cultural Revolution. A desire for

Figure 3.1 Large-Scale Poverty Reduction in China: Uneven
Progress (poverty head count index, 1981–2001)

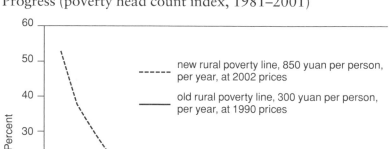

Note: The head count index indicates the percentage of the population living in households with per capita income below the official poverty line. The rural consumer price index is used as the deflator.

Source: Ravallion and Chen 2004.

change, a thirst for learning and "catching up" extending from the top leaders to villagers, motivated the initial opening up and early domestic reforms. In 1976–1977, a debate took place on the "optimal paths of reforms" based on the experiences of Eastern European countries—Hungary and Poland—that started on this path earlier than China. But the true reform started at the grassroots level—the villagers in Anhui Province who initiated the Household Responsibility System, which achieved great benefits. Pragmatism prevailed when the authorities realized that the best path of reform starts with unleashing people's initiative and learning from experience. This was when Chinese leader Deng Xiaoping proposed to "cross the river by groping stones at the bottom," and encouraged institutional reform through experimentation. Since 1978, economic reform and openness have become two main strategies for growth and poverty reduction, which have been consistently implemented for more than 25 years.

The reforms started in rural areas and, over the years, experiments have been initiated using homegrown Chinese institutions; these experiments—which are not perfect market institutions—have been scaled up when considered positive. They included the Household Responsibility System, Township and Village Enterprises (TVEs), and Special Economic Zones (SEZs). They were innovative experiments at the time of inception and appropriate to the political situation.

As Francis Fukuyama, professor of international political economy at Johns Hopkins University, has pointed out, "Perfect institutions cannot be supplied to a country ex ante." China is an example of introducing second-best but homegrown institutions. Qian (2000) divided China's reform into two periods. In the first period (1978–1993), China introduced incentives and competition by adopting indigenous but imperfect institutions, decentralizing government, and adopting a dual-track approach to liberalization that incorporated the simultaneous use of plan and market. In the second period (1994–present), China aimed to learn and develop best-practice market institutions, bringing its laws and regulations into conformity with World Trade Organization (WTO) principles, reforming the government, and beginning to privatize the state-owned enterprises (SOEs).[4] Table A3.2 in the chapter annex lists some of these homegrown and indigenous institutions, some of which were not covered in the eight case studies.

In addition to the importance of institutional transformation that led to growth, there has been a debate on the importance of factor accumulation versus productivity growth in explaining China's growth. Some have focused on the high savings rate and rapid accumulation of capital, asserting that China's growth would slow down because of low productivity growth, just like that of the former Soviet Union (Krugman 1994; Young 2000). Others suggest that it is the rapid institutional reform and the openness to trade and foreign direct investment (FDI) that drive the rapid growth in total factor productivity (TFP) (Lin, Cai, and Li 1996; Qian 2002).

As shown in table 3.1, first, with human capital incorporated, the growth of TFP contributed significantly to output growth, accounting for 24.3 percent of growth between 1978 and 2002. The contribution of TFP growth was consistently negative for the prereform period and positive for the reform period in the sensitivity analysis using different assumptions. A significant part of the TFP growth so far, however, has resulted from sectoral reallocation and, if China is to maintain the growth momentum, TFP growth within sectors will have to come to the fore. Second, the accumulation of human capital in China, as measured by the average years of schooling in the population aged 15–64 years, was quite rapid and it contributed significantly to growth and welfare in the prereform as well as in the postreform periods. However, the pace of human capital accumulation slowed after the reforms, partly because of inadequate provision of education and health services in the rural areas. Third, physical capital accumulation contributed significantly to economic growth, accounting for more than 50 percent of growth in gross domestic product (GDP), and more so in the postreform period.

What this analysis cannot show, however, is that rapid capital accumulation in physical capital is not the sufficient condition for rapid growth and poverty reduction. A country needs an accumulation of all forms of capital—physical, human, natural, and social—as well as a favorable policy environment that empowers people, unleashes their creativity, opens the country to new ideas, and allows institutional reforms and experimentation. China's case studies show clearly that without the institutional reforms that empowered farmers, entrepreneurs, and local governments, economic take-off would have been only a dream.

Importance of Having the "Right" Pattern of Growth

The pattern of growth, or sectoral composition of growth, matters for poverty reduction. Many studies have found that rapid growth in agricultural or rural income is the driving force of poverty re-

Table 3.1 Sources of Economic Growth, 1953–2002 (average annual growth rates in percent)

Item	Prereform period (1953–1978)	Reform period (1979–2002)
Average annual growth rate		
Output	6.12	9.36
Physical capital stock	6.14	9.99
Labor	2.24	1.96
Human capital stock	5.46	2.22
Total factor productivity	−0.80	2.28
Contribution to GDP growth (%)		
Physical capital stock[a]	50.2	53.3
Labor[a]	18.3	10.5
Human capital stock[a]	44.6	11.9
Total factor productivity[b]	−13.1	24.3

Notes: Factor shares used are 0.50 for capital, labor, and human capital. Physical capital assumes a depreciation rate of 5 percent.

a. Ratio of input growth, weighted by factor share to GDP growth.

b. Ratio of TFP growth to GDP growth.

Source: Wang and Yao (2003), updated by the authors.

duction. China's economic reform started in the rural areas through the introduction of the Household Responsibility System, providing equitable land user rights on a 15-year basis, later extended to 30 years. Meanwhile, the procurement prices of grain were lifted significantly. With equitable access to land and less distortion in prices, farmers had the right incentives to increase their productivity. From 1978 to 1985 total agricultural output and productivity grew rapidly and rural net per capita income grew at an annual rate of more than 15 percent (Qiu 2005).

An econometric study showed that 46.9 percent of the total output increase in this period can be attributed to the Household Responsibility System (Lin 1992). Ravallion and Chen (2004) found that nearly half of the poverty reduction that happened before 1985 was the result of the rural reform, which led to a clearly defined property (user) right, more equitable access to land, and less distortion in agricultural prices.

A "make-or-break" issue was the strong focus on rural income growth. China has been taxing farmers for more than 50 years, but the extent of taxation was significantly reduced after the rural reforms in 1978, thanks to the increases in procurement prices of agricultural products and the decreases in the prices of agricultural inputs. However, the focus on rural income growth was on and off over the last 25 years, and this had significant effects on poverty reduction outcomes . Poverty reduction was rapid when the focus was on rural reform and strong policy support to agriculture (1979–1984 and 1994–1996). Poverty reduction slowed in two periods (1985–1993 and 1997–2002), when this rural emphasis was lacking. Instead there was an urban bias in fiscal allocation and public service provision, leading to worsening terms of trade and lowering income levels for farmers, and to worsening income inequality (Chen and Wang 2001; Qiu 2005). In fact, it was the divergence between growth and poverty reduction in the period 1985–1993 that was the motivation for China to launch a national, targeted poverty reduction program in 1994 —the 8-7 Plan (see box 3.1).

The focus on agriculture and a labor-intensive export sector allowed China to better use its comparative advantages. Before the economic reform, China's development strategy was to make significant investments in the heavy industrial sector by taxing farmers. To catch up, China studied the experience of East Asia's tigers. Some Chinese economists characterized their export-oriented strategy as a "comparative advantage strategy" that fully uses the potential of a country (Lin, Cai, and Li 1996). Learning from this ex-

Box 3.1 8-7—An Overarching National Plan for Poverty Reduction

To intensify the poverty reduction efforts that had begun in the second half of the 1980s, in 1994 China introduced the *8-7 National Plan for Poverty Reduction*, aspiring to lift a large proportion of its 80 million poor people above the government poverty line in seven years, from 1994 to 2000. Perhaps the largest poverty reduction initiative in the world, the plan was China's first national program of poverty alleviation that had specific objectives, measures, targets, and deadlines. It aimed to enhance the ability of the poor to develop their own capacities; thus the plan stands for a decisive break in China's poverty reduction approach, a break from relief to development—and from an exclusively government-led to a broad-based approach involving the non-state sector, including the nongovernmental organizations. Under the plan, the annual central government outlay on poverty programs was RMB113 billion ($13.6 billion), accounting for 5–6 percent of total government expenditure.

The 8-7 Plan focused on three main programs: subsidized loans for enterprises and later households with activities in industry and agriculture, food-for-work programs that used surplus farm labor to develop infrastructure, and government budgetary grants to support investment in poor areas across sectors. (The plan also included targeted multisectoral poverty reduction projects and innovative initiatives, such as East Supports West.) Agriculture and industry each received approximately 30 percent of the funds and infrastructure received approximately 35 percent. Given the plan's short time horizon and the enormous infrastructural needs in rural areas, it emphasized investment in physical facilities far more than education and health. Another reason for the relatively low attention to human capital development under the plan relates to the very low returns on education associated with the severe labor market distortions in China until the late 1990s.

The effects of the plan have been immense and varied. It delivered growth rates of farm output and income for the targeted poor counties that were higher than the national average. Measured by the $1-per-day income standard, the total number of poor people in China dropped from 266 million in 1993 to 111 million in 2000—an annual rate of poverty reduction of 11.7 percent. It is, however, difficult to isolate the effect of targeted poverty programs from that of other antipoverty measures, such as the government procurement reform of 1994–1996 that boosted farmers' incomes, and from the impact of overall economic growth—which was in any case partially supported by the plan. Analysis indicates that the impact of special poverty reduction investments on the actual number of poor people does not appear to be strong. This suggests that nonpoor people may have enjoyed a greater share of the growth in household income, the subsidized-loan component being the most susceptible for capture by the nonpoor populace. The poverty reduction effect of the plan might have been stronger with greater clarity in objectives (poverty reduction, rather than development and fiscal revenue generation), better geographical targeting (poor villages, even poor households, rather than poor counties as the focus), greater emphasis on social security and health, and more participatory approaches (for example, microcredit).

In spite of its uneven success in poverty reduction, the 8-7 Plan has been invaluable as a learning experience and as a virtual laboratory for experimentation with novel practices, such as the functioning of a multidepartmental coordinating mechanism, ways of knowledge sharing and dissemination, extensive use of pilot studies, public bidding in procurement, special account management, a reimbursement system, and monitoring and transparency features. An awareness of the ineffectiveness of subsidized loans and the complexity of the needs of poor villages prompted the government to launch multisectoral rural development projects, such as the Southwest Poverty Reduction Project (see box 3.2).

The 8-7 Plan has proved to be an effective launching pad for the next round in the fight against poverty: the New Century Rural Poverty Alleviation Plan for 2001–2010. In addition to the 592 poor counties, the new plan targets 148,000 poor villages (thus covering poor villages in nonpoor counties) that were excluded in the 8-7 Plan. The new plan also emphasizes participatory village planning and multisectoral approaches, basic health and social security schemes, rural-urban migration, and education services in the rural areas.

perience, China rightly stressed rural reforms and involvement with international trade early on in the reform process. With gradual price reforms and unilateral trade liberalization that accelerated in the 1990s, the subsequent growth of manufacturing and trade became closer to China's comparative advantages. Reallocating resources to these productive sectors led to rapid productivity growth. The rapid growth of TVEs (case 2) along with heavy investments in infrastructure further stimulated rural income growth through diversification to nonfarm activities and remittances from migrant workers.

Improving the Distribution of Opportunities

Improving the distribution of opportunities is also crucial for a better shared economic growth. A country may have several assets crucial for growth: physical capital, human capital, natural capital, and social capital. For growth to have an impact on poverty, the assets of the poor, especially their human capital and land, need to be augmented and shared more equitably. Asset distribution represents the distribution of opportunities and is a precondition for increasing individual productivity and income (Wang 2000, ch. 3). Equitable access to land and education are equally important.

The main asset of most poor people is their raw labor power. Investing it with human capital is a powerful way to augment their assets, redress asset inequality, and reduce poverty. Yet, inequality in educational attainment is staggeringly high, reflecting market failures and underinvestment in the human capital of the poor.

China is a good illustration of both aspects: rapid progress and large disparities. Even before the economic reform in 1978, China had provided more equitable access to basic education and health services than other developing countries at the same income level.[5] The adult literacy rate, an outcome of past cumulative investment in education, rose from 60 percent in 1960 to 74 percent in 1994 and to 85 percent in 1999. The average education attainment for the population aged 15+ years rose from less than 1 year in the 1950s to 4.3 years in 1975 and 6 years in 1999. In 2000, China was well on its way to achieve its Millennium Development Goal in education, 6.3 years of schooling being the average. Official data show a similar picture (case 6). This relatively more equitable access to education at the beginning of reforms represents a more equitable distribution of opportunities. However, the pace of progress has slowed since reform started and there have been increasing regional disparities in education attainment among urban and rural, coastal, and western regions. The difference between years of schooling for a child born in Beijing and a child born in a remote region could be as great as 8 years (Wang and Yao 2003).[6]

Although access to quality education is important in that it enhances people's capability to generate income, this is not enough to ensure increased productivity and thus reduced poverty. To be more productive, people need to be able to combine their human capital with other productive assets, such as land and equity capital, and with job opportunities in an open market. However, job opportunities are far from being equally accessible because of the household registration (*hukou*) system and restrictions on rural-urban migration, which will be discussed below.

Openness and Improved Investment Climate

At the same time that China was instituting rural reforms, it opened its trade regimes through unilateral trade liberalization, cutting tariffs and nontariff barriers, and introduced international competition in manufacturing sectors, leading to rapid growth in coastal regions. The average tariff rate was cut from nearly 50 percent in the 1980s to 36.3 percent in 1994, and to 16 percent in the 2000s, with the process being speeded up in the 1990s (Ianchovichina and Martin 2004). The number of trading companies grew 10 times, from 800 to 8,000.

After the success of the initial four SEZs, hundreds of cities and development zones were opened to foreign investment. The climate continued to improve, which led to an investment boom in several large growth centers along the eastern coast and to the creation of millions of nonfarm job opportunities for the poorest populations. Thanks to rising rural income and freedom of entry, millions of TVEs were established in the early 1980s, competing with the SOEs and eventually outgrowing them. The number of TVEs mushroomed from a few thousand in 1980 to 1.5 million in the 1990s. They employed more than 135 million rural workers in nonfarm employment in 1996 and maintain this level today(figure 3.2).[7]

Figure 3.2 Employment in TVEs, 1985–2003 (millions)

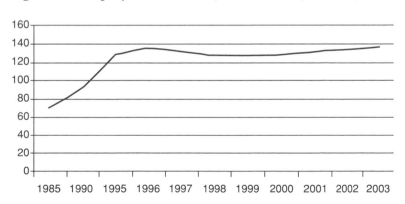

Source: China Statistical Yearbook, National Bureau of Statistics, various years.

Arguably, public spending and tax concessions imparted an urban and coastal bias to China's growth to an unwarranted degree,
leading to increased disparities across regions and a spatially uneven pattern of poverty reduction. Also, restrictions on migration
from rural to urban areas, albeit gradually relaxing, prevented the

---

Box 3.2 The China Southwest—Commitment and Participation in the Multisectoral Project for Poverty Reduction

Poverty results from diverse elements. Despite its ease of implementation and management, a single-sector approach to poverty reduction does not lead to enduring outcomes. Multisectoral projects also
have generally failed to live up to their potential. The China Southwest Poverty Reduction Project (SWPRP)—the first World Bank
Group–supported project in China to use an integrated multisectoral
rural development approach to attacking absolute poverty in an area
severely deficient in resources—has been spectacularly successful in
achieving its objectives. It is instructive, therefore, to examine the
factors behind the Southwest Project model.

SWPRP, implemented in 1995–2001 as part of the 8-7 Plan (see
box 3.1) in Guizhou and Yunnan provinces and the Guangxi autonomous region, covers 35 of China's poorest counties, with about
2.8 million primary beneficiaries. The project area is dominated by
the picturesque *karst* topography of irregular limestone mountains,
caverns, underground streams, and little arable land, which unfortunately makes for harsh conditions for people living in the rural areas.
The three principal objectives of the project were to tap the potential
of a multisectoral, participatory approach to poverty reduction targeted at the poor townships and villages; to develop a market-friend-
ly program to find employment for the rural poor in the rapidly
growing urban areas of China; and to upgrade poverty monitoring
at the national and local levels. The project had six components: (1)
social services, including education and health; (2) labor mobility;
(3) rural infrastructure; (4) development of both land and farmers;
(5) development of town and village enterprises; and (6) institution
building and poverty monitoring.

On completion, the project had a significantly favorable impact
on many dimensions, including income levels, agricultural output,
food security, access to infrastructure, and social indicators governing the overall well-being of the majority of the poor households in
the project area. By helping roughly 280,000 people secure off-farm

jobs, the labor mobility component of the project was notable in benefiting the extremely poor population in the project area and in having significant policy implications at the national level. The project was also found to have beneficial effects on women and on the environment.

The following are some of the key factors undergirding the success of the project:

- The top leadership of the country, including the president and the State Council, signaled their commitment to the project through letters and meetings, thus creating a political atmosphere for mutual coordination from and among governments and departments at various levels and for the smooth operation of the project.
- By design, the extensive participation of poor households in all phases—project selection, implementation, contribution of voluntary labor and matching funds, and training activities—was a fundamental characteristic of the initiative.
- From the outset, great emphasis was placed on capacity building, flexibility (with midcourse adjustments in project components and policy), transparency, and the incorporation of sustainability features (especially follow-up project management).

In terms of poverty reduction impact, the project has demonstrated new approaches to labor mobility, village development planning, and poverty monitoring. The key lessons of the project have now become part of China's national poverty reduction policy and have been extended to poor counties throughout the country. The Southwest Project model has been adopted for a number of World Bank–assisted poverty relief efforts in China and elsewhere—for example, the Northern Mountains Poverty Reduction Project in Vietnam.

benefits of globalization from being shared more widely by the rural poor. Several studies documented the significant wage gaps between rural and urban workers with comparable background and ability (Zhao 1999; Sicular and Zhao 2004). China has started to come to grips with this issue in a systematic manner, as indicated by the introduction of a labor mobility component in the Southwest Poverty Reduction Project (case 2). It may be noted, however, that the labor mobility component led to positive outcomes because of the openness and growth in the eastern coastal section of China.[8] Nationally, more than 100 million rural migrant workers already are working in urban areas and sending remittances worth more than RMB (renminbi) 10 billion to their rural homes. This has started to change the entire landscape of urban and rural communities.

The How of Poverty Reduction

China approached the huge challenge of reform and development pragmatically and with humility. The initial motivation for opening up was to learn from the outside world and to catch up with the rapid development in the East Asian countries. This section aims to provide a general framework of learning and knowledge acquisition, emphasizing *who* was empowered and mobilized to learn and experiment, *what* incentives motivated them, *from whom* and *where* they learned, and *how* an open and enabling environment has been conducive to learning and innovation. The case studies will be used as examples to support these ideas.

A Framework of Learning

Learning or acquisition of knowledge is determined by both demand and supply factors, and labor market incentives and macroeconomic environment play an important role, according to the human capital production model. An economic agent, be it an individual or a firm, is motivated to learn if the expected rate of return from learning is higher than the financial cost and opportunity cost of time spent in learning, after controlling for endowments and other external factors. The expected rates of return would then be affected by the macroeconomic environment and labor market conditions of a country. The supply side of learning opportunities is determined by the public and private provision, freedom of entry, access to information/technology, regulatory or ideological barriers, as well as the macroeconomic condition—whether the country is open to trade, investment, and ideas. Human capital cannot be produced—capacity will not be enhanced—without the intersection of both demand and supply side factors (Kaufmann and Wang 1996).

In the initial stage of the reforms there were long debates on what belongs to socialism and what does not belong. However, ideological barriers were replaced by pragmatism as the earlier outcomes of rural reforms and opening up demonstrated that "trial and error" is a good approach. A reflection of the pragmatism is the combination of a centralized political structure and the decentralization and competition between localities and subnational governments that prevails in China. The senior Chinese leader

Deng Xiaoping said, "No matter black or white, the cat who can catch the mouse is a good cat." This gave the green light for trial and experiment regardless of ideological barriers. Local governments, individuals, and firms were empowered to learn, experiment, and innovate. Risk taking was encouraged and innovative approaches deemed successful were rewarded.

Decentralization of Authority

In 1979 China started the process of decentralization, which devolved government authority from central to local levels, including provinces, prefectures, counties, townships, and villages. The devolution of authority was accompanied by fiscal incentives, and local governments were encouraged to adopt innovative approaches to reforms and were rewarded for promoting the development of their local economies. At the beginning of the 1980s, a fiscal contract system replaced the system of unified revenue collection and unified spending. Under this fiscal contract system, local governments can enter into long-term fiscal contracts with higher-level governments and retain some of the incremental revenues at the margin. This system, albeit imperfect and eventually replaced by a tax assignment system in 1994, provided a huge incentive for local governments to develop local economies through learning, trying new ideas, and opening to foreign trade and attracting foreign investment. The case study on the Sunan and Wenzhou models illustrates clearly the role of local government in learning and experimentation (box 3.3).

The balance between central government and the local governments has thus been a major reason for the ability of China to implement its programs and projects for poverty reduction. The central government sets policies and decides on priorities for allocation of government funds, but programs and projects are implemented by the local governments. For example, each of the nearly 2,000 counties has its own specialist bureaus in agriculture, water, health, education, and poverty reduction. The local government leaders are rotated periodically; this ensures impartiality, avoids favoritism, and facilitates learning across provinces and localities.

This structure of government has provided a sound framework for the realization of the Southwest Poverty Reduction Project (case 2) and the Loess Plateau Watershed Rehabilitation Project (case 3). They were implemented within the existing system with Leading Group for Poverty Reduction and Project Management Offices (PMOs) at each level of government, and a Central PMO at the central government level. The work at each level was checked and verified by the next level of government to ensure project quality and the accuracy in claims for disbursement. The case studies on water supply (case 4), rural roads (case 5), and education (case 6) show a similar approach to project management.

Box 3.3 Institutional Innovation, Improvement of Investment Environment, and Poverty Reduction— Models of Sunan and Wenzhou

This case study describes the different paths taken by two regions engaging in institutional innovation through township and village enterprises in their journey from abject poverty to prosperity. The Sunan region has a population of approximately 14 million people, and includes the cities of Suzhou, Wuxi, and Changzhou and their surrounding areas in the Yangtze River Delta. Sunan has been China's industrial base since the 19th century. In the 1960s and 1970s, however, its economy stagnated because rural people were not allowed to develop industry or move to cities. By the late 1970s, farmers' net annual income per capita was only RMB204 and had not changed in the previous 20 years. When the central government gave opportunities to develop rural industry, Sunan was quick to respond. The strategy was to develop collective-owned TVEs in labor-intensive processing industries. The new collective firms grew rapidly because of the comparative advantages of a high-quality labor force, openness to trade and investment, and the local governments' social mobilizing power. Sunan now attracts the largest share of foreign direct investment in China. Its rural per capita annual net income, at RMB5,657 in 2001, has grown to more than twice the national average, and most of that growth is attributable to the TVE-based economic development model.

Wenzhou, in the south of Zhejiang Province, has a population of 6 million. With little state investment in the three decades before 1979, the region was traditionally known for its poverty, with farmers' annual net income per capita (RMB113) lower than that in 1952 in real terms. But Wenzhou's access to the sea and a fine natural harbor had given rise to a well-developed handcraft industry and to commerce. The Wenzhou people developed an unorthodox local culture that emphasized both trade and commerce and risk taking in traditional agriculture. Using their heritage of aggressive risk taking, the Wenzhou people developed private industrial and commercial businesses and gradually formed specialized production bases. They were helped by the local government, which protected individual property rights, ensured the sound operation of market forces, and provided a favorable social atmosphere for privately owned business. By 1986 a third of Wenzhou's farm households were earning more than RMB4,000, and by 2001 Wenzhou's rural net per capita income was RMB4,680.

A virtuous cycle of learning and experimentation enabled Sunan and Wenzhou to achieve success relatively quickly. In Sunan this cycle was driven by government; in Wenzhou the dissemination of experience has been a spontaneous, self-organized process driven upward from the grassroots.

The case of Shanghai helping Yunnan (case 8) is unique in the sense that it featured learning across regions as the driving force of growth and poverty reduction. This program was initiated by the local governments. Shanghai, being the largest manufacturing and commercial center in China, is endowed with a good human capital base, a large export sector and manufacturing center, and rapidly increasing municipal fiscal revenue. Shanghai's official aid program focused on investing in the human capital of the poor and providing technical assistance and facilitating capacity building through a staff exchange program with Yunnan province. This facilitated learning across different regions and supplemented for the inadequacy in leadership and capacity in the provincial government of Yunnan.

Government officials are evaluated on the basis of their performance indicators, which are often linked to GDP growth and other indicators of the local economy. These officials are sometimes promoted vertically as a reward for innovation and excellent performance in developing the local economies. In Sunan (case 7), an exemplary model of attracting FDI with export-oriented growth, several heads of Suzhou City have been subsequently promoted to the central and provincial governments.

Introduction of Free Market Elements

Under some conditions, learning and self-discovery are also enhanced by freedom of entry and market competition. China introduced freedom of entry and market competition early on (in the 1980s) in the reform process, while delaying the privatization process. Essentially this approach allowed new enterprises and institutions to grow and compete with existing state enterprises, and gradually imposed a hard budget constraint on the SOEs.

Along with unilateral trade liberalization and China's accession to the WTO, market competition became relentless.[9] A "change-or-die" mentality was established and widely accepted, which forced the state enterprises to restructure themselves through mergers and acquisition or through corporatization. Li Rongrong, who heads the powerful State Asset Commission, told the SOEs, "If you cannot be one of the top three firms in your sector, be prepared to be acquired by some other firm." This explained why large state enterprises became more eager to restructure themselves when they expected to face fierce international competition after China's WTO accession.[10] For China's millions of entrepreneurs, freedom of entry and competition are great opportunities for self-discovery in finding their market niche. The change-or-die approach is as true for the state or private firms as it is for individual citizens and local governments.

With increased global integration, China's labor market has become more flexible and skill premium has been rising, providing higher rates of returns to skilled workers, high-tech gurus, and managerial talents. Unskilled workers faced with the pressure of unemployment are eager to seize opportunities for on-the-job training or higher degrees. Given a strong incentive and pressure, there has been a rapid rise in the education level of China's regional leaders. As U.S. scholar Cheng Li (2003, p. 3) observed, in 1982 only 20 percent of China's provincial leaders had attended college. In 2002 this number was 98 percent. The number with postgraduate degrees grew from 12.9 percent in 2001 to 29 percent in 2003. Among the younger leaders, those "fourth-generation" leaders under age 54, two-thirds hold master's or PhD degrees.

With openness to foreign capital inflows, local governments are competing with each other to attract foreign direct investment. Freedom of entry and market competition also allowed local government to find their local comparative advantages. Some local government allowed market forces to motivate the development of private enterprises (case 7, the Wenzhou model); other governments used a more interventionist approach in taking a leadership role to attract foreign investments.

Many different models were competing with each other, and the best performance was rewarded. In recent years, local governments have started to compete to improve the investment climate, based on international investment climate surveys (Dollar and others 2002). Transparency and freedom of media also have helped hold local governments accountable for their actions. Reports on indicators of air pollution and environmental degradation have provided pressure for improving government performance.

Partnership with External Agencies

At its best, the relationship between developing countries and international and bilateral development agencies is one of partnership in a learning process. Learning has often been a two-way street, with, for example, the World Bank learning from the country client, and the country client learning from the World Bank. Two cases illustrate this point that learning is mutual. First, in the Loess Plateau Watershed Rehabilitation Project, the World Bank's task manager learned about the utility of grazing bans from local indigenous people. He went on a field visit to see what had worked and found a small village that banned grazing. This ban was incorporated into the project design and expanded. The project led to such positive outcomes conducive to poverty reduction and environmental rehabilitation that the Chinese government provided an award to the task manager (box 3.4).

Second, in the Southwest Poverty Reduction Project, local governments in Guangxi Province initially had a county-targeting approach: They wanted to build manufacturing facilities in the counties and were not keen to target poor households. After long discussions and a field visit to the remote villages, the local leaders were finally convinced by the World Bank that targeting poor households was the way to go. In the design of the same project, the World Bank was willing to listen to the demands of the local indigenous people. A labor mobility component, which was to prove very effective, was added to the project later, upon receiving demands from surveys of local poor people who wanted to find job opportunities for their sons and daughters.

Learning and capacity building were featured in the 8-7 National Poverty Reduction Program (case 1). After the joint work on a poverty assessment report of 1992 and several international conferences and training workshops, China's poverty reduction strategy was heavily influenced by international best practices, shifting from targeting the poor counties to targeting the poor households as a complementary measure. The participatory approach was introduced to village-level poverty planning, allowing villagers to vote in selecting the subprojects they would like to have. Now, more than 140,000 villages have completed participatory village-level planning for poverty reduction investment projects.

Box 3.4 **The Loess Plateau Watershed Rehabilitation Project—Learning from the Beneficiaries**

How to break the vicious cycle of environmental deterioration and poverty and to realize nature-friendly development are pressing challenges in many parts of the world. The success of the Loess Plateau Watershed Rehabilitation Project offers valuable lessons on meeting the challenges. The Loess Plateau in China covers 640,000 square kilometers in the upper and middle parts of the drainage basin of the Yellow River. Unsustainable farming practices, combined with huge population pressure, have led to massive soil erosion, downstream flooding, and widespread poverty in the region. Earlier efforts at soil erosion control were unsuccessful. The current project did not aim solely at soil erosion control, nor solely at poverty reduction. It aimed at sustainable and coordinated social, economic, resource, and environmental development of small watersheds. It integrated harnessing of small watersheds with economic development and improvement of people's living standards.

The project had two parts: The first part was to conserve land, control sediment, and enhance farm income through terracing, afforestation, orchards, grass growing, construction of sediment control dams, and roads; the second part involved capacity building through training, scientific research, and technique promotion. The project planning and implementation involved developing detailed maps of current and projected land use, accomplished iteratively with the farmers' full participation. Sustainability was enhanced by giving farmers long-term contracts—a minimum of 30 years—for all land developed under the project.

The project has benefited more than 1.2 million farmers and changed their lives fundamentally. The population living under the poverty line in the project area has declined significantly as a result of the project and the government's other poverty alleviation measures. In addition, the project was successful in three respects: It replaced unsustainable crop cultivation on steep slopes with sustainable cultivation on high-quality, broad, flat terraces. It planted the slope lands with a variety of trees, shrubs, and grass to stabilize the land and produce fuel, timber, and fodder. It substantially reduced sediment runoff from slope lands and gullies. Moreover, because some 70 percent of the laborers on the farmland are women, the diversified income sources and the improvement of production efficiency have been particularly beneficial for the women.

Free grazing of goats and sheep has been a major cause of soil erosion on the plateau. A major breakthrough in the project was the decision to ban grazing—initially by the village committees in the project area, but eventually on a countywide basis by many counties. A grazing ban was not part of the original project, but rather the result of the demonstrated effect of villagers' voluntary actions. This has led to pen-feeding in place of free grazing and to the introduction of improved breeds of livestock. The policy is now being adopted widely beyond the project counties. Thus, we are witnessing a revolution in land and livestock management.

Monitoring and Evaluation

Better data collection, access to information, and transparency facilitate learning and evaluation. China has invested in transforming and upgrading its system of data generation and monitoring, with assistance from international financial organizations (Chen and Ravallion 1996). The National Statistical Bureau conducts household surveys that are publicly available and monitors progress in poverty reduction. Cross-country empirical analysis shows that countries with better information flows indeed have better-quality governance (Islam 2003).

Special efforts were made to improve monitoring systems and transparency in SWPRP (case 2). A computerized Farmers Monitor and Management System for the Comprehensive Poverty Reduction Project was developed to track and evaluate project benefits. In 1995, with World Bank support, the National Bureau of Statistics (NBS) and the Leading Group Office on Poverty Alleviation and Development (LGOPAD) jointly set up a poverty-monitoring and project impact evaluation system in the SWPRP area. From 1995 to 2001 the rural survey team of NBS conducted annual surveys, and independent evaluations were made on the poverty reduction performance in 35 project countries in three provinces. This has greatly increased the transparency and accountability of project officials.

More generally, incentives, merit, and accountability are being improved in China. Through institutional innovation, China is able to align the incentives for central, provincial, and local government officials with its development goals, and implement a merit system with accountability for civil servants. Officials are made responsible for the performance of the local economy and welfare of the people. There are reports that officials were forced to resign or were demoted for poor performance. From 1996 to 2003, more than 16,000 civil servants were fired and 30,000 resigned (Bolin 2005). This is a results-oriented system with clear and credible rewards and penalties that make the administrative system effective. Information within the system is transmitted quickly and policies can be implemented effectively.

External Environment

Creating and learning from an external environment that is open to and supportive of new ideas and innovation are crucial for poverty reduction. Table A3.1, the taxonomy of the eight case studies on China, indicates the unique features in learning and innovation, the driving factors in terms of conventional growth theory, as well as the degree of progress in scaling up for poverty reduction. From this table one can see that learning and innovation have been facilitated by openness to China's external environment:

- Openness to international trade and investment and new ideas have been key to learning and innovation, including willingness to try ideas that are "foreign," with less regard to ideological barriers; in other words, there is freedom of entry in accessing knowledge and high technology.
- Transparency has been introduced in many sectors and all aspect of life. There is a fierce competition not only among firms but also among regional and local governments. If a firm is not learning fast enough it cannot survive. If a local government is not learning from new ideas, its local economy will suffer and the officials' promotions will be affected.
- Risk taking has been encouraged during the reform process. Regional and local governments are empowered or encouraged to try their own methods. If they find a new way to answer urgent issues, they will be rewarded. One example is the "Zhucheng Model" of privatizing the small SOEs managed by local governments. These loss-making, inefficient, small state enterprises were big burdens on local government finances and governments were eager to sell them. The Zhucheng Model is a way of selling or privatizing the small state enterprises through management buy-out and other methods. When it was successful, former premier Zhu Rongji visited the site and confirmed this model as useful; the approach was scaled up nationally. However, there are many other failed attempts—a sign that risk taking has been encouraged.
- Learning with an open mind and due humility from small as well as large countries, from poor as well as high-income

countries, from successes as well as failures has also been encouraged. Examples of these are the adoption of the export promotion strategy of the East Asian small tigers, and the adoption of the participatory approach learned from other low-income countries. Microfinancing in Bangladesh informed China. Lessons from the East Asian financial crises in 1997 were intensively studied.

- Competition has been introduced in the selection of civil servants through entrance examination and merit and promotion systems. There is competitive selection for promotion, considering many criteria, including practical experience in one of the poor provinces. At the time of writing, 60 percent of the 6 million civil servants are selected and promoted through competition (Bolin 2005). The rotation of civil servants facilitates the spread of new ideas, as in the Shanghai helping Yunnan initiative, where many officials and managers were sent from Shanghai to Yunnan, bringing with them new ideas and practical experience from an advanced coastal region (case 8).

- Team building and training have been stressed because institutional capacity depends on teams. In Guangxi province under the SWPRP (case 2), the objectives were set to "establish a set of institutions and regulations, build a strong and capable work team, and lift a large population out of poverty." Project Management Offices/stations have been set up at several levels and a set of behavioral standards publicly posted. And the project organized training of 10,000 person-sessions. With a PMO team of 169 staff members in the counties, and 487 staff members in the townships, this means training opportunities of 10 to 15 sessions per person. Training is institutionalized and, nationally, some 2 million civil servants participate in training each year. Through training, new approaches and behavioral standards have been implemented. Without this tremendous effort to build a strong team and strong institutions, the objective of "lifting a big population out of poverty" can only be an empty promise.

Challenges for the Future

There are both positive and negative lessons from China's past experiences; some policies have worked and others failed. Old issues remain to be resolved as reflected by recent pro-poor policy reforms. In addition, China is facing new challenges in the new millennium. The pace of poverty reduction has slowed significantly and inequality has been rising rapidly (Qiu 2005). This section briefly reviews the old issues and new challenges, and the policy measures adopted recently to address them.

Old Issues and New Pro-Poor Reforms

China's new leadership recognized the critical importance of agriculture and rural (*san-nong*) issues, and proposed the new ideology of "putting people first" and building a "harmonious society with five balances." In an effort to build such a society, a series of new policy measures was adopted in 2005 to remove some urban-biased policies, and resolve some of the old issues. Four examples are provided here:

1. China has taxed farmers since the 1950s and these taxes are now considered regressive. In January 2005, the government of China announced that agriculture taxes will be reduced annually and be eliminated within five years. According to vice minister Liu Jian, LGOPAD, the 592 counties under the national poverty program will be exempted from the agricultural tax. In addition, many eastern provinces have reduced or eliminated agriculture taxes ahead of schedule.

2. The allocation of public expenditure does not adequately address the issue of poverty and regional disparity. Regional allocation of public expenditure had an urban bias and was pro-rich—rich regions got more public expenditure per person than the poor regions. This situation is gradually changing. A number of policy measures have been taken, including direct subsidies to farmers who grow grains, subsidies to farmers who use improved varieties, and a floor price for the purchase of important grain products. These measures have led to a sharp, 22 percent increase in the central government's fiscal expenditure on agriculture, rural residents, and rural areas (Gao 2005).

3. Fees and tuition for rural primary schools are relatively high compared with income levels, reflecting inadequate government financing for social services such as basic education in the rural areas. This year, the students from poor families in the 592 key poor counties will be exempted from book fees and extra fees during their compulsory education period. The residential students will get subsidies

for school living expenses. The effort to train young rural workers and help them move to nonagricultural sectors will be accelerated (Gao 2005).

4. Rural microcredit is inadequate. Until the late 1990s, for example, Wenzhou's nonstate or collective enterprises received no more than 7 percent of aggregate bank loans, even though they were generating more than 90 percent of GDP. Microcredit has not been very successful in China for many reasons; one is excessive intervention and subsidization by the government and state-owned banks. Useful lessons can be learned from other countries, such as Bangladesh.

New Challenges and Policies in Response

China is facing a number of new challenges in the 21st century. First, the pace of poverty reduction has slowed down significantly. The number of rural poor declined by 13.7 million annually during the 1980s, by 6.2 million in the 1990s, and by only 1.5 million in the new century. Second, income inequality continues to worsen and regional gaps have widened significantly. The income Gini index rose from 30 percent to 44 percent (without adjusting for cost-of-living differences) and from 28 percent to 39 percent with adjustment for these differences. Other challenges include managing scarce natural resources such as land, water, and energy; and the need to create jobs for landless rural residents, redundant workers, and migrant rural workers. Several new policies are being adopted to meet these challenges (based on Qiu 2005 and Gao 2005). The government plans to

- reform macroeconomic policies that are inconsistent with the target of poverty alleviation, including tax and transfer systems, and increase input into agricultural and rural development to continue promoting rural productivity growth and reduce rural poverty;
- strengthen public service provision in the rural areas by revamping rural health and education systems and reducing tuition and fees;
- transform the pattern of growth to focus more on people, job creation, productivity, and efficiency, developing urban centers to "pull and propel" the growth of rural and poor areas. Barriers for labor mobility and rural urban migration will be farther removed, and young farmers will be trained to facilitate their migration and find nonfarm jobs;

- adjust the poverty lines and incorporate the "low-income line" (*di shou ru*) as the new poverty line, addressing the issues related to people living under or around the low-income line, including the urban poor. For the existing "core groups" of poor people under the current extreme poverty line, mostly people living in remote mountainous areas, the sick, and the old and vulnerable groups, government will provide social relief rather than relying solely on "reducing poverty by economic development" (*kaifa fupin*); and
- invest further in capacity development for poverty alleviation, and in monitoring and evaluation. Several new initiatives are being carried out, including the Sunshine project, which promotes labor mobility among young rural workers. An International Poverty Reduction Center in China also was established recently to provide a platform for South-South peer learning and exchange experiences, and to promote training and capacity building in China as well as in neighboring countries.

Annex

Table A3.1 Taxonomy of Chinese Case Studies Focusing on Growth and Learning Aspects

Case title	Type	Period	Growth factors in production function	Degree of success	Degree of scalability in other settings	Strengths	Weaknesses	Learning and innovation main features
The 8-7 National Poverty Reduction Program	National program	1994–2000	Physical capital, human capital, and TFP	Successful but uneven progress	Conditional	Commitment; institutional innovation; two-way learning between client and donor; and learning by doing	Lack of clarity of goals; poor targeting in some cases; participatory approach is weak; human development aspects were weak	Introduced a new coordinating agency, LGOPAD, and new approaches in project design, fund allocation, and management; introduced targeting at household level; participatory approach in village planning, albeit at initial stages
The China Southwest Poverty Reduction Project	Targeted program	1995–2001	Physical capital, human capital, labor mobility, and TFP	Significant	High	Multisectoral, multiyear; participatory approach; targeting; commitment; capacity building; transparency	Insufficient definition of property rights; sustainability issues (repairs, medical cooperatives); pros and cons of some World Bank rules	Two-way learning in the project design stage; introduced targeting at the household level and participatory approach in village planning; capacity development (both project team and villagers) is part of the project; emphasized team build-

Continued

Table A3.1, Continued

Case title	Type	Period	Growth factors in production function	Degree of success	Degree of scalability in other settings	Strengths	Weaknesses	Learning and innovation main features
								ing, training, and accountability of PMO officials; flexibility in policy and project management; implemented a good system of data collection for monitoring and evaluation
The Loess Plateau Watershed Rehabilitation Project	World Bank project, natural capital management	1994–2002	Natural capital and TFP	Significant	High	Harmonization of goals; commitment; participatory approach; property rights; capacity building; monitoring	Water supply component is missing	Learning from villagers in the project design stage; introduced grazing ban (an indigenous approach) on a large scale; capacity building was part of project; introduced new products, approaches, and technology
Rural Water Supply and Sanitation in China	Four World Bank sectoral projects	1985–2005	Human capital	Significant	High	Participatory approach; cost recovery; commitment; coordination	Health and hygiene-education is not stressed	Introduced decentralized service delivery and total cost recovery (unique feature of this case); involved cross-sectoral collaboration

82

								to promote "three-in-one" approach, competitive hiring of water plan staff, and participatory management; implemented lifetime skill training approach for project staff and facilities operation
Infrastructure, Growth, and Poverty Reduction in China	World Bank project: road improvements for poverty alleviation	2001–2002	Physical capital	Significant	Conditional	Participatory approach; diverse sources of funds; sustainable (provision for maintenance)	Insufficient funding from higher levels of government; over-reliance on voluntary labor	China introduced the World Bank's modern project management approaches after 1980s (including international competitive bidding) and trained a group of highly professional project managers—this project is no exception
Universalizing Nine-Year Compulsory Education for Poverty Reduction in Rural China	National/sectoral program	1985–present	Human capital	Successful but uneven progress, education gaps are high	High	Commitment; mobilization; monitoring; involvement of NGOs and mass media	Inadequate funding; low private returns to primary education	Incorporated international best practices; professionalization; extensive piloting before expansion

Continued

Table A3.1, Continued

Case title	Type	Period	Growth factors in production function	Degree of success	Degree of scalability in other settings	Strengths	Weaknesses	Learning and innovation main features
Instititu-tional Innovation: Model of Sunan	Reional strategy	1984–present	Physical capital, human capital, and TFP	Significant	Conditional	Local government initiative and commitment; openness to trade and foreign investment; improved investment climate; social security for both urban and rural areas	Local government involved in picking winners, being both "a referee and an athlete"; over-interventionist approach; unclear property rights in some cases	Continuous process of institutional innovation and adaptation; collective enterprises initiated and supported/run by local governments; opening to foreign trade and investment led to successful scaling up and technological upgrading; significant capacity and skill enhancement resulted from opening up to foreign technology and market competition
Institu-tional Innovation: Model of Wenzhou	Regional strategy	Early 1980s–present	Physical capital, human capital, and TFP	Significant	High	Private initiative within favorable environment created by local government; property rights are clearly defined	Initially low level of technology and small scale; upgrading issue; governance and regulatory issues (against low-quality products and intellectual property rights infringement)	Initiated by private entrepreneurs; encouraged and facilitated by local government via hands-off approach; extensive experimentation and piloting before scaling up;

The East Helping the West Reduce Poverty: Shanghai Helping Yunnan	Subnational government initiative to supplement national strategy for poverty reduction	1996, ongoing	Physical capital, human capital, and TFP	Adequate	Limited	Valuable adjunct to other plans and projects; enhances available resources; brings many different social layers into play	Low level of participation by the poor in decisions; needs efficient administration to be effective	Designed according to the "flying geese" hypothesis, the program aimed to allow learning from the successes of the coastal regions; one of the key components is sending civil servants, officials, and managers from Shanghai to Yunnan to enhance capacity in poor regions; investment in education and skill building are key components

significant capacity enhancement through opening to foreign investment and international market competition

Source: Compiled by author based on case studies.

Table A3.2 Institutional Innovations That Were Crucial for Poverty Reduction: The Sequence of Introducing New Institutions

Institutional innovation	Year started and scaled up	Scaling up accomplished	Degree of complexity in learning	Results/outcome in brief
Initial stage of reforms (1978–1993): indigenous institutions				
The Household Responsibility System in the rural areas	1978–1983	From a village in Anhui, to nationwide in 1983	1	Provided incentives for farmers; rural productivity rose rapidly
The Special Economic Zones, high-tech development zones, dual approach in regional development	1978–present	From 4 in 1978–1980, to 12 coastal cities, and to hundreds of special and high-tech zones	2	Facilitated experimentation and learning from own experiences
Township and village enterprises	1980s	Mushroomed; employed 135 million workers	3	Empowered entrepreneurs; promoted private sector development later
Fiscal decentralization: Chinese style (pre-1994 reforms) and tax assignment system after 1994	1980–1990	Experimentation followed by a top-down nationwide scaling up	4	Empowered local governments and motivated them for experiments
International competitive bidding and other project management approaches introduced and implemented	1980s–present	Scaled up through training, learning by doing, and learning by implementing projects	5	Improved the efficiency in project implementation and impacts

Second stage of reforms (1994–present): establishing modern/best-practice institutions

Modern corporations/share-holding companies have replaced state-owned enterprises, and TVEs were privatized	1990–present	Zhucheng Model has been scaled up nationwide	10	Reform is ongoing
Deeper integration with the global economy; as China joins WTO, hundreds of laws are redrafted to comply with the WTO principles	1990–present	Top-down implementation of WTO-consistent laws and regulations at the national level	10	Reform is ongoing; continued learning by doing and learning by exporting; and learning from international best practices
Unfinished reforms: financial sector reforms, for example, in the banking sector	1990–present	Introduced domestic competition first, followed by foreign entry; more needs to be done	20 (more complex)	Ongoing

Notes

1. The official poverty line is low, at 300 RMB yuan at 1990 price, since China started at a low income level in 1978. In 2004 the poverty line rose to 668 RMB yuan, or $0.78 at official exchange rate (NBS 2005). This line is used here to have the longest time series data, from 1978 to 2004.

2. The case studies cited in this chapter are the following: *case 1*—W. Sangui, L. Zhou, and R. Yanshun, China's 8-7 National Poverty Reduction Program—The National Strategy and Its Impact; *case 2*—W. Guobao, Q. Yang, and C. Huang, Southwest Poverty Reduction Project: A Multisectoral Approach; *case 3*—C. Shaojun, W. Yue, and W. Yije, Loess Plateau Watershed Rehabilitation Project; *case 4*—M. Shuchen, T. Yong, and L. Jiayi, Rural Water Supply and Sanitation in China; *case 5*—D. Yan and F. Hua, Infrastructure Growth and Poverty Reduction in China; *case 6*—Z. Tiedao, Z. Minxia, Z. Xueqin, Z. Xi, and W. Yan, Universalizing Nine-Year Compulsory Education for Poverty Reduction in Rural China; *case 7*—Y. Peng, S. Boyuan, and Z. Min, Institutional Transition, Improvement of Investment Environment, and Poverty Reduction in Sunan and Wenzhou; *case 8*—X. Zuo, H. Quan, T. Wang, and G. Shen, The East Helping the West to Reduce Poverty—Shanghai Helping Yunnan.

3. This focus is chosen because, whereas China's circumstances are in many ways quite unique in the developing world and many approaches adopted by China are country specific and not replicable, the approach of learning and experimentation for innovation is replicable across countries.

4. Qian (2000) drew the following conclusions: that a country can achieve rapid growth if it adopts sensible, albeit imperfect, institutions; that incentives and hard budget constraints should be introduced not just for firms but also for governments; and that it is possible and politically desirable to implement reforms without creating losers. China's incremental reform using a dual-track approach to liberalization is conducive to maintaining a stable growth path and avoids creating many losers—the new poor—during the historical transition to a market economy (see the third section of this chapter).

5. Sen (1992, p. 126) noted, "In the case of China, the big surge in life expectancy and decline in mortality rates took place before the economic reforms of 1979, and occurred actually in a period of very moderate economic growth."

6. In some not-so-poor regions in the western part of China, primary enrollment varies from village to village, and the drop-out rate remains high. Inequality in education attainment is staggering. The education Gini index, an indicator of inequality in education, declined in China from 0.55

in 1975 to 0.38 in 2000, which is still high compared with Korea's 0.19 (Thomas, Wang, and Fan 2001).

7. As shown by the case on Wenzhou and Sunan (case 7), these new enterprises initially did not have a clearly defined property right—some were collectively owned and others were later restructured into private enterprises. They provided higher and diverse income to rural households and directly helped them out of poverty. In the late 1990s, some of the TVEs were restructured into private firms, partnerships, or corporations.

8. During the field visit to Dongguan County in Guangdong, participants were told that 14,000 foreign enterprises were operating, employing 5 million migrant workers. Among them, 100,000 laborers came from Guangxi Hechi City to Dongguan under the labor mobility component, with remittances of around RMB300 million.

9. John Sutton (2005) vividly presented a case where globalization and competition have forced firms to compete through learning and capacity building, without which the firms will die.

10. Consequent to WTO accession, there is likely to be a slight decline in rural wages and incomes. The resulting adverse effect on poverty is likely to be small and it can be addressed by measures such as improving rural technology and infrastructure, expanding educational opportunities in rural areas, and reducing the barriers to migration out of the rural sector. On the other hand, accession has the potential for a favorable impact in the rural economy over the longer term. As a key member of the WTO, China can press for reduction of the barriers against its agricultural exports. The barriers facing China's exports of agricultural products are at least four times as high as those facing its nonagricultural exports (Martin 2001).

Bibliography

Ahmed, Etisham, and Yan Wang. 1991. "Inequality and Poverty in China: Institutional Change and Public Policy, 1978–1988." *World Bank Economic Review* 5 (2): 231–57.

Bolin, Zhang. 2005. "Speech by the Minister of Personnel." Presented at the China Reform Summit: Promoting Economic Restructuring by Focusing on Administrative Reform, Beijing, July 12–13, 2005.

Bourguignon, Francois, and C. Morrison. 1998. "Inequality and Development: The Role of Dualism." *Journal of Development Economics* 57 (2): 233–57.

Cao, Yuanzheng, Yingyi Qiao, and Barry R. Weingast. 1999. "From Federalism Chinese Style to Privatization, Chinese Style." *Economics of Transition* 7 (1): 103–31.

Chen, Shaohua, and Martin Ravallion. 2003. "Hidden Impact: Ex Post Evaluation of an Anti-Poverty Program." Policy Research Working Paper 3049, World Bank, Washington, DC.

———. 1996. "Data in Transition: Assessing Rural Living Standards in Southern China." *China Economic Review* 7: 23–56.

Chen, Shaohua, and Yan Wang. 2001. "China's Growth and Poverty Reduction: Trends between 1990 and 1999." Policy Research Working Paper 2651, World Bank, Washington, DC.

Dollar, David, Mary Hallward-Driemeier, Anqing Shi, Scott Wallsten, Shuilin Wang, and Lixin Colin Xu. 2002. *Improving the Investment Climate in China.* Washington DC: World Bank.

Dollar, David, and Aart Kraay. 2002. "Growth Is Good for the Poor." *Journal of Economic Growth* 7 (3): 195–225.

Gao, Hongbin. 2005. "Opening Speech on Behalf of LGOPAD." Conference on Pro-Poor Growth and Scaling Up Poverty Reduction," Beijing, May 18–19, 2005.

Hausmann, Ricardo, and Dani Rodrik. 2002. "Economic Development as Self-Discovery." Working Paper 8952, National Bureau of Economic Research, Cambridge, MA.

Ianchovichina, Elena, and Will Martin. 2004. "Impacts of China's Accession to the WTO." *World Bank Economic Review* 18 (1): 3–28.

Islam, Roumeen. 2003. "Do More Transparent Governments Govern Better?" Policy Research Working Paper 3077, World Bank, Washington, DC.

Kaufmann, Daniel, and Yan Wang. 1996. "Macroeconomic Policies and Project Performance in the Social Sector: A Model of Human Capital Production and Evidence from LDCs." *World Development* 23 (5): 751–65.

Krugman, Paul. 1994. "The Myth of Asia's Miracle." *Foreign Affairs* 73 (December): 63–78.

Li, Cheng. 2003. "Education and Professional Backgrounds of Current Provincial Leaders." *China Leadership Monitor* 8.

Li, David D. 1998. "Changing Incentives of the Chinese Bureaucracy." *American Economic Review* 88 (2): 393–97.

Lin, Justin Yifu. 1992. "Rural Reforms and Agricultural Growth in China." *American Economic Review* 82: 34–51.

Lin, Justin Yifu, Fan Cai, and Zhou Li. 1996. *The China Miracle: Development Strategy and Economic Reform.* Hong Kong: Chinese University Press.

Liu, Jian. 2005. "Speech on Behalf of LGOPAD." Conference on Pro-Poor Growth and Scaling Up Poverty Reduction," Beijing, May 18–19, 2005.

Martin, Will. 2001. "Implications of Reform and WTO Accession for China's Agricultural Policies." *Economics of Transition* 9 (3): 717–42.

NBS (National Bureau of Statistics). 2005. "Communiqué on 2004 Rural Poverty Monitoring of China." Beijing.

———. Various years. *China Statistical Yearbook*. Beijing.

Qian, Yingyi. 2000. "The Institutional Foundations of China's Market Transition." In *Annual Bank Conference on Development Economics 1999*, ed. Boris Pleskovic and Joseph Stiglitz, 377–98. Washington, DC: World Bank, .

Qian, Yingyi, and Barry R. Weingast. 1997. "Federalism as a Commitment to Preserving Market Incentives." *Journal of Economic Perspectives* 11 (4): 83–92.

Qiu, Xiaohua. 2005. Speech of the Vice Commissioner, National Bureau of Statistics. Conference on Pro-Poor Growth and Scaling Up Poverty Reduction, Beijing, May 18–19, 2005.

Ravallion, Martin. 2005. "Externalities in Rural Development: Evidence for China." In *Spatial Inequality and Development,* ed. Ravi Kanbur and Tony Venables. Oxford: Oxford University Press.

Ravallion, Martin, and Shaohua Chen. 2004. "China's Uneven Progress against Poverty." Development Economics Research Group, World Bank, Washington, DC.

———. 2001. "Measuring Pro-Poor Growth." Policy Research Working Paper 2666, World Bank, Washington, DC.

Sen, Amartya K. 1992. *Inequality Reexamined*. Cambridge: Harvard University Press.

———. 1980. "Equality of What?" In *Tanner Lectures on Human Values,* vol. I, ed. S. McMurrin. Cambridge: Cambridge University Press.

Sicular, Terry, and Yaohui Zhao. 2004. "Earnings and Labor Mobility in Rural China: Implications for China's Accession to the WTO." In *China and WTO: Accession, Policy Reform, and Poverty Strategies,* ed. D. Bhattasali, S. Li, and W. Martin. Washington, DC: World Bank.

Sutton, John. 2005. "Competing in Capabilities: An Informal Overview." First Development Economics Lectures, Development Economics Vice Presidency, World Bank, Washington, DC.

Thomas, Vinod, Yan Wang, and Xibo Fan. 2001. "Measuring Education Inequality: Gini Coefficients of Education." Policy Research Working Paper 2525, World Bank, Washington, DC.

Wang, Yan. 2000. "Improving the Distribution of Opportunities." In *The Quality of Growth,* eds. Vinod Thomas and others. New York: Oxford University Press.

Wang, Yan, and Yudong Yao. 2003. "China's Sources of Growth: Incorporating Human Capital Accumulation, 1953–1999." *China Economic Review* 14: 32–52.

World Bank. 2005a. *Economic Growth in the 1990s.* Washington, DC: World Bank.

———— 2005b. *World Development Report on Equity and Development.* Washington, DC: World Bank.

————. 2003. "China: Promoting Growth with Equity: Country Economic Memorandum." Report 24169-CHA, October, World Bank, Washington, DC.

————. 2000. *World Development Report: Attacking Poverty.* Washington, DC: World Bank.

————. 1997. *China 2020: Sharing Rising Income.* Washington, DC: World Bank.

Yang, Dennis Tao. 1994. "Urban-Biased Policies and Rising Income Inequality in China." *American Economic Review* 89: 306–10.

Young, Alwyn. 2000. "Gold into Base Metals: Productivity Growth in the People's Republic of China during the Reform Periods." Working Paper 7856, National Bureau of Economic Research, Cambridge, MA.

Yusuf, Shahid. 2003. "Innovative East Asia—The Future of Growth." Washington, DC: World Bank.

Zhao, Yaohui. 1999. "Labor Migration and Earnings Differences: The Case of Rural China." *Economic Development and Cultural Change* 47 (4): 767-82.

4

Thematic Analysis

Kim Cuenco, Roberto Dañino, Waleed Malik, Anne Ritchie, Lisa Taber, Egbe Osifo-Dawodu, Gift Manase, and Karen Lashman

INFRASTRUCTURE

The impact of infrastructure on growth and poverty reduction is widely documented. Overall, the literature suggests that transport, telecommunications, and electricity are very important for growth and poverty reduction, whereas rural roads, water, and sanitation are critical for improving the living standards of the very poorest people.[1]

The Shanghai infrastructure examples and the ongoing reform initiatives to which they refer provide a broad base for developing a strategy to tackle the increasingly complex challenges in the in-

The five thematic sections of this chapter were written by these authors: infrastructure, Kim Cuenco; judicial reform, Roberto Dañino and Waleed Malik; microfinance, Anne Ritchie and Lisa Taber; health, Egbe Osifo-Dawodu and Gift Manase; and education, Karen Lashman.

frastructure sector—to further the mutually reinforcing objectives of growth and poverty reduction. This section is based on 12 case studies. These cases are varied, ranging from 5 cases covering broad infrastructure strategies and policies, 3 on access to water, 2 on transportation, and 2 on integrated urban development. The lessons on scaling up poverty reduction through infrastructure investments are drawn from this set of cases.[2]

The specific impact of infrastructure on poverty has been studied in a number of ways. Infrastructure can lead to a real increase in real incomes of the poorest people. It also can improve their access to education and health services.[3] The widest definition of poverty focuses on how infrastructure enhances social inclusion, human capabilities, and freedom. One finding from these studies is that increases in infrastructure investments do not always translate into greater access by the poor to basic services and improved quality of life. Studies have shown that although the broad-based impact on poverty may often be positive, the local socioeconomic effects from infrastructure development sometimes can be negative unless deliberately mitigated (hydropower projects, for example).

Focusing on Inclusive Infrastructure Development

Providing safe, reliable, and cost-effective infrastructure services is an important contributor to raising living standards and improving the quality of life. Nevertheless, increasing infrastructure investment and ensuring that the benefits of those interventions are shared by the poorest people have remained daunting challenges for many countries. The case studies illustrate some key lessons for ensuring that the outcomes of infrastructure interventions address their welfare objectives.

The Morocco Rural Roads Project demonstrates two key factors that have enabled the project to achieve a bigger impact on poverty reduction—adopting a focus on outcomes (accessibility) and promoting local government participation. The effect of these factors on central government processes has led to scaling up the project at the country level. During the project conception, the government made the strategic decision to focus on accessibility rather than physical outputs to ensure that road services benefit the less-accessible populations, which normally include a higher proportion of the poorest people. A key factor that contributed to the implementation of this approach was the active participation of lo-

cal governments in the planning process, even as the responsibility
for developing and implementing the program remained vested
with the national highway agency. This participatory process was
strengthened by the financial contribution made to the roads program by local governments at various levels. This process will be
further strengthened in the follow-up project, which envisages a
stronger and more focused contribution to the improvement and
maintenance of rural roads at the local level. At the same time, the
government's emphasis on improving accessibility to rural infrastructure has influenced the national highway agency to change its
focus from physical targets to targets based on the number of people who will benefit from improved accessibility to reliable roads.

A key lesson to take away from this study is that infrastructure
interventions can go beyond the sector because the spillover of investments in one sector, such as roads, is often broad and touches
on a variety of sectors and services. Although these effects can be
predicted, others are more difficult to anticipate and are dependent
on local conditions. Nevertheless, these unintended consequences
can present a great opportunity to exploit the positive externalities
that come with investments in one sector and expand the coverage
of the benefits to other related services.[4]

Piloting and Risk Taking

Keeping poverty reduction as a central goal may involve an element of piloting. During the piloting phase, a model is tested to see
if it can be replicated on a larger scale. Often the introduction of a
new way of doing things involves an element of risk taking, experimentation, and pilot testing. To trigger impact on poverty reduction, the lessons from this phase can be embedded in a national
program. In Ghana, the rural water and sanitation sector was
transformed over the last decade from a centralized supply-driven
model to a system in which communities operate and maintain systems, and the private sector provides the goods and services. As the
study relates, the reform started with a dialogue among major
stakeholders, and was then implemented in several large pilot projects. The lessons from the pilots were eventually incorporated into
a national program.

Risk taking can pave the way. In India, where investment in infrastructure is considered a high-risk venture for the private sector,
the state government of Tamil Nadu broke new ground by launching several innovative private sector infrastructure projects in an

attempt to establish the viability of private sector participation in an otherwise risk-averse, public sector–dominated environment. The state established three important umbrella institutions in partnership with the private sector: the Tamil Nadu Water Investment Company; the Tamil Nadu Urban Infrastructure Financial Services, Ltd.; and the Tamil Nadu Road Development Company. Each has been innovatively structured with broad mandates on the design and development of projects with private sector participation.

The Asian Development Bank has developed criteria for ensuring that infrastructure development speaks to the needs of the poorest populations; these criteria are summed up in box 4.1.

Scaling Up across Different Dimensions

Scaling up through infrastructure intervention has different dimensions. This section will look at how the effects can be *accelerated* with the right economic and political conditions in place, such as occurred in China and Vietnam. There is also a *spatial* dimension, as demonstrated in the citywide slum upgrading program in Rio de Janeiro and in regional infrastructure projects supported by the Asian Development Bank in the Greater Mekong Subregion. The third dimension is illustrated by the City-to-City Challenge in which *municipality-to-municipality networking* on poverty-oriented programs provides a potentially powerful form of cooperation for disseminating good practice, sharing knowledge, and advocating for cities.

Scaling Up through Broad-based Growth

Countries such as Vietnam and China have succeeded in dramatically reducing poverty by sustaining the pace of accelerated growth, combined with deliberate policy and institutional reforms to stimulate growth while building human capacity. Investment in infrastructure combined with complementary poverty reduction interventions has been an essential ingredient in the design of this development strategy. To illustrate, during the last decade Vietnam's economy grew at an annual average rate of 7.6 percent, one of the fastest in the world. This growth has been remarkably pro-poor, lifting about 20 million people out of poverty in less than a decade. Infrastructure investment has been the main engine for poverty reduction, complemented by targeted poverty reduction programs.

Box 4.1 ADB—Lessons from Infrastructure Projects

Under favorable circumstances, infrastructure projects can significantly assist in reducing poverty. Evaluation studies by the ADB in the road and transport sectors have identified the following key drivers for improved poverty effects from infrastructure projects:

1. *Commitment to pro-poor development:* In countries with pro-poor policies and programs, better infrastructure led to expansion of economic and social development opportunities and poor people were often able to take advantage of the opportunities both directly and indirectly. Without such a pro-poor policy commitment, the infrastructure created might not have affected as much the lives of the poor.

2. *Complementary infrastructure pricing and service policies:* Use of cross-subsidies, support for initial connection fees for the poor to ensure access, and varying tariff bands are examples of policies that can help crystallize the poverty reduction spillovers of infrastructure investments. In the absence of appropriate policies, there is a risk of resources being hijacked by nonpoor and vested interests. Similarly, affordable transport tariffs can make improved road infrastructure accessible to the poorest people if a competitive environment is fostered in the transport services.

3. *Open and competitive institutional setting:* Infrastructure services fare better in the context of openness and competition, which foster a good market environment leading to increased production, trade, and growth. An important driving factor in infrastructure provision in the regional context, as evidenced in the Greater Mekong Subregion, has been the strong commitment to improved functioning of markets and increased trade and investments for fostering growth.

Large-scale regional transportation projects have played a critical role in creating links between growth centers and their surrounding rural areas. At the same time, investments in water, sanitation, and transport, in particular, have had a large positive effect on poverty reduction at the provincial level.

Similarly, China invested heavily in transportation to provide access to markets, facilitate domestic market integration, lower the cost of production and transportation, and allow the country to compete internationally. Besides driving growth, this investment has helped reduce poverty by increasing access to services and economic opportunities. As the returns to infrastructure investment decline over time, however, China will have to consider a broader strategy to sustain its economic growth and poverty reduction programs.

Scaling Up in Space and Time

Counted among the best-known stories in urban improvement programs in Latin America, the Favela Bairro program is considered a reference for slum upgrading projects. The achievements of the project can be attributed in large part to its integrated approach, both in terms of investments and interventions, combined with the use of transparent selection criteria and participatory implementation processes. Since its implementation, the standard of living of residents within these informal settlements has improved; health conditions have been enhanced; the value of real estate has increased; and poverty-related risks among the most vulnerable groups have been reduced. Factors crucial to the program's accomplishments include efficient and sound financial and managerial controls, use of transparent selection criteria, a high degree of community involvement, and clear communication of the benefits of the program to the community. The Favela Bairro program launched a scaling up model in Brazil that has drawn interest from other countries, such as Argentina, Bolivia, Ecuador, and Uruguay, which have begun similar initiatives. Other programs within Brazil were influenced by the design of this program. The Favela Bairro study demonstrates the importance of adopting an integrated approach that combined both physical and social improvements with a high level of community participation. Single-sector solutions do not solve complex urban problems.[5]

Increasing inequality between rural and urban areas is also raising new infrastructure challenges, and rapid urbanization is placing significant strain on urban infrastructure and the capacity of urban managers to keep up with demand. New pockets of poverty are emerging in peri-urban settlements. Sustaining and expanding the welfare effects of infrastructure investments will require consideration of the spatial dimension of poverty and a prioritization of investments, taking into account limitations in resources. This will involve trade-offs that will need to be carefully considered. One of the key lessons that cut across the different cases is the need to provide a framework where decisions regarding the prioritization and sequencing of interventions can be made.

Scaling Up across Regions

Although infrastructure support often has been provided in the national or local context, regional initiatives in infrastructure have enabled many countries to reduce poverty on a larger scale by exploiting cross-border economies of scale, scope, and networks. This is particularly evident in the road sector. Networking of transport channels has significant scaling up potential for poverty reduction (box 4.2).

In Asia and the Pacific, regional economic cooperation has facilitated such networking across select countries, thereby making it easier to share lessons more widely. A good example is the Asian Development Bank's Greater Mekong Subregion (GMS) Program. Since 1992, when the six member countries of the GMS first embarked on the program, there have been many accomplishments. Economic

---

**Box 4.2 Assessment of Large-Scale
Transport Infrastructure in Northern Vietnam**

Among Vietnam's most important large-scale infrastructure programs is the improvement of National Highway No. 5 (NH5) in the Red River Delta region. NH5 is the only road connecting the national capital of Hanoi with the port city of Haiphong, and it carries much of the economic and social activity of Vietnam's northern region. In 1992, the governments of Vietnam and Japan agreed to improve NH5 and rehabilitate Haiphong port. The project focused on expanding business activity in the areas along the highway, developing high-value agricultural production, improving access to higher education, and advancing medical services. The outcomes of this massive project were significant at both the household and regional levels. Foreign direct investment (FDI) to major industrial zones increased dramatically, and a survey of more than 70 FDI firm managers suggests that nearly 90 percent of new investments were spun directly from this improvement. At the same time, provinces along the corridor also experienced faster growth rates in per capita income and reduction in the number of poor households compared with the average for the Red River Delta of the whole country. The benefits from growth have spread to neighboring areas with similar transformation in the rural economy. Improved transportation has also increased tourism in Ha Long Bay.

linkages have been strengthened through a series of infrastructure
and other related projects. In turn, the emergence of a new trade
area has attracted investor interest, promoting economic growth and
social development in the region while contributing to improved relations among member countries. Investment in transport infrastructure was complemented by changes to the regulatory framework. All
these have led to higher trade and investment flows within the region
accompanied by early signs of an emerging trade-investment nexus.
Especially for landlocked countries, integration through regional infrastructure links is critical for development. The GMS Program has
spun off initiatives that now cover the entire Asia-Pacific region, including the Central Asian Regional Economic Cooperation and the
Central and South Asia Trade Forum initiatives.[6]

International Scaling Up

The story of the City-to-City Challenge demonstrates the feasibility
of international and municipal cooperation to achieve the Millennium Development Goals (MDGs) through the networking of
cities. Two pairs of cities—Tamale, Ghana, and its sister city
Louisville, Kentucky; and Dushanbe, Tajikistan, and Boulder, Col-
orado—agreed to focus on the MDGs as part of the Sustainable
Cities Program of Sister Cities International, an international nongovernmental organization (NGO). The two pairs of cities are part
of a network of 1,500 cities in Asia, Africa, and Latin America that
are in sister-city relationships with 750 cities in the United States.
The project is unlike the others presented at the Shanghai Conference. First, the project is fundamentally a result of horizontal cooperation at the municipal level that is already operating on a very
large scale—on the order of thousands of cities—in much of the
world. This municipal cooperation project is a potentially powerful form of cooperation for disseminating good practice, sharing
knowledge, and advocating for cities.

Factors That Promote
Scaling Up in Infrastructure

Political Leadership and Commitment

Champions—politicians, policy makers, NGOs, donors—play a
crucial role in reaping the positive benefits of infrastructure on
poverty reduction and growth.

> ## Box 4.3 When Scale Is Achieved
>
> Scale is achieved when
>
> - positive pilot tests are embedded in practice—for example, regional expansion of water supply in rural areas of Ghana, Lesotho, and South Africa
> - processes derived at one level cascade into other levels—for example, Morocco's rural roads and poverty reduction project
> - integrated operations are used to solve multiple problems—such as Brazil's Favela Bairro project
> - decisions on sequencing and prioritization are done right, as portrayed in all cases considered in this section of the chapter.

Scaling up requires a long-term vision and sustained efforts over time. In particular, political commitment at the highest level, supported by the allocation of resources and enabling legislation, is critical to the implementation of poverty reduction programs. Two cases stand out: China and Vietnam. The Chinese government has been investing intensively in public infrastructure during the last 20 years, with targeted investments in transportation, water supply, and sanitation constituting an important component of its poverty reduction program. In particular, rural water supply and sanitation were regarded as important components of poverty reduction. In the government's view, this was not simply a technological and economic issue, but a political priority as well. Accordingly, the government set ambitious targets, aiming to provide 95 percent of its rural population with access to improved water supply (70 percent with piped water supply) and 65 percent with access to sanitary latrines by 2010.

At the core of this initiative, however, was the belief that strong leadership and commitment were required not only at the national level, but also at the provincial and local levels. For a country the size of China, decentralization was essential to the rapid development of infrastructure. To support this program, the government not only allocated the necessary resources, but also streamlined the institutional framework to reduce duplication and improve coordination among agencies at different tiers of government. Without these conditions in place, scaling up in the rural water supply and sanitation sector would have presented insurmountable challenges. All these initiatives require a high degree of commitment from political leaders and policy makers. However, the government also needs the political and administrative power to push through this agenda. China stands out in this respect.

In Vietnam, clear political commitment proved essential to poverty reduction in the rural economy. Its Comprehensive Poverty Reduction and Growth Strategy provided the context for the National Highway No. 5 project (box 4.2). With this strategy, central and provincial governments have provided comprehensive support to poor farmers. A good example is the increase in rural credit offered by state banks. Without these complementary interventions, farmers would not have been able to make use of the business opportunities provided by improvements in transport infrastructure. This transport project demonstrates the broad range of roles that infrastructure can play in stimulating economic growth and directly contributing to poverty reduction through multiple channels. But it would not have happened without strong and clear political commitment by government.[7]

The initiatives in Albania and Africa demonstrate the importance of top-level commitment and clear legislation in expanding interventions in the water and sanitation sectors. In Albania, political support for institutional reform and implementation of a legal framework, in order to enable local governments to assume full responsibility for water service delivery, has been the driving force for change. By including the right to basic water and sanitation as part of an extensive social, economic, and environmental package of rights, South Africa's 1996 constitution ensured that national rural water supply and sanitation programs became an integral element of the whole nation's legislated human rights program. In Lesotho, the legal framework evolved as the sanitation program evolved from the pilot stage to a nationwide operation, notably through the formation of a national rural sanitation program in 1987. Similarly, in 2000 the government of Albania approved a new law on local government that transferred the responsibility for water supply to communes and municipalities.[8] Although many bylaws are still required to enforce it, this law is a major step forward because it will create ownership and place incentives to improve services at the local level.

Although studies have consistently emphasized the leadership role of national governments, empowerment and involvement of communities and local civil society groups are prerequisites for effective outcomes. Community management principles have been important in Ghana and Lesotho, and in a few aspects (notably sanitation) in South Africa. In Albania, farmers and water users as-

sociations were important to scaling up the benefits of these programs.

Power of Innovation

Learning and innovation can break the vicious cycle of a low-
performing infrastructure sector. The Pamir Private Power Project
in Tajikistan was driven by the need to find innovative ways to
provide essential services in a country where public resources are
extremely limited and where the public sector is reluctant to enter.
The institutional innovation consisted of the creation of a fully
functional regional utility, which unbundled the monolithic national utility in a geographic sense;[9] the creation of a fully funded social protection mechanism, monitored and administered by a credible third party (in this case, the World Bank); and participation of
the International Development Association (IDA) in the financing
of a project company in which the International Finance Corporation (IFC) has a 30 percent share. Tariffs were gradually increased
over a 10-year period, and an escrow account was established to
ensure that the government pays its bills for electricity consumption over time.

Although some aspects of this project are unique (for example, a
development-oriented private investor), Tajikistan is also unique
from the perspective of poverty and risks. If this form of public-
private partnership can structure a viable infrastructure project with
private sector participation in one of the poorest countries in the
world, it should be applicable elsewhere. In Tajikistan, strong political commitment, combined with openness to innovation, experimentation, and learning, and supported by external financial and aid organizations contributed to the implementation of the program.

Mobilizing Resources for
Infrastructure Investments

Adequate and certain long-term financing is a vital prerequisite. In
East Asia alone, it is estimated that close to $200 billion will be re-
quired annually over the next five years. A major constraint to the
expansion of infrastructure is the low levels of current spending on
infrastructure combined with the inefficient use of scarce resources
to maintain existing stock and expand resources. Underperfor-
mance in the sector, in turn, results from inadequate investment
planning, coordination, and resource mobilization, and from a decrease in private sector participation.

Meeting the resource requirements to scale up infrastructure development will require governments to have a long-term economic vision that recognizes the need for sustainable infrastructure financing mechanisms. This raises issues of user fees and subsidies, sharing of risks and rewards between public and private sectors in infrastructure financing, and leveraging donor financing to stimulate innovation and experimentation. The Tamil Nadu initiative on public-private partnerships; the example of fiscal support and risk sharing for the power sector in Tajikistan; and the example of cost recovery for basic services in China (box 4.4), including water supply and sanitation, illustrate the importance of this issue.

Role of External Catalysts

The contribution that external assistance for infrastructure can make to poverty reduction can be important (box 4.5). The keys are how to focus and leverage official financing (which is small compared to the magnitude of need to introduce reforms); build institutions and skills; attract private investment; promote innovation; and introduce new technology, management techniques, and approaches to operation and maintenance.

Box 4.4 Cost Recovery for Rural Water Supply in China

In China, high levels of investment in infrastructure were supported with policies promoting cost recovery at the lower level. The adoption of a more open and market-oriented economy has played an important role in changing the mindset on cost recovery policies for water supply and sanitation. The principle of full cost recovery within the limits of what residents can afford has been well accepted by provincial, county, and township governments, village committees, and rural residents. In most cases, the operation and maintenance of rural water plants are also fully financed by rural residents through water tariffs that are regulated by county price bureaus. These financing policies have been implemented for many years and have proved to be quite effective. The benefits from infrastructure investments cannot be realized in the absence of the political will and consumer willingness to devote resources for new investments and for operation and maintenance.

Box 4.5 Scaling Up with Donor Assistance

In China, about 80 percent of foreign funding for the rural water supply and sanitation sector has come from the World Bank. The first World Bank–supported project in this sector was started in 1985 and was followed by three others, each building on lessons from previous experience. The four projects involved 72,000 water supply subprojects in 178 counties across 18 provinces, reaching nearly 23 million beneficiaries. The World Bank–supported sanitation projects have built 64,500 sanitary latrines. Projects have also taught a large number of rural residents about water supply, health care, and hygiene. In addition to the benefits that typically accompany expanded water consumption and sanitation coverage, there is evidence that World Bank projects have increased local incomes and investments.

Where Do We Go from Here?

How can infrastructure promote and reinforce inclusive development? Although the Shanghai cases limit the discussion to specific interventions, they offer evidence that, under the right conditions, infrastructure can lead to growth and the sharing of benefits that extends to the poorest members of society. The East Asia and Pacific Infrastructure Flagship Study completed in 2005[10] illustrates well these linkages.

However, this requires strong pro-poor policies that underpin the processes of growth, new partnerships with local constituencies and private sector groups, and political commitments to regional initiatives. Finally, infrastructure investments are lumpy and extend across multiple geographical areas. Achieving sustainable impact at scale is a major challenge. As the magnitude and complexities of the infrastructure challenges multiply, so will the urgency for scaling up increase. The cases reviewed present options that seem to be transportable across regions and sectors.

SHARED EXPERIENCES IN JUDICIAL REFORM

It is widely held that effective legal and judicial systems are key pillars of development. This reflects growing evidence that effective legal frameworks and institutions can contribute to poverty reduction by improving investment climates and access to the benefits of development by poor people.[11]

Experience gained through judicial modernization and reform activities has helped establish the linkages between judicial reform and high-level development objectives. The challenges ahead are to leverage these experiences, harness good practices, and share knowledge so as to develop strategic approaches that can make those linkages operational and enhance impact on the ground.

Although no single approach can be applied to the challenges faced by judiciaries, one of the clearest lessons of the Shanghai Conference was that valuable dividends can be reaped from an examination of cross-cutting strategies, priorities, and other innovations that lend themselves to local applications. The representatives of four countries, Guatemala, Rwanda, the Philippines, and Russia, with markedly different histories and traditions, shared their experience in judicial reform at the conference.[12] The purpose of this section of the chapter is to present a few of the experiences shared in that context.

Judicial reform is a long-term process. "There is certainly no 'one size fits all approach' to judicial reform. It is, however, important to focus attention on four dimensions—institutions, enforcement of decisions, legal framework, and societal commitment."[13] How long does it take to change the (judicial) culture? How long does it take to reeducate judges? How can leaders and stakeholders expand and evaluate programs? These are open, unanswered questions with which experts and practitioners must grapple.

Many countries have implemented judicial reform projects over the past two decades with donor support. The World Bank, "since initiating its work in this field in the early 1990s, has supported 1,300 legal reform efforts as part of its regular loan operations; and today has approximately 30 loans dedicated exclusively to judicial reform."[14] The World Bank's 2005 *World Development Report* on investment climate demonstrated that accountable, trustworthy, and efficient court systems help reduce barriers to investment and can advance economic and social development. Also, confidence in a country's judicial system ranks among the indices measured by the World Bank Investment Climate Surveys, along with the effects of policy uncertainty, corruption, and crime. (Significantly, all of these factors can be correlated with the strengths of the rule of law and the judicial system.)[15]

The importance of judicial institutions in the context of development priorities has traditionally been understood as deriving from their roles as arbiters of social conflict and dispute resolution, and guarantors of civil and human rights and the rule of law. The social consequences of well-functioning judiciaries are well established. Their economic impacts, however, have only begun to be measured (May 2005).

There are at least four means through which strengthening judicial systems can contribute to the sustainability of poverty reduction. They are

- *empowering the poor* by providing them with means to address their social, civil, and economic grievances, resolve disputes peacefully, and adjudicate questions of rights in the appropriate forum;
- *improving governance* by strengthening accountability, transparency, and efficiency of judicial actors, and by increasing civil society's participation in the modernization of governance;
- *enhancing a secure environment* for human, social, and economic development; and
- *encouraging domestic and foreign investment* by reducing the uncertainties of engaging in legitimate commerce. This involves all aspects of commerce from creating a business, to hiring people, to enforcing contracts, to obtaining credit, to purchasing inputs and exporting goods and services.

Implementation Factors Affecting Judicial Reform

The context and challenges of judicial reform for each of the four countries were diverse: Guatemala's judicial modernization process follows a transition to democracy as part of the implementation of the Peace Accords that ended a 36-year internal war. Rwanda's reform is an attempt to administer large-scale indigenous justice and create a stable environment for social and economic development in the wake of a genocide. Both countries' justice systems played central roles in restoring order, instilling democracy, and preventing further violence.

The Philippines has significant, long-persistent development challenges, and is attempting to update and change its traditional judicial system to enhance its performance. Russia's judicial reforms follow a sweeping attempt to install democracy in place of communism, and to create the requisite conditions for a viable market economy. To some degree, all of these experiences exempli-

fy the problems of establishing or restoring the legitimacy of judicial institutions and controlling violence in these societies.

The judiciary's role in these circumstances is not difficult to ap-
preciate, especially in the arguably "transitional" cases where the
state is challenged to depart from one political, economic, or social
reality and to build a new one, such as open markets, democracy,
and peace building. It is very difficult for judicial systems in these
situations to respond to their new (as well as ongoing) challenges.

Commitment and the Political Economy of Change

In most of the countries examined, the need to reform judicial systems was driven by strident domestic demand and international
backing for changes, after decades of war, strong discontent with
conditions of widespread impunity and corruption, and the population's entirely inadequate access to judicial services.

Judicial modernization and reform are important to improve accountability, transparency, and performance. It is relevant, then, to
consider the extent of ownership and consensus building around
this issue of judicial reform in the population, and what factors can
expand and deepen the circle of stakeholders and reduce resistance
to change (especially among judges). The experiences shared provide valuable insights.

A participatory design and implementation methodology, together
with partnerships with stakeholders, helped sustain the Guatemalan
judicial modernization program by both widening and deepening
ownership of a continued reform program. This broad ownership is
particularly important in Guatemala, where the Supreme Court is replaced every five years and justices elect a president every year to
manage the administration of the courts. Judges, NGOs, the media,
the business community, indigenous groups, and law schools participated fully in the planning process for reform. Legislative and executive branches were generally supportive and this support has lasted
over changes of government administration since the Peace Accords
were signed in December 1996. Constitutional guarantees for secur-
ing the judiciary's budget as well as a commitment of the government's own resources to the project all helped to demonstrate broader buy-in. Changes in judiciary and executive branch leadership have
had no major negative impact on the implementation of this project
(Wanis-St. John 2004).

In Rwanda, political leaders and executive branch officials made
the decision to overcome the sad legacy of intertribal strife by not
waiting for the formal judicial system to perform its usual role.

Rather they encouraged the use of traditional justice mechanisms and adapted them to the volatile situation. They moved quickly in an attempt to address the major backlog of conflict cases. In view of this approach, the formal system remained weak and still continues to impede development. It bears noting, moreover, that the traditional family mediation mechanism, the *gacaca,* which relies on community leaders and other elders, has been questioned because it does not meet the standards of formal justice procedures.

The Philippine Action Program for Judicial Reform (APJR) is led by the head of the judicial system, the chief justice Hilario G. Davide, who provides high-level input and leadership for the various aspects of modernization work. Justice Davide explicitly recognized that the Philippine system is undergoing a change in its organizational culture. The APJR therefore has built in a Reform Support Program that is meant to harmonize the justice needs of different sectors and stakeholders in the Philippines and sustain their support as the judiciary undergoes changes (Davide 2004).

Russia has focused on judicial reform by creating a legal framework from scratch and then entrusting the judicial leadership with the main task of adopting these changes within their institutions. In this case, it entailed setting up a new commercial court system (arbitrage courts) with existing human resources and complementing them with an induction of other new judges and staff largely from law enforcement and other justice sector agencies. Given that the reforms (mostly law reforms) were driven from outside leadership in the executive branch and the parliament, ownership of reforms has not developed to a significant extent. Implementation progress has been patchy. Resistance to change from some justice system stakeholders, the legal community, prosecutors, and bailiffs has also slowed the reform process and limited its effects.

Institutional Development, Innovation, and Capacity Building

Each of the four countries relies heavily on building up its judicial system via staff training, technical assistance, and policy improvements. In no case was the existing system adequate to address either the ongoing or new needs of the state, regardless of whether the challenge was postconflict trauma, war crimes, a poor investment climate, lack of public confidence, or the need for new market systems.

The judicial branch modernization work in Guatemala is nothing less than a top-to-bottom reinvention of the justice system and the way in which the population interacts with it. Integral to this process is the institutionalization of a full judicial career, judicial training, re-training of administrators, right-sizing of the civil service portion of the system, and bridging the gap between the formal and indigenous justice systems.

The Rwandan case is very different: No classic approach to modernization would suffice to meet the extraordinary needs created by the hundreds of thousands of severe criminal and genocide-related cases. In this instance, training and capacity building were necessary but simply insufficient. "At the pace of conventional courts, it would take 150 years to try the genocide suspects in Rwanda's jails. For most of 2003 there were over 100,000 prisoners in Rwanda, 85 percent of whom were awaiting trial for genocide-related crimes.... Over 100 projects have been established, including the training of lawyers, judges, investigators, and police, and exercises on the reform of the court and administrative procedures. However, by early 2000 only around 3,000 suspects had been through the conventional court system and it was clear that the justice system could not work any faster to clear the backlog of cases" (Musoni 2004).

Instead of relying on the formal judicial system of courts, the Rwandan experiment with *gacaca* required the creation of a national infrastructure to address the high numbers of detained persons and to create the opportunity for truth telling, accusation, punishment, and reconciliation. This required training of both administrative personnel and judges to expand the *gacaca* program at the national scale.

The Philippine judicial reform program takes a holistic approach, in which institutional development is a key objective for the achievement of better service delivery, integrity of infrastructure, accountability, and disciplinary mechanisms. It depends heavily on increasing the personal and institutional skill levels throughout the judicial system. Support systems, transparency, and technology are upgraded to respond to information gaps in performance measurement and to reach citizens in different parts of the country. Mediation and community outreach are key elements of the program. So, too, are conscious efforts to learn from other countries and draw on international good practices. Field visits of judges have been carried out in Asia and Latin America.

The creation of commercial courts in Russia involved setting up a new framework of laws and codes; selecting, hiring, and training new judges and staff; providing space and other tools for the operation of courts; building linkages and communication mechanisms with other actors in the justice sector; and informing businesses and other users about the operation of these courts and their responsibilities. Presently, about 4,100 commercial court judges handle 7 percent of the total cases of the overall justice system annually. They are widely dispersed in Russia.

In all the countries examined, "learning while doing" played an important role. Guatemala's long-standing exclusion of the Mayan people (especially women, who are poorest) has been addressed in part by explicitly creating mediation centers; these are often operated by indigenous community members and conducted in one of the more than 20 Mayan languages spoken throughout the country. Some of the mediation centers are situated in new Centers for the Administration of Justice; experimentally, others are being housed in mobile units that drive to remote communities that the state has long underserved. About 6,000 people benefited during one mobile court's first year of operation. Women judges and staff who speak the local language have also been hired.

Since the Shanghai Conference, the chief justice of the Philippines visited Guatemala and directly observed the Guatemalan mobile courts. He quickly demonstrated the value of experiential learning by creating the Philippines' own Justice on Wheels program, which emulates the Guatemalan model by providing youth justice services in Manila.[16] The Philippines, capitalizing on the experience of other Asian neighbors with a diverse, pluralistic population, has also been instituting cultural sensitivity programs for ethnic populations.

The arbitrage courts initiated in Russia were not new from a global perspective, but were untested in Russia. The new system is operational and reviews indicate that businesses are better served now than before these reforms were started. It is important to note here that the overall justice system of Russia is extremely large, and the general jurisdiction courts that handle the bulk of the workload of the justice sector are cumbersome. But several initiatives and reforms have been under way with starts and stops over the last decade.

The monitoring and evaluation aspect of capacity building has generally lagged in these countries, but for some exceptions in the Philippines. The other countries have shied away from this or are only now developing appropriate methods and tools. This area appears to be one of the main gaps in reform programs that were shared (a view generally consistent with other findings on this topic for the judicial sector).

External Catalysts

The Peace Accords signed in 1996 were the key catalyst for justice reform in Guatemala. The United Nations Development Programme (UNDP), human rights groups, and the international donor community (including the World Bank) helped build momentum for this reform. The locally led judicial reform process and international community involvement continues. This partnership has helped promote the demand and supply linkages for access to justice service, and helped gradually extend the service to the urban and rural areas. This has also helped keep pressure on issues of corruption and accountability in the system. But much more needs to be done. Rwanda's internal devastation was so extensive and reported so widely that change was demanded from all sides. Large-scale donor support has continued to flow for capacity building and the promotion of postconflict reconstruction.

In the Philippines, judiciary-led efforts have been supported by the World Bank and Asian Development Bank, and brought to the attention of bilateral donors. The system seeks concessionary resources for the judicial program to reduce the fiscal impacts of reform. Many donors fund activities and this has helped maintain the support and collaboration of the other branches of government and NGOs. About 20 percent of the technical assistance needs of the judiciary are being funded out of grant resources.

In Russia, there has been generous donor support to help build the rule of law. This has produced overlapping programs, conflicting advice on priorities, and donor coordination problems. Given that judicial ownership has been low and champions have generally been outside the system (for example, parliament and academia), these catalysts have not been fully productive. There is increasing recognition among the judicial policy makers that the earlier approach of law reform needs to be revised and complemented by proactive judicial leadership, institution building, and citizen education to enhance reform outcomes and gain the confidence of the citizens.

Looking Forward

Although it seems clear that in these "four countries, each with different considerations, each with challenges and each saying that if you want to deal with poverty reduction you must deal with the question of the judicial system,"[17] the approaches have been different, reflecting local motivations and realities. Guatemala and the

Philippines have implemented significant, systemwide moderniza-tion projects and invested heavily of their own resources and peo-ple in their ongoing efforts. They have constantly learned from others and among themselves. The Rwandan experience stands out with regard to the grave condition of its judicial system and repre-sents a notable response to the overwhelming consequences of genocide. The Russian effort focuses on one major innovation that affects the entire commercial arena.

Guatemala and the Philippines are positioned to create opportu-nities for the empowerment of the poorest people while increasing the overall investment climate of their countries by continuing and increasing their efforts. Rwandan efforts to modernize the judicial system will advance and benefit from the lessons of other judicial reform programs, such as those mentioned here, in the measure that the extraordinary genocide cases are cleared and make way for focusing on the ordinary administration of justice.

At the inception of these reforms, the institutional capacity it-self—as well as the concrete activities, human resources, financial resources, infrastructure, and services—were, in many senses, inad-equate to the challenges of helping create the conditions for pros-perity and peace. For this reason it is not surprising to find that the reforms and programs have all involved significant political com-mitment, learning and experimentation, serious capacity building, and an engagement with external facilitating factors.

This look at the record indicates that experiential learning can be a crucial complement to the informed preparation and planning of development projects, including the essential work of improving governance as a pillar of economic development. But experiential learning can take time; reformers often need to wait until an expe-rience is well under way before being able to fully analyze it for les-sons learned. One way to reduce time to learning is to harness the experience of similar projects in different national contexts.

MICROFINANCE

There is robust evidence that countries with better-developed fi-nancial systems experience faster reductions in income inequality and faster rates of poverty alleviation (Beck, Demirguc-Kunt, and Levine 2004). Whereas the development of an efficient financial system is associated with pro-poor growth, the immediate benefits derived from credit, savings, and payment services accrue only to

those who have direct access to the financial system. These benefits
include the opportunity to accumulate productivity-enhancing capital that can increase income, the means to safely put money away
in a savings account for use in an emergency, and the ability to efficiently access transfer payments from relatives working away from
home.[18]

In Kenya, for example, poor people use savings and loans to invest in business activities (inventory, salaries), save for the future
(education, medical costs), manage household cash flow needs
(rent, food), invest in assets (land, housing, appliances), and cope
with crises or life events (illness, marriage, funerals). Evidence from
Tanzania (Beegle, Dehejia, and Gatti 2003) shows access to credit
at the household level substituting for child labor; and studies conducted in Zimbabwe, Bangladesh, and India have pointed to a link
between improved health and education outcomes for microfinance clients and their children (Littlefield, Morduch, and Hashemi 2004). Microfinance thus supports the MDGs by providing
poor people with resources to build their income-generating capacity, which in turn provides them with the opportunity to improve
their family's nutrition, health care, and schooling, and to avoid or
ameliorate deprivation when income suddenly declines.

The efficient and sustainable provision of financial services for
poor people is developing with great promise in many countries
throughout the world. This section highlights the features of five
country experiences that were implemented by diverse types of organizations: a state-owned development bank in Mongolia, private
and public commercial banks in Kazakhstan, specialized microfinance institutions (MFIs) in Bangladesh, an NGO in Kenya that
was transformed into a microfinance bank, and financial cooperatives in Mexico.[19] The section discusses implementation factors
that helped these organizations reach their goals, and concludes by
drawing lessons that can inform the process of globally scaling up
financial services for poor people to help achieve the MDGs.

Enabling the Poor to Gain Greater Access to
Financial Services: Country Examples

The country examples outlined below demonstrate the variety of
organizations that can deliver financial services to a broad range of
the population that has not previously had access to the formal financial system. The examples illustrate how commercial banks
have profitably expanded their clientele to include lower-income

households and enterprises; how NGO MFIs achieved nationwide outreach to the poor; and how financial cooperatives can professionalize and expand their coverage to the poor through a comprehensive approach that includes improvement of government regulation and oversight, as well as development of organizational and technological networks.

Mongolia: Turning Around and Privatizing a State-owned Development Bank

After its inception in 1991, Mongolia's Agricultural Development Bank was steadily drained of resources throughout the early part of the decade as local managers, appointed by provincial and county-level authorities, regularly made lending decisions based on political criteria. In 1996, the high level of nonperforming loans and operating deficits forced the Central Bank to appoint a receiver for the insolvent institution. The degree of politicization and high cost to the government of the Agricultural Development Bank's dismal performance made it an obvious candidate for liquidation. However, the bank was the only formal financial institution with branches throughout Mongolia's vast rural areas, and closing it would have had a devastating effect on the rural economy. In 1999, in conjunction with a World Bank–financed program to strengthen the financial sector and with financial support from the U.S. Agency for International Development (USAID), the government decided to reform the institution.

Eliminating political interference in the bank's operations was critical to effecting a turnaround. The government agreed to replace the bank's board of directors with independent members, and charge them with overseeing the institution's return to profitability and eventual sale. Even with a change of government in 2000, from the Democratic Party to the former Communist Party, it was clear to Mongolia's new leaders that little opportunity for sustainable provision of financial services in rural areas existed short of a commercially driven approach.

In July 2000, following an internationally competitive process, the newly selected management team began the work of restoring the Agricultural Development Bank to financial soundness, expanding services to the country's rural population, and preparing the bank for independent operation followed by privatization. The team focused on enhancing the revenues of unprofitable branches, rather than closing them, by launching the development of new products, revamping the bank's policies and procedures, decentral-

izing accountability for decision making to branch managers, upgrading staff performance by rolling out a bankwide training program and providing staff with substantial incentive pay for financial performance, and soliciting external marketing expertise to
improve the bank's image and to attract new clients.

The reform and privatization process led to impressive growth in
outreach and sustainability. From July 2000 through February 2004,
deposits grew by 740 percent; the number of loans approached 1
million, with small clients forming the bulk of borrowers (average
loan size was $382 in February 2004); and 90 percent of all loans
were made in rural areas. Profitability was achieved in 2001, and
two years later the bank was sold to a Japanese firm. The new own-
er contributed equity and reinvested earnings of nearly $7 million in
its first year of ownership, more than doubling the bank's capital
base, and intends to continue expanding outreach among the bank's
target market—lower-income and rural households.

Kazakhstan: Building Microenterprise Units within Commercial Banks

In 1997, the Kazakh government made an urgent request to the
European Bank for Reconstruction and Development to help it develop a sound lending program for micro and small enterprises
(MSEs). At that time, a four-year-old credit line to banks for MSE
lending had disbursed only a third of the funds available. Portfolio
quality was poor, and a bank failure had cost the government $9.5
million for its guarantee of the MSE portfolio. The Kazakhstan
Small Business Program (KSBP) was the result of efforts to develop
a more effective approach to sustainable MSE lending. The previous program had failed in large part because the credit line was not
coupled with technical assistance—banks lacked interest or knowledge on how to develop a viable MSE loan operation. The new
program aimed to transfer know-how to the participating banks
from professionals with extensive MSE lending experience, and
build incentives for the banks to go after this market segment by
demonstrating its profitability.

The program selected partner banks based on strict eligibility criteria, including financial health and commitment to MSE lending at
the highest levels of management, and required them to set up separate MSE departments run by KSBP staff. International experts who
were contracted to manage these MSE departments selected and
trained local teams of loan officers. The program was launched in
eight branches of five banks, and initially offered a limited number

of MSE loan products. KSBP concentrated on building the lending procedures and management information systems needed to efficiently manage an MSE portfolio, and on training staff, aligning incentive structures with portfolio performance objectives, and piloting new products. The strategy was to build the MSE departments into profitable, independent entities within each bank, and then to gradually expand the product line and range of operations to include more cities, using the first batch of experienced loan officers to lead training efforts and set up MSE departments in the new locations.

Within two years, the experience of the first MSE units had bred enthusiasm and ownership of the program within the participating banks, and consequently motivated bank management to expand the concept to other branches in other locations. Moreover, the success of their competitors convinced additional banks to participate. KSBP then focused on scaling up outreach, adding new products such as an "express" micro loan with no collateral requirements and rapid disbursement, integrating the MSE departments into the banks' organizational structures, and gradually handing over management responsibility from the external experts to the trained and seasoned local staff. Training for bank staff who were not MSE specialists was well received because, by this time, the banks had begun to perceive MSEs as valuable customers in the increasingly competitive financial markets of Kazakhstan.

By February 2004, KSBP partner banks had opened MSE windows in 185 locations in more than 40 cities. The MSE portfolio of $162 million included more than 35,000 loans, with only 1 percent of these loans having arrears of more than 30 days. Fully 90 percent of KSBP clients had never before had a bank loan. The profitability of the MSE units has motivated partner banks to gradually increase the portion of MSE loans financed from their own funds, rather than donor-financed credit lines, to 40 percent.

Bangladesh: Massive Outreach through Specialized Microfinance Institutions

Following the country's independence in 1971, Bangladeshi MFIs started experimenting with ways to empower the poor socially and economically. By the late 1980s, many of these organizations had realized that economic empowerment of the poorest populations necessitated credit for the start-up and expansion of small economic activities. The major MFIs—Grameen, Bangladesh Rural Advancement Committee (BRAC), Proshika, and the Association for

Social Advancement (ASA)—adopted an approach to microcredit that focused on the provision of loans to individuals organized into groups. Group members provided guarantees of each other's loans, and received strong support and monitoring from field staff in branch offices. Most organizations offered an inflexible loan product, with standardized loan sizes and repayment periods. By the early 1990s, several MFIs had acquired sufficient management capacity and field-based expertise to undertake massive expansion. This growth was facilitated by a methodology that was well understood by both staff and clients and by high population density, which enabled MFIs to provide services to the largely rural population at a reasonable cost. It was also fueled by large amounts of funding from donors for both capacity building and the capitalization of loan funds; by high levels of loan repayments, which enabled the MFIs to recycle their loan funds; and by commitments from the MFIs to move toward full cost recovery and eventual independence from donor subsidies.

In 1990, a public-private financial apex called the Palli Karma Sahayak Foundation (PKSF) was created to channel loan funds to MFIs. In addition to providing funds for expansion, PKSF has played an important role in increasing the professionalism of the microfinance industry in Bangladesh by establishing eligibility criteria that include progress toward financial sustainability, helping to build the capacity of many MFIs, and advocacy on issues affecting the whole industry (such as the development of an appropriate regulatory framework). However, many MFIs had a relatively strong retail capacity at the time that PKSF was formed. Apex bodies in other countries have failed when they provided large amounts of funding to MFIs that did not have the retail capacity or the incentives to absorb it.

Over the past decade, product diversification has become an important area of innovation for Bangladeshi MFIs as it has become clear that the standard loan product does not meet the needs of many clients. Rules such as minimum loan floors, fixed weekly loan repayments, and loan guarantees of the poorest by those who are less poor have often constrained the expansion of access. The big MFIs have introduced new products to mitigate some of these constraints: ASA has a flexible loan program with loan sizes and repayment schedules that are more flexible than their standard loan. Grameen offers loans with zero interest to beggars, and BRAC's Income Generation for Vulnerable Group Development program combines food aid with microcredit and training for the poorest people.

As a result of these efforts over more than two decades, some 1,200 MFIs now reach 13 million households. Every district in the country is covered, although there are still a few isolated areas with little or no coverage. The scale of outreach to the poorest sectors of the population and the geographical reach into all parts of the country are remarkable.

Kenya: Transforming a Nonprofit Organization into a Bank

The Kenya Rural Enterprise Program (K-Rep) started as a USAID project in 1984, was transformed into an NGO in the late 1980s, and then became a commercial bank a decade later. The main reason for the transition to a bank was to enable the organization to increase its outreach by tapping into commercial sources of funding, including equity capital and deposits. As an NGO, K-Rep could not attract funds from investors or savers. The compulsory savings traditionally collected from clients could be used only as security for loans, and had to be banked in formal financial institutions that did not serve the poorest people. This was not advantageous for either K-Rep or its clients. K-Rep could not intermediate client savings into client loans, and clients could not access their savings when they most needed them.

Transformation from an NGO to a bank brought about many issues and challenges. Finding the right investment partners who shared K-Rep's vision of profitable provision of financial services for the poor, and who could assist with overcoming the reservations of the Central Bank of Kenya, was paramount, as was finding the right ownership structure, including ownership of the considerable assets that had been acquired over the years by the NGO. The transformation eventually required the creation of four legal entities: K-Rep Group, a holding company that owns the largest number of shares (28.8 percent) in K-Rep Bank; K-Rep Bank, Ltd., a private for-profit company; K-Rep Advisory Services (Africa), Ltd., a private, for-profit consulting firm fully owned by K-Rep Group; and K-Rep Development Agency, an NGO also wholly owned by K-Rep Group, which focuses on microfinance research and innovation.

A significant challenge has been developing human capacity and commitment. New staff, including bankers, had to be hired to handle new functions created as a consequence of the transition to a bank: additional front- and back-office operations, clearing functions, regulatory compliance, and treasury management. A culture clash erupted between the old staff of K-Rep, who had a strong commitment to social goals, and the new bankers focused on profitability. Morale and commitment were eventually restored through actions that included the creation of an employee stock ownership program and reaffirmation of the bank's vision. Fear of mission drift to higher-income clients has not materialized. The deposits sought from the nonpoor have been used as a base for expanding coverage of services to the poor, and new products that benefit the poor, as well as the nonpoor, have been added. These include individual loans, bank overdrafts, consumer loans, health loans, passbook savings, current accounts, and time deposits.

Difficulties have been faced introducing many of these new products, especially savings products, and with data migration from old information systems to new ones. Despite all the difficulties, however, increased outreach has been achieved quickly. In the four years since its transformation, K-Rep's clientele has increased from 15,000 to more than 90,000 clients. This includes the 48,000 shareholders of autonomous financial services associations created and managed by K-Rep Development Agency.

Mexico: A Comprehensive Approach to Strengthening Financial Cooperatives

A recent survey conducted in Mexico's cities showed that about three quarters of the adult population (and 85 percent of entrepreneurs) do not use the services of formal financial institutions (Caskey, Ruiz, and Solo 2004). In rural areas, fewer than 6 percent of households held any savings or loan accounts with financial institutions in 2000. Among those with access to financial intermediaries, 7 percent of the economically active population, or 3 million people, relied on small financial cooperatives and NGOs to safeguard their savings or provide them with loans. The majority of these organizations were unregulated, and depositors lost millions of dollars in savings when a number of poorly or unscrupulously managed financial cooperatives failed in 1998–2000. Moreover, these small, community-based institutions could not provide their customers with access to the national payments system, or provide the types of products of larger, more technologically advanced financial institutions.

In this context, the government of Mexico and a number of cooperative institutions began working on the development of the Popular Savings and Credit Act, which was passed in 2001. It established regulations and supervision arrangements for all nonbank savings and credit institutions, using federations or groups of cooperatives to perform some oversight functions. At the same time, a state-owned savings bank was transformed into the National Savings and Financial Services Bank, or BANSEFI, to provide the newly regulated financial cooperatives with access to liquidity, back-office services, and a shared technology platform that allows access to payment systems and automated reporting to the banking supervisor. BANSEFI is also contracting with specialized technical assistance providers to strengthen hundreds of financial cooperatives as well as their federations and confederations, which play important roles under the new supervision framework.

The goal of this nationwide effort is to help the financial cooperatives meet the legal and regulatory standards mandated by the new law and offer safer, more efficient financial services to the lower-income clientele they tend to serve. BANSEFI is a unique development bank because its mission and methods exclude lending, and its aim is ultimately to be sold to the cooperatives. The government's massive investment in the sector thus seeks to put the country's financial cooperatives in a position to build scale on a sustainable basis through strong network institutions at many levels.

The Secretariat of Agriculture, Livestock, Rural Development, Fisheries, and Nutrition (SAGARPA) has developed a companion initiative to ensure that smaller, geographically isolated, and, in many cases, weaker financial cooperatives operating in marginal rural areas also receive assistance to bring their accounting, risk management, and governance practices up to the standards set in the new law, and to expand their outreach among especially vulnerable populations in those areas. SAGARPA provides small, in-kind grants and contracts to international organizations that work with local professionals to provide technical assistance to cooperatives to build a sustainable membership base, including people from very poor rural areas and many different indigenous communities. The effort to strengthen cooperatives in these marginal rural areas focuses on developing *conciencia, confianza, y compromiso* (awareness, trust, and commitment) between new members and their financial institutions so that the benefits, rights, and responsibilities of each member are understood and they share a sense of mutual investment. As of January 2004, SAGARPA's program had helped about 35,000 people in Huasteca, Chiapas, Veracruz, and Guerrero gain access to safe and responsive financial institutions. More than 80,000 people from Mexico's poorest, most marginalized groups are expected to gain access to the financial system through this effort by 2007.

Implementation Factors

Several factors account for the expansion of financial services to the poor people in the countries reviewed above.

Commitment and Leadership

As illustrated in the country examples, many types of financial intermediaries now operate in accord with commercial business principles to profitably serve low-income markets. However, a fundamental change in institutional culture is often required: either a shift toward the poorest populations or a shift toward commercialization. Therefore, institutional commitment and leadership are essential, from the boards of directors to the field staff providing services to clients. In Bangladesh, the visionary leaders of the country's principal MFIs have been a powerful force for the development of the industry internationally, as well as for the strength and vibrancy of the sector in that country. In Kenya, the readiness of the organization's leaders to respond to challenges, and the ability of staff to continuously learn about and respond to the needs of clients, were critical to the transformation of K-Rep from a nonprofit organization to a commercial bank.

The commitment and leadership of policy makers is also critical to the development of broad-based access to financial services. Government must create a stable macroeconomic environment, support the development of a regulatory framework that promotes fair and vigorous competition among financial institutions, and demonstrate leadership in eliminating political influence within financial institutions. In Mexico the government made a major commitment to financial cooperatives that is improving their performance and enhancing their long-term viability. In Mongolia, government commitment was critical to the turnaround of the state-owned Agricultural Development Bank.

Experimentation, Innovation, and Learning

Microfinance is a field where continuous experimentation, innovation, and learning over many years have led to a revolutionary conclusion: The poor are indeed bankable. Despite small transactions that are expensive to process, it *is* possible for financial institutions to cover the costs of service provision to this population. Thus, the poor can be mainstreamed into a country's financial system without long-term subsidies.

Experimentation and innovation have shown that there is no distinct organizational form that best lends itself to successful microfinance. For example, although state-owned banks are considered difficult to reform, a number of public institutions have now profitably introduced banking services for the poor people, including the Agricultural Bank of Mongolia and Halyk Bank in Kazakhstan. Implementation drivers common to these—and all financial institutions—include good governance and management, coupled with demand for responsive products, effective information systems, and incentives that motivate staff to choose borrowers carefully and to recover all loans.

However, adequate provision of services to poor households, as well as MSEs, requires products, processes, and systems that are quite different from those in conventional banking. For example, experimentation with products and services that meet clients' needs is crucial to capturing the low-income segments of the financial services market. In Mongolia, a focus on revenue-generating activities revealed that product diversification can have multiple benefits for both the institution and its clients. The bank increased revenues from its underutilized and loss-making branches by creating products for new types of clients, such as nomadic herders. The demand for this and other new products turned many of the rural branches into profit-making units.

Technological innovation also has allowed microfinance institutions to overcome many of the difficulties inherent in delivering financial services to large numbers of small-scale clients who are often geographically dispersed. In Kenya, Equity Building Society's mobile banking technology allowed it to efficiently serve clients in thinly populated areas that cannot support the fixed costs of a branch office. In Mexico, the use of a shared technological platform is enabling small or decentralized organizations to enjoy scale efficiencies, as well as to obtain such services as treasury management and portfolio risk analysis at reduced cost.

The development of management information systems that carefully track customer data has enabled microfinance institutions to improve portfolio quality and to learn about what works and what does not work in their organizations. Managers use these systems to identify and follow up at an early stage with clients who have problem loans. The converse is also true: Excellent clients can be easily identified and rewarded with better loan terms. In addition, clients often benefit from improved management information systems. For example, Equity Building Society's new system reduced customer turnaround time at the counter from 30 to 5 minutes.

External Catalysts

Donors have been instrumental in supporting the growth and development of the microfinance industry over the past 25 years. They have financed much of the experimentation that has led to the practices used by many MFIs today. They have capitalized the loan funds of nonprofit organizations; financed technical assistance for the development of organizational processes and information systems; established exchange programs for lateral learning among microfinance practitioners; and helped build industry infrastructure, such as associations of microfinance institutions, training centers, and shared credit information systems.

Lessons for Scaling Up

Build Retail Capacity

A strong capacity for retail service delivery should be developed before extensive scaling up can take place. This also depends on the many good governance and management practices highlighted throughout this section, such as development of internal staff capacities through on-the-job and formal training. The outcomes also depend on establishment of meaningful performance incentives; good communication between branches and head office; a culture of service excellence; and systems that provide timely information for decision making, transparency, and accountability. In other words, the organization must have a set of financial products that clients are willing to pay for, as well as processes and systems that enable it to deliver them profitably, before it can scale up. The process should then take place in phases, deploying profit center accounting so that the performance of the microfinance unit or program can be monitored. As the institution grows, decentralization of responsibility to the lowest tier of the administrative structure at which accountability can be ensured is likely to facilitate results.

Develop a Favorable Policy and Enabling Environment

No matter how well positioned an organization may be, its ability and incentive to scale up depends also on favorable market conditions. This is to a great extent dependent on government policy. Government should create an environment that encourages the productive growth of economic activities of all sizes, including agricultural activities. It should develop a regulatory framework that fosters competition and allows for the selective entry of new financial institutions. It should also facilitate the development of financial infrastructure, including efficient payment and credit information systems.

Ensure Effective Donor Support

Donors are most effective if they work together in a coordinated way. Uncoordinated donor missions, disparate disbursement arrangements, and different reporting requirements are inefficient, and unpredictable resource flows to MFIs inhibit sound business planning. To help create a level playing field that facilitates competition among different types of financial institutions, donors need to harmonize the conditions attached to their support and refrain from providing unfair advantages to one class of organization over another. In addition, donor staff responsible for microfinance programming should be grounded in the basic elements of sustainable microfinance, and the need for innovative and flexible approaches.

Evaluate Scaling Up Strategies

The context within a particular country will determine which organizational approach is most promising for the purpose of massively expanding financial services to reach poor households and MSEs. In countries that have private or state-owned banks with large pre-existing branch networks, it makes sense to consider whether these banks could introduce microfinance because their branch networks could be used to roll out products to a new clientele more quickly than new or small microfinance specialist institutions. In some countries, large cooperative networks or large financial NGOs with branch infrastructure could offer the same potential. There are also international networks of microfinance institutions that have well-developed methodologies and systems that have been fine-tuned over a long period in a wide variety of settings. These institutions might be able to quickly replicate their particular methods.

In countries or regions with large numbers of small institutions, such as small savings and loan associations, financial cooperatives, or financial NGOs, federations and networks can provide economies of scale in many areas, including product development, shared technological infrastructure, and the contracting of external audits. They can provide credibility by establishing norms, setting performance benchmarks, certifying compliance, and establishing a "brand" that recognizes participating institutions that comply with agreed standards.

A financial apex institution can help manage liquidity, as demonstrated by BANSEFI in Mexico and PKSF in Bangladesh. It should be kept in mind that a country must have sufficient retail capacity for a financial apex to succeed because the capacity to absorb funds can be easily overestimated. In most cases, the major factor constraining growth is institutional capacity rather than funding constraints.

Take Up the Challenge

Microfinance providers have reached only a tiny fraction of the population in most countries. The challenge is to multiply access from the few households that have services today to the many who do not. Governments must foster dynamic financial markets, donors must continue to finance innovation, and pro-poor financial institutions must achieve a scale of operation large enough to generate efficiency and profitability. As the world's poorest people are increasingly able to invest in productive economic activities and better manage their household finances, they will be able to earn income that enables them to pay for food, shelter, education, and health care. In this way, microfinance will continue to play an important role in the achievement of the MDGs.

HEALTH

Half of the MDGs are directly related to health. In 1990 more than 10 million children under the age of 5 died in developing countries—the vast majority of them from preventable causes such as poor nutrition and diarrhea associated with unsafe drinking water; more than 500,000 women died from complications of pregnancy and childbirth; more than 2 billion people practiced open-air defecation; and HIV/AIDS together with malaria and tuberculosis claimed more than 5 million lives. Combined, these problems have had—and continue to have—a particularly devastating effect on the welfare of households and economies in developing countries.

Achieving the MDGs for health is a daunting task, requiring 270,000 new water connections per day for the next 10 years, and providing 2 billion people with access to basic sanitation (WHO 2003; World Bank 2004b). The requirements for combating

HIV/AIDS are even more formidable. Of the 5 million to 6 million people needing HIV treatment in low- and middle-income countries, only 400,000 (7 percent) had access to treatment in 2003. The difficulties encountered in meeting the MDGs are reflected by slow progress toward the set targets. For example, no region is on track to reduce by two thirds the mortality rate of children under 5 years of age by 2015—except possibly Latin America and the Caribbean. Similarly, all the regions—except the Middle East and North Africa—appear to fall short of achieving the 2015 target of reducing by three quarters the maternal mortality ratio. Generally, at the current pace of improvement, the majority of countries will not accomplish most of the MDGs—especially those related to health (World Bank 2004c).

Thus, meeting the MDGs for health requires innovative approaches and efforts beyond business as usual. Evidence from cases presented at the Shanghai Conference shows that with political commitment, appropriate policies, and external support, great strides can be made toward achieving the MDGs for health. The challenge is how to scale up such initiatives to expand health care to the poorest populations.

Background to Scaling Up Health Services

The objective of this section is to draw out lessons from the global learning process that can inform efforts to trigger positive health responses, basing the lessons learned on six case studies presented at the Shanghai Conference.[20] To realize the MDGs for health, local innovations in the delivery of health services need to be extended to reach more people. This subset of cases on health illustrates the following two dimensions of scaling up: in space and time, and across countries.

Scaling Up in Space and Time

Innovations on a local scale can be extended to other regions or can reach more people within a region through widespread adoption and adaptation. The case of India's HIV/AIDS outreach among injecting drug users (IDUs) in Manipur vividly illustrates scaling up in space and time. Initiated by three grassroots organizations with limited external support, the outreach response based on the harm-reduction approach was initially limited to a few communities and targeted at IDUs. However, as information about the remarkable outcomes of the initiative spread, communities, donors, and the government became involved. The Manipur State AIDS Control Society, a state agency, endorsed the harm-reduction approach and formulated a policy to mandate its statewide implementation, thus paving the way to expand the response to other regions within the state. By the end of 2002, the initiative reached 18,000 IDUs, compared with 6,000 when it started. In 1998 the response was enlarged to cover seven states through the formation of the North East Network.

However, there are numerous examples of positive local initiatives in the health sector that did not progress partly because of a lack of support from policy makers. Advocacy, sensitization, and demonstration of results can be used to get support from policy makers. Scaling up of India's HIV/AIDS outreach program, for example, can be attributed to demonstration of achievements and to sensitization and engagement of policy makers in an informed and sustained manner.

Scaling Up across Countries

The case of riverblindness, for example, started with village-level vector control in the 1940s, and expanded to cover river systems in 7 countries, before being systematically extended to 11 and then 30 countries in West, Central, and East Africa. Commitment at the highest political level and coordination are indispensable for scaling up health responses across countries.

Factors Underpinning the Scaling Up of Health Responses

Cases presented at the Shanghai Conference demonstrated remarkable achievements in improving health outcomes, especially among poor people. Factors that could be extrapolated to other countries and regions include leadership and political commitment, institutional innovation, learning and experimentation, and external catalysts.

Leadership and Political Commitment

How the government perceives the nature and extent of the health problem (acute or chronic) appears to influence the intensity of its response. This is illustrated by differences in responses to the HIV/AIDS epidemic (an acute health problem) and to child mortality (a more chronic problem). When the governments of Thailand and Uganda realized that HIV/AIDS was not just another disease limited to a particular group of people but an emergency threatening the entire population and the development process, the responses were intensive, urgent, and massive. Policies and institutions to deal with the problem were put in place, resources were mobilized, and massive awareness campaigns were conducted. For example, mandatory 30-second HIV/AIDS advertisements were played every hour on TV and radio in Thailand.

This intensive and disease-focused approach is in sharp contrast to the Islamic Republic of Iran's gradual and broad-based response to chronic disparities in health status, especially child mortality rates, between rural and urban populations.

It is generally recognized that political commitment at the highest level plays a crucial role. The major challenge facing project implementers is how to secure this commitment when it is not already mobilized. The country experiences presented at the Shanghai Conference offer some significant insights on this process and demonstrate three ways through which political commitment can be fostered: smart data presentation, engagement of political leaders, and community demand (box 4.6). These factors alone, however, are not enough to initiate and sustain results. In addition, the government should be willing to accept change, to formulate pro-poor policies based on evidence provided through research or health information systems, and to be accountable.

Political commitment can be demonstrated by formulation of appropriate policies and strategies to guide responses, active participation by political leaders, and budgetary support to execute the policies.

Once the government acknowledges the threats to welfare and national development posed by a disease or health condition and agrees to tackle the problem, appropriate national policies and strategies need to be formulated to guide responses. Experiences from Cuba, the Islamic Republic of Iran, and Thailand demonstrate this point. Cuba set a national policy for universal and free access to social services with expansion of free health care to rural and low-income urban groups as one of its primary goals. Iran adopted a constitutional mandate to provide universal access to basic health services, whereas Thailand developed the AIDS Prevention and Control policy administered from the prime minister's office.

Box 4.6 Methods of Securing Political Commitment

Smart Data Presentation

Presentations of compelling research findings or statistics from surveillance surveys attracted political attention and led to subsequent
prioritization of HIV/AIDS in Thailand, tuberculosis in Nepal, and
riverblindness in West Africa. Political commitment needs to be
based on a solid understanding of the nature, extent, and socioeconomic effects of the health problem. The first HIV/AIDS case in
Thailand was identified in 1984 but government response was mut-
ed, based on the belief that the epidemic would remain limited to
groups practicing high-risk behavior—IDUs and men having sex
with men. This view changed drastically, however, when findings
from the first national epidemiological survey showed that the pandemic was spreading rapidly among the general population—44 percent of sex workers in Chiang Mai province were infected, leading
initially to high rates of infection among their male clients and subsequently among the general population. These survey results, brought
to public attention by NGOs, made it difficult to deny the reality of
the disease and prompted the government's strong, swift, and comprehensive response.

Similarly, riverblindness had been endemic among the poor communities in West Africa, but this disease was invisible to the colonial
administrations who thought it affected only the poorest of the poor
living in the most remote rural areas and so did not affect their interests. However, scientific research revealed astonishing and disturbing
facts—60 percent of the population in the savanna carried the para-
site, 30 percent of the people were visually impaired, and 10 percent
of the adult population were blind. The socioeconomic consequences
were devastating. High prevalence of blindness among adults reduced labor for agricultural activities. Food shortages and the subsequent collapse of these agrarian economies forced residents to abandon the fertile river valleys for dry, infertile, and overpopulated
highlands. Ultimately, riverblindness pushed prosperous communities into abject poverty. Presentations of the extent of its prevalence
and devastating economic impact made it a priority issue among
governments and development workers, first in West Africa and subsequently in Central and East Africa.

Engaging Political Leaders in Discussion of Health Issues

Linked to the point made above is that statistics can generate discussions among political leaders and policy makers. Discussions among
heads of state can be particularly effective in conveying messages and
convincing their fellow leaders to act. This was the case of Uganda's

fight against HIV/AIDS when President Museveni was warned by the president of Cuba, Fidel Castro: "You have a problem. Your army is going to be wiped out, not by the bullets of the enemy, but by HIV" (World Bank 2004b). This prompted President Museveni to personally lead the country's initial efforts to combat the disease. Lobbying at regional and international gatherings of heads of state can be used to raise awareness among political leaders and persuade them to prioritize health issues and apply pressure on one another to achieve as much progress as possible.

Community Demand

In environments that allow communication between communities and policy makers, poor communities can demand health services and cause governments to adopt *pro-poor* policies. The Islamic Republic of Iran, for example, enshrined the goal of providing basic social services to the poor—health care included—in the national constitution. This, combined with campaign promises of better services and greater influence of rural communities, led to high demand by the rural population for the same publicly supported health services enjoyed by their counterparts in urban areas. The Primary Health Care system was, in effect, the government's pragmatic way of responding to this demand.

Another way to demonstrate commitment is through active participation by the political leadership in the execution of policies. In Thailand the AIDS policy was put under the Office of the Prime Minister, and he chaired the multisectoral National AIDS Prevention and Control Committee. In Uganda, the AIDS Control Program met weekly under the chairmanship of President Museveni himself. This direct involvement of political leaders gave a sense of urgency and ensured that government and other development workers treated the problem as such. In Thailand the number of new infections was reduced significantly from an estimated 200,000 new cases in 1991 to 17,000 cases in 2003. Uganda managed to reduce HIV prevalence among antenatal mothers from more than 20 percent in 1992 to 6.5 percent in 2001.

Given the scarcity of resources in developing countries and competition for the same resources between health and other sectors, the human and financial resources required to address health problems can be secured only if there is political commitment at the highest level to make health a priority. This is vividly illustrated by the case of Cuba where, in spite of experiencing a severe economic

crisis that at its worst saw gross domestic product (GDP) plummet
by 35 percent, government expenditure on social services (health,
education, pensions, and social assistance) actually increased in
real terms and as a percentage of GDP from 15.8 percent to 20.7
percent, between 1989 and 2000. Similarly, Iran allocated 38 percent of public expenditure to health in 2001/02 in pursuit of its
policy of universal access to basic health care. However, increasing
public expenditure alone is not enough. Simply increasing public
spending without improving efficiency and targeting is unlikely to
improve health outcomes substantially. Most public spending on
health benefits the nonpoor and much of it fails to reach the front-
line service providers (World Bank 2004c).

Institutional Innovation: Decentralization

It has long been recognized that institutional arrangements have a
great bearing on the success or failure of health delivery systems.
Over the past 20 years, decentralization—defined as the transfer of
political power, decision making, and resource mobilization and allocation from central government and its agencies to subnational
levels—has gained popularity.[21] Arguments for decentralization include improved efficiency in allocating resources, responsiveness to
local needs, and accountability.[22] The main challenge facing project
planners and implementers is how to initiate institutional reform.
This requires major shifts in policies, which government workers
and politicians may resist. The task is further complicated by lack of
empirical evidence on the effectiveness of the various types and
forms of decentralization. Although not providing a panacea, the
cases of the Islamic Republic of Iran's Primary Health Care (PHC)
system, Nepal's Directly Observed Treatment Short-Course (DOTS)
program, and riverblindness control in West Africa demonstrate
simple decentralized institutional innovations that can effectively
and sustainably roll out health services, especially in the context of
limited human and financial resources (see box 4.7).

However, decentralization per se neither facilitates nor guarantees
the sustainability of health initiatives. In addition to the decentralized structure, the service level and technologies should be appropriate, and there should be capacity building and close coordination
among the various agencies.

Iran's remarkable experience in sustaining health services among
the rural poor can be attributed to a combination of decentralized institutional arrangements, focus on preventive care (immunization,
public health, antenatal attention, and so forth) as opposed to curative care, use of appropriate technologies and manpower (*behvarzan*,

not physicians), and establishment of integrated health information systems (see box 4.7). This system contrasts sharply with Cuba's centralized health system, which emphasized curative care, relied on high technology and physicians, and was thus unsustainable.

Box 4.7 Institutional Innovations

To improve access to health care services in remote rural areas, and given its limited human and financial resources, the Islamic Republic of Iran embarked on an innovative Public Health Care system that is simple but adequate and cost effective. The institutional arrangement for the PHC comprises Rural Health Houses (RHHs) established in remote villages—at most an hour's walk from the farthest household in its catchment. These houses are staffed with health workers recruited from local communities. Communities participate in the selection of local health workers, known locally as *behvarzan*. The second level of the system is the Rural Health Center (RHC) designed and located to support five RHHs and staffed by a medical doctor, nurses, and laboratory technicians. The third referral level is the District Health Center, which, among other things, is responsible for training *behvarzan* in the district, supervising RHCs, and providing tertiary care to referred patients. At the provincial level, universities of medical sciences and health services are responsible for planning and administering all health service delivery in the province. Although some other country development may have played a critical role, the accomplishments derived from this system are often associated with the decline in child mortality rates and narrowing of the gap between rural and urban areas. In 1974, when the Islamic Republic of Iran embarked on the PHC program, the infant mortality rate per thousand live births was 120 and 62 for rural and urban areas, respectively. By 2000 the respective rates were 30 and 28. Today, the country is one of the few on course to achieve the MDGs concerning child mortality and maternal health.

Nepal was confronted with high morbidity and mortality rates from tuberculosis. In the mid-1990s the detection and treatment success rate for tuberculosis was very low. However, adoption of innovative institutional arrangements to implement DOTS in 1996—initially as a pilot in 4 districts and subsequently expanded to all 75 districts—increased the cure rate to the internationally set indicator of 85 percent and a case detection rate of 70 percent by 2003.

The same is true for riverblindness control in Africa, where innovative, community-based drug distribution networks in 16 countries have expanded treatment from an initial 60,000 people (using the formal health system) to a staggering 35 million people—the majority of them living in remote rural areas where government health services are weak or nonexistent.

Capacity building plays a critical role in ensuring quality services at the various levels of the decentralized health delivery systems and in overcoming the chronic shortage of health workers, particularly in Africa.[23] Nepal's DOTS program has a strong capacity-building component to ensure competent staff at the various levels. The Japan International Cooperation Agency (JICA) has sponsored training of National Tuberculosis Control Program officials in Tokyo; annual tuberculosis seminars facilitate exchange of knowledge and experiences; and manuals, guidelines, and formats offer easy reference material to practitioners.

Although a decentralized institutional arrangement as well as a multisectoral approach are apt and desirable (see outcomes in box 4.7), close coordination is also necessary among the various players. Establishment of lead institutions such as the National Tuberculosis Control Centre as the national focal point played a pivotal role is Nepal's DOTS program. Given the cross-cutting effects of HIV/AIDS, responses are multisectoral, involving numerous organizations with a variety of approaches. To coordinate HIV/AIDS responses, Thailand and Uganda established National AIDS Committees in line with the "Three Ones" principle—one action framework that provides the basis for coordination, one national coordination authority, and one agreed monitoring and evaluation system.

More than 80 partners are involved in the riverblindness program, including 26 donors, 30 African countries, a major pharmaceutical firm, 12 major NGOs, and tens of thousands of local communities. Although creating synergies and enormous advantages as evidenced by the program's remarkable achievements, this broad coalition is difficult to maintain. A comprehensive international agreement (memorandum of understanding) that clearly delineates the roles and responsibilities of each part has fostered coordination in this 30-year program.

Learning and Experimentation

Learning and experimentation occur when different strategies are tried on a local scale first and, based on results, systematically integrated into the most promising national or regional strategies. The types of action learning illustrated in the country experiences range from institutionalized scientific research to ad hoc trials by communities (box 4.8).

Flexible Program Design in Implementation Flexibility in program design and monitoring are crucial in learning and experimentation.

Box 4.8 Learning and Experimentation

Scientific Research in West Africa

Scientific research is imperative in action learning because it provides much-needed scientific information about disease or health conditions, as illustrated by the riverblindness initiative in West Africa. That initiative started with spraying an area of 660,000 square kilometers—an area initially thought to be large enough to contain the blackfly that spreads riverblindness. However, after three months of successful spraying, there was invasion by migrant blackflies from untreated areas. New scientific evidence revealed that the blackfly can travel a distance of up to 600 kilometers. This new scientific evidence showed that to ensure effective control, spraying had to cover all the endemic zones. This, together with the knowledge that the lifespan of the female worm is 10–15 years, meant that even with instant and complete transmission control, the disease would not die out naturally for 15 years. These findings in turn led to a regional and long-term design.

In 1980, research and experiments indicated that the blackfly was developing genetic resistance to the sole larvicide used in the program. Scientific research and experiments yielded an innovative strategy that used seven different larvicides in rotation—a strategy that has become the standard model for vector control. Through research, the project has also developed rapid epidemiological mapping of onchocerciasis, a technique vital to rapid mapping and to accelerating the scaling up process. The initiative now invests 10 percent of its budget in operational research.

Community-based Action Learning in India

The Indian case study illustrates the importance of supporting local innovation. The Centre for Social Development's (CSD's) HIV/AIDS outreach intervention among injecting drug users in the state of Manipur, India, actually started as an agricultural project aimed at encouraging terrace cultivation, tractor hiring at low rent, as well as low-cost housing and latrine construction. However, progress was hampered by the debilitating effects of drugs and HIV/AIDS—just one year after the first case of HIV/AIDS was reported in the state in 1989, prevalence among IDUs rose to 50 percent, reaching 80 percent by 1997. Faced with this problem and in the absence of government mechanisms, CSD, with two other grassroots organizations—one formed by a local medical doctor and the other by former drug addicts—initiated innovative and unprecedented interventions to arrest drug use and the transmission of HIV/AIDS. Initial approaches applied by the three grassroots organizations emphasized abstinence.

Continued

Box 4.8 Continued

However, based on the assessment of the situation in Manipur and its experience elsewhere, the Swedish International Development Cooperation Agency recommended the harm-reduction model as opposed to the prevalent abstinence model. This approach involved providing IDUs with new injection needles and bleach to clean their injecting equipment. As expected, the harm-reduction approach faced critical opposition from the communities and law enforcement agencies. However, the three organizations responded by extending their activities to include educating and sensitizing the community and law enforcement agencies to the link between harm-reduction therapy and prevention of HIV/AIDS transmission. Their efforts created an environment free from any form of reprisal, condemnation, or pressure on IDU drop-in centers.

This initiative was so successful that in 1998 the Manipur State AIDS Control Society endorsed the harm-reduction approach and formulated policies to mandate its implementation across the state. The society also provided much-needed government leadership and commitment.

Flexibility allows for innovation and action learning. Communities learn from their innovations by systematically assessing and sharing information about what works and what does not. Activities are adjusted to changing circumstances and better understanding of the health problem. This is the case with riverblindness control in West Africa, which started with village pilot programs but found that the nature of the problem required a long-term and multicountry approach. The program evolved from a vertical, categorical vector-control program to community distribution of treatment and now to community mobilization to provide other health services. Although Nepal's DOTS program had guidelines and manuals, implementation was flexible to allow adaptation to local situations, and to give NGOs space to investigate new and more effective approaches. Similarly, Uganda has guidelines and manuals for combating HIV/AIDS but the government maintains a liberal policy that allows actors an opportunity to try innovative approaches.

Monitoring   Monitoring plays a crucial part in action learning.[24] Through monitoring, the effectiveness of the new approach can be assessed and feedback provided to make improvements. In Nepal's DOTS program, monitoring enabled the district and regional teams to review their performance regularly and take corrective action immediately. More important, monitoring generates information that can be used to influence decision making at the policy level. As alluded to earlier, an extensive serological surveillance of the general population, sentinel surveillance of groups whose members practice high-risk behavior, and surveillance of risky behavior generated information that changed the perception of Thailand's political leaders about HIV/AIDS, and allowed that country to identify the problem early and take measures to control the epidemic. Therefore, simple but effective health information systems are indispensable because they provide an information flow channel through which positive local innovations can be identified.

External Catalysts

Donor funding provides the extra resources required to scale up responses. In 2002, official development assistance was $57 billion with about 13 percent going to the health sector (Joint Learning Initiative 2004). In almost all the health cases—with the exception of the Islamic Republic of Iran and to some extent Cuba—direct external funding helped expand responses. The case of riverblindness in West Africa provides positive lessons on donor aid volatility—an issue generating heated debate, especially in countries expected to receive substantial amounts of aid for HIV/AIDS. Figure 4.1 shows oscillations in donor commitments that make it difficult for governments to set long-term plans. In the case of aid for HIV/AIDS, as an example, ministries of health cannot hire additional health staff to scale up activities because they are not certain

Figure 4.1 Donor Commitments as a Percentage of Total Health Expenditure, Selected Countries

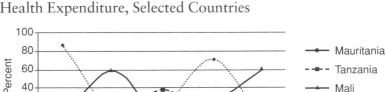

Source: Gottret and Schieber 2004.

about the duration of donor commitment and disbursements are unpredictable.

For external funding to be effective in improving and sustaining the health status of the recipient communities, it has to be long term, disbursement should be predictable, and the procedures to access aid should be simple. When the riverblindness program started in 1974 there were 18 donors. Today—31 years later—15 of the original donors are still actively supporting the program. Donor contribution to the initiative increased from $63 million when the program started to $157 million when the disease was defeated in West Africa in 1991. In West Africa, the initiative managed to increase labor productivity, prevented 600,000 cases of blindness, and made 25 million hectares of abandoned land safe for human settlement. After 1991, donor aid declined as the initiative moved to other parts of Africa where riverblindness, though present, is not as critical as it was in West Africa. Between 1974 and 2004 the initiative received more than $500 million. The long-term commitment of donors to this initiative was maintained through openness, regular feedback, and a clear definition of roles and responsibilities.

External support in the form of technical assistance is instrumental in scaling up responses, as demonstrated by the cases of Nepal and India. In 2003 bilateral agencies spent some $2.5 million on technical assistance in the form of training, personnel, and equipment in health and other sectors (OECD 2005). Technical assistance from the JICA in the form of equipment and advice on policies and institutional arrangements played a pivotal role in Nepal's DOTS initiative. Similarly, the Swedish International Development Cooperation Agency's technical assistance on the harm-reduction approach as opposed to the predominant abstinence model fostered greater adoption among UDIs and proved more effective in combating HIV transmission.

Looking Forward

The world is working to achieve the Millennium Development Goals related to health. Achieving these goals is a challenging task and the situation is further complicated by the current environment, which is characterized by shortages of human resources for health, tight budgets for the ministries of health, donor aid volatility, and the devastating socioeconomic effects of the HIV/AIDS pandemic. However, the task is by no means insurmountable, as shown by the case studies produced and shared at the Shanghai

Conference. Those initiatives reported remarkable achievements in providing adequate responses to health crises.

In discussing the main factors (leadership, innovation, learning, and external catalysts) considered imperative to roll out health services, especially to the poorest people, the health case studies shed light on *how* to secure these inputs. For example, effectively using data, engaging political leaders, and creating demand for health services among communities through awareness campaigns are some of the tools that can be used to secure political commitment and enhance accountability. The cases also show that there is a need to adopt pro-poor policies, use appropriate technologies and service levels, build capacity at the various levels, establish effective mechanisms for coordination, create a conducive environment for external support, make donor aid more predictable, and establish simple but effective health information systems. Based on evidence demonstrated by the country initiatives, we can conclude that, with these factors in place, nations can make significant progress toward the MDGs for health.

EDUCATION

Education, development, and growth are inextricably linked, with the major distributive and poverty amelioration effects of education well researched and extensively documented worldwide.[25] Education investments reap strong, positive economic, political, and social benefits, with girls' education demonstrating particularly high returns to individuals, their families, and societies.[26]

Despite substantial global improvements over the past few decades in increasing access to quality primary education for all (EFA), attainment of universal primary completion by 2015 remains a major challenge for many countries. An estimated 104 million children presently are out of school worldwide, including 58 million girls. Progress toward this Millennium Development Goal has been far slower than expected, given current per capita GDP growth rates in South Asia, the Middle East, and North Africa, and the target is likely to be widely missed in Sub-Saharan Africa unless efforts are sharply accelerated. Children who are poor, live in rural areas, or have special needs are at highest risk of noncompletion.[27]

Notably, girls' enrollments are increasing at a faster pace than those of boys in most countries. Nevertheless, the MDG of gender parity in primary and secondary education by 2005 will be missed. Moreover, amid continuing significant gender disparities in their enrollments, numerous countries may not reach this goal even by 2015 without a major push by their governments as well as support from the international development community. Support should be provided not only in terms of expanded resources but also of exploration and introduction of innovative approaches, contextualized to each setting, to address pervasive demand as well as supply constraints that limit girls' school enrollment and retention.

Moreover, hundreds of millions of children globally receive poor-quality education. Far too many schools lack basic inputs needed for good teaching practice and high learning outcomes, including qualified, well-deployed, and properly remunerated teachers; sufficient quantities and quality of textbooks and teaching materials; skilled school leadership and administration; and adequate physical infrastructure. Significant internal inefficiencies exist in many systems, often with high rates of teacher as well as student absenteeism contributing to excessive repetition and drop-out rates, thus precluding achievement of these students' full potential academically, economically, and socially.

Yet selected countries have made remarkable accomplishments in providing quality education services, particularly at the primary level and for highly vulnerable children. Many of these stories were captured for the Shanghai Conference.[28] They reveal several common distinguishing features of positive education reform efforts across countries of widely disparate economic and social development status, size, political systems, and organizational structures. Moreover, many experiences emerge from strikingly diverse local contexts, with social and cultural differences within each country commonly at least as great as between countries. These examples thus suggest several promising policy levers that the many other countries still facing slow progress in educational development may apply to accelerate attainment of education for all.

Factors Contributing to Scaling Up

Strong Leadership, Sustained Political Commitment, and Sound Strategies

Strong effective leadership and commitment to reforms of policies, institutions, and investments played a crucial role in virtually all countries studied, consistent with findings in other sectors. An essential corollary is commitment to the "right" policies. This underscores the importance of learning, experimentation, monitoring, and evaluation to guide scaling up, as is discussed later in this chapter.

The genesis of such strong commitment to EFA varies widely. In Kenya, Lesotho, Malawi, and Uganda, where attainment of universal primary education had long been constrained by political opposition and in some cases political instability, newly elected multiparty democratic governments made provision of free primary education a major tenet of their political platforms. Leaders sensed an inviolate social contract with their electorates and immediately abolished school fees—widely viewed as the principal obstacle to universal primary enrollment, especially among the poorest children.

Elite groups in Bangladesh, attributing their own ascent from rural areas to national prominence to their access to quality education, became major supporters of EFA. Touting the vital importance of education to national development goals, these leaders helped forge a shared commitment across divergent party boundaries and administrations. Recognizing the importance of education for economic competitiveness and global integration, political leaders of the Arab Republic of Egypt effectively transformed EFA into a national priority; as a result, budgetary allocations were redistributed from other sectors to support needed investments.

Similarly, spurred by a landmark 1993 Supreme Court decision affirming the right of every child to education, and the ensuing EFA-9 Summit that year in New Delhi, the central government of India launched a major initiative in partnership with states to attain its long-elusive goal of universal primary education—the District Primary Education Project (DPEP). Given the diversity of the country, including special challenges to service provision presented by small, remote communities, DPEP promoted experimentation with not only formal but also nonformal schooling models such as that adopted in the late 1990s in Madhya Pradesh, India. The Education Guarantee Scheme (EGS) became the flagship mission of that state government, assigned highest political and budgetary priority by its chief minister.[29]

Continuity of reform leadership also helped sustain program momentum in at least two studied countries—El Salvador and India (Madhya Pradesh). Core teams in each case remained in power for at least a decade, providing their nascent reform movements with the stability needed to stay the course and manage popular expectations—crucial factors given the inherently slow change process.[30]

Analysis suggests, however, that the defining determinant of the pace, breadth, and depth of positive experiences was the locus of leadership, particularly the extent to which education reform strategies attained an equilibrium between centralized and decentralized approaches, appropriate to the given country context and with clearly defined roles and responsibilities for each level of the system. The right sequencing of reforms also proved crucial. These presented substantial challenges for many countries, as underscored in experiences shared at the Shanghai Conference.

Centralized Leadership and the Big-Bang Approach Among studied countries that launched highly centralized reforms, designed and instituted largely via top-down leadership, several also represented "big-bang" approaches, with multiple reform components instituted simultaneously. These led often to a relatively rapid initial expansion of access to educational services to a level at which the vast majority of school-age children were enrolled (net enrollment rates of 70 to 80 percent). The often highly visible, immediate, positive effects of rapid, highly centralized reform efforts helped gain at least short-term political buy-in from the general population.

Turkey's Rapid Coverage for Compulsory Education (RCCE) Program is a key example. Conceived during a period of severe economic crises, political instability, and short-lived coalition governments, its early survival appears attributable in part to conscious adoption of a highly centralized, big-bang approach, thus reducing potential for opposing interest groups to undermine it. The intensity of the government's education reform efforts, coupled with promulgation of a new law permitting tax-deductible donations to education, also awakened a strong public fervor to contribute. Ensuing substantial inflows of private sector donations, particularly those from the Istanbul Stock Exchange (ISE), helped accelerate the scaling up process.[31]

The frequent lack of adequate, upfront, broad political and social consensus, or in-depth planning and management in such top-down reforms, including often weak attention to strengthening institutional capacity, can lead to unforeseen and negative consequences that threaten their medium- to long-term sustainability. All such studied reform countries ultimately had to mobilize support of major stakeholder groups in order to continue. Most important, these experiences suggest that models purely led from the center often are less effective in reaching the most vulnerable subgroups, such as the rural poor, minorities, girls, and people with disabilities.

Local Participatory and Incremental Approaches Several countries mobilized strong local government and community participation in their education reforms. These countries facilitated the relatively rapid adaptation of education reform models to unique local needs and contexts, thereby advancing progress toward universal primary completion.

Community-generated or -led bottom-up reforms, such as the Education with Community Participation (EDUCO) program in El Salvador and the EGS in India, represent models of strong partnership with the state and the benefits that may accrue from adoption of more incremental reform approaches. Their stepped, sequential reform process allowed for more careful planning and management than those launched with a big bang. From the outset, both central governments assigned key leadership roles in the development, implementation, and monitoring of education service delivery to local communities and civil society. This proved crucial to reach the most vulnerable children in a timely and effective manner. Moreover, the strong sense of local ownership these measures generated appears instrumental in sustaining reforms over the longer term.

EDUCO dramatically altered the role of El Salvador's central education ministry in rural education. The central government remained the principal financier and overseer of public education, and assumed a key local capacity-building and technical assistance role. Service delivery, however, became the domain of local communities via elected, autonomous community education associations (ACEs), comprising the parents of students, contracted by the ministry to deliver a given curriculum to an agreed number of students. For the first time, school management authority was totally decentralized to the school itself. By 2003, the more than 2,000 ACEs operating in the country directly administered in aggregate $50 million or some 12 percent of the national education budget.

This model not only profoundly changed rural education service delivery but also catalyzed development of strong community social capital. Devolution of school control to parents empowered them to assume for the first time a leading role in their children's education and encouraged them to augment their own educational attainment. Significant operational efficiencies were realized. The agility of the new model reduced start-up time for new schools from the traditional average of three to four years to mere months in most cases, facilitated by the common conversion of much existing local community infrastructure to education facilities. The results framework adopted had high returns. Performance-based contracts by which community associations recruited teachers significantly reduced their absenteeism: ACE-contracted teachers av-

eraged five days per week in school versus the three days previously typical in rural schools. Further, some evidence exists that the
EDUCO-managed educational services are of better quality than
those offered by traditional schools.

The well-documented experience of this community-based model led the central government to establish by law nationwide school
boards to manage funds transferred from the central level in all traditional public schools.[32] EDUCO also encouraged substantive reforms in the central education ministry, instituted with financial
and technical support from both the Inter-American Development
Bank and the World Bank.

The EGS of Madhya Pradesh exemplifies a similar radical shift in
that state's education paradigm catalyzed and guided by the DPEP
program that the central government of India launched in 1994.
Though planned and financed from the top down, DPEP promoted
the adoption of decentralized, flexible, and innovative models of
service provision, responsive to the country's diversity-based demand to contextualize program design and management to local
needs. It specifically targeted districts with low female literacy rates.
These districts became the locus of education planning, drawing on
the substantial accumulated experience and expertise outside the
traditional education system, including NGOs, for new ideas and
approaches to enhance system capacity, expand coverage, and increase gender equity of educational opportunities. In sharp contrast
to the formal system in India, and similar to the EDUCO approach,
these schools were totally owned by the community, with DPEP
transferring education budgets directly to school management committees composed of local villagers. Communities also decided
school calendars appropriate to local agricultural cycles and seasonal needs for child labor. As in China's primary education universal-
ization process, an integral component of the DPEP approach was
the interstate transfer of reform knowledge and skills.

Madhya Pradesh benefited directly from DPEP-led analyses to
guide its state education reform movement. The EGS scheme also
was informed by a 1996 household survey revealing that almost
one in four boys and more than one in three girls of primary school
age were out of school, most of them never having enrolled. The
ensuing reform reshaped the Madhya Pradesh education system,
moving it from an historically highly centralized one to a unique
and mutually supportive partnership among the community, local
government, and the state.[33]

Through the EGS initiative, the state government provided a unilateral, legally bound guarantee to respond within 90 days with req-

uisite funding to every local self-government institution—the *pan-chayat*—that generated demand for a primary school within walking distance of its community. The pledge included state funding for school construction, textbooks and other core learning materials, as well as pre- and in-service training of new teachers identified by communities. These new schools were predominantly single-teacher, multigrade classrooms. The state government also maintained responsibility for supervision, monitoring, and evaluation of community-run primary schools, to ensure their parity with traditional primary schools in terms of inputs, outputs, and student learning outcomes. Local communities in turn provided land or space for new schools and managed the midday school meal. Most notably, the EGS introduced for the first time formal mechanisms for communities and *panchayats* to participate directly in local school management, supervision, and educational quality improvements.

Thus, the EGS "effectively flipped the accountability pyramid" with the education system answerable to the local village and the school totally owned by and accountable to the Village Education Committees and parent-teacher associations—all members of which were elected by the villagers. Education coverage rose rapidly under the EGS, with 1.2 million children enrolled in primary schools between 1997 and 2002. The overwhelming majority of students were from socially disadvantaged, rural families, and almost half were girls, thus closing the gender gap and significantly raising female literacy rates—coveted achievements for much of India. Substantial human and physical infrastructure investments underpinned these increased enrollments.[34]

Seeking Equilibrium among Central, State, and Local Initiatives
Highly decentralized models can result in significant inequities in education services among regions, districts, and communities within countries because of these entities' highly variable fiscal and institutional capacity, among other factors. Further, as reform experience elsewhere highlights, rapid implementation that permits early visibility of outcomes can be crucial to secure political support and thus sustain momentum in outer years. Slower-paced reforms thus face the inherent danger of being undermined by opponents before they take sufficient root and establish requisite wide stakeholder trust and confidence. Hence, close monitoring of the political climate as well as of these systems' performance is essential to swiftly address potential problems as soon as they emerge.

Central governments thus typically must continue to play key roles in promoting equity through such measures as setting overall system education standards; monitoring and evaluating system and student performance, including learning outcomes; and channeling subsidies where fiscal gaps threaten disparities in inputs, outputs, and outcomes. Achieving and maintaining the optimum balance between top-down and bottom-up leadership continues to be a major challenge.

Bangladesh is a prime example of the value of highly centralized policy formulation and planning in the initial stages of the reform process, and then the adoption over time and of necessity of a more integrated, collaborative centralized and decentralized model including a markedly pluralistic approach to education service provision. The original big-bang initiative spurred rapid increases in overall national enrollment levels but proved less effective in reaching those at highest risk of being out of school—rural children and girls. Thus, the original policy framework and program design had to be modified not only to permit but also to strongly encourage participation of alternative service providers. These new actors included local districts and communities, as in several other education initiatives highlighted at the Shanghai Conference, as well as NGOs offering nonformal primary education programs and new public-private partnerships in secondary education. Such diversification of the education service model resulted in the operation, nationally, of at least 11 distinct types of official primary schools in Bangladesh.

This diversification of the education landscape in Bangladesh occurred, however, without any significant devolution of central government authority over education policy and planning. Thus, the central government remains a major provider of education services, directly managing and providing all resources for about half of all official primary schools, and a major force in the subsidization of their operations and oversight to ensure that all schools meet national curriculum standards.

China similarly adopted a "stratified, categorized centralization" strategy for its Universal Nine-Year Compulsory Education Program for Poverty Reduction. This unique incremental, phased reform was guided by a centrally formulated master plan. Achieving rapid progress toward universal primary enrollment, however, required government willingness (particularly in rural areas) to adopt differentiated interventions and reform time frames, developed in close collaboration with regional and local governments based on in-depth analysis and mobilization of substantial community resources. These responded directly to recognized, highly variable regional and local education status and capacity for reform.

Focusing on Strategy The studies reveal that the choice of reform strategies pursued by leaders can profoundly affect progress toward scaling up education programs. Those strategies that appear to yield better reform outcomes include (1) articulating well-defined objectives and the division of responsibilities to achieve those objectives, as well as widely and effectively communicating them to key stakeholder groups; (2) prioritizing and targeting investments and interventions, including contextualizing them to local conditions, particularly in large countries with federal systems; and (3) addressing pervasive, continuing demand constraints to student enrollment and retention in school, including quality issues, concomitant with expansion of supply.

Effective reforms generally had clear, overarching objectives (often highly selective) derived from careful prioritizing and targeting of investments to subgroups and interventions that promised high payoffs. Many country reform programs thus focused on the hardest-to-reach students, typically rural poor children and girls, as was the case in China, the Arab Republic of Egypt, Turkey, and Bangladesh.

China had long recognized that expanded access to basic education was central to its development, particularly for the majority of its population residing in rural areas. Its education program for poverty reduction, launched in 1986, responded to lagging progress toward this goal. Its overriding objective was to ensure that all children completed at least nine years of basic education and all youth and adults were literate. A tightly circumscribed strategy was pursued with investments heavily concentrated in two main areas—upgrading all school facilities to meet at least minimum standards, and enhancing teacher quality via a comprehensive certification process. Solid improvement has been reported for both efforts.

Over the initial 15 years of China's program, net enrollment in nine-year compulsory education nationwide reportedly reached 85 percent; and illiteracy among young adults fell to less than 5 percent. Among key contributing factors was a significant increase in the proportion of qualified primary and lower secondary teachers (to 94 percent and 88 percent, respectively). The indicated outcomes of these reforms led to their continuation as integral components of China's Tenth Five-Year Plan (2000–2005).

Egypt similarly prioritized its investments, emphasizing improvements in school quality that national research revealed most affected girls' enrollment and retention, particularly smaller class sizes, lower student-teacher ratios, closer proximity and improved physical conditions of schools, teaching and curriculum that were not gender based, and more extracurricular and home economics activities. Further, strict parameters were set, such as maximum school walking distances and mandatory attendance follow-up mechanisms, and school performance indicators were specified.

Between 1999 and 2003, both female and male school drop-out rates in Egypt reportedly were halved, to 4 percent; average class sizes decreased to some 41 students or roughly the world average; and double and triple shifts almost were eliminated. Underlying these achievements were major investments in new schools, predominantly in poorer governates; in pre- and in-service teacher training, including instruction in gender sensitivity; and in provision of school uniforms and supplies to some 46,000 disadvantaged students, including 15,000 who returned after having abandoned school. These efforts culminated in national attainment of gender equity in primary schooling in 2005. Assuming reforms are sustained, as expected, Egypt is well poised to achieve universal primary education by 2015.

Turkey's RCCE program, launched in 1997, had one dominant goal—enrolling the last and hardest-to-reach 35 percent of students, mostly rural children 11–14 years of age and girls. Interventions were identified and prioritized via an in-depth analysis of the target group by the National Planning Office, and precise strategies were outlined. Delineation of quantitative and qualitative education sector performance indicators in Turkey's 15-Year Master Plan helped build wide public confidence in the program's potential for results. This well-targeted investment strategy had high apparent returns. Total enrollment increased by 1.5 million students after 1998, and net enrollment for the eight-year compulsory cycle rose to 95 percent. After a 162 percent increase in the program's first year, rural girls' enrollments in grade 6 continued to register sharp annual gains.

Experience also reveals, however, that tightly circumscribed reform agendas can exact a high toll on excluded groups. Bangladesh's virtually exclusive focus on expanding enrollments of rural poor children, and especially girls, led to considerable bypassing of other marginalized subgroups, including *chor,* tribal minorities, and urban slum children, whose distinct needs have only recently begun to be addressed (largely by NGOs). Such service provision patterns reflect common tendencies by governments to rely on alternative providers and modalities, including nonformal services to help reach more geographically and socially marginal groups.

Throughout the studied countries, as in much of the developing world, positive reform strategies addressed not only the need to rapidly and substantially increase the supply of education but also, and often most importantly, significant demand side constraints to attainment of universal primary education goals. Major sociocultural barriers to school entry and retention emerged, particularly relating to girls' education. These often reflected widespread parental questioning of the value and relevance of curriculum to traditional roles of females within their societies. The typically high direct and indirect costs of schooling including outlays not only for school fees but also for textbooks, materials, examinations, uniforms, school meals, sports and cultural activities, and at times even supplements to teacher salaries, represent a significant financial burden, especially for the poorest households.

The experiences of Malawi and Uganda—early education reformers in Africa—reveal the importance of pursuing EFA as an integral part of systemic, sectorwide programs, as was the case in infrastructure, as earlier discussed. Systemic approaches must be coupled with clear definition of priorities to guide decision making on where best to initiate the reform process. In this context, these Sub-Saharan African studies highlight the close interaction between quality of education and demand for schooling. The unprecedented pace of growth in enrollment following introduction of free primary education (FPE) policies suggests that fees were major obstacles to raising coverage levels. Their elimination resulted in severe "access shock" as education systems strained to meet multiple demands. These demands included redressing acute shortages of teachers, textbooks, and other educational materials. Also required were major changes to teaching practices to respond to learning needs within a far more diverse classroom than in the past, one encompassing students with a wider range of abilities and socioeconomic backgrounds, those with special education needs (consistent with more inclusive education policies), and large numbers of over-age pupils who had never enrolled or were re-entering after dropping out of school.

In Malawi and Uganda, early initiatives failed to sustain primary enrollment increases. Numbers of drop-outs rose rapidly as education quality waned amid increasing dependence on double and triple shifts to meet such unprecedented levels of demand for schooling. The failures proved to be powerful lessons for subsequent reformers, such as Kenya and Lesotho. Both nations gained valuable insights from field visits to countries already instituting FPE policies, and subsequently adopted more planned, phased, and integrated strategies to improve enrollments and enhance quality simultaneously. These more incremental approaches also afforded them time to consult and negotiate with key stakeholder groups, thus helping forge strong local ownership of reform processes. Drawing on earlier experiences, later reformers also embarked on intensive consultative processes with the international community to close financing gaps, thus helping stabilize these education systems.

Eliminating school fees catalyzed numerous other systemic reforms in Kenya, Lesotho, Malawi, and Uganda. These ranged from curriculum and textbooks to new modalities of teacher training and classroom practice, and even to the introduction of local languages to facilitate learning in the early primary years.[35]

These experiences also reveal the need to protect against potentially negative consequences of introducing FPE policies. Review of several Sub-Saharan African countries by Kattan and Burnett (2004) suggested that FPE policies at least initially may have undermined long-standing, strong parental commitment to education in these countries, and created new expectations that the central government would henceforth assume all responsibilities and costs for children's education. This led to major government efforts since 2000 to re-ignite community participation in such key areas as school construction and teacher contributions. Although phased grade-by-grade introduction of FPE greatly facilitated most systems' adjustment to the inherent shocks of rapid expansion, it also led to distortions in enrollment levels at discrete grades in at least one country—Lesotho. A surge occurred in first grade as many families enrolled very young children to avoid paying fees for preschool that were not covered in FPE policies and in the final year of primary school (with some parents withholding their children from promotion to higher grade levels that were not free).

Over time, and with needed policy adjustments, institution of FPE reportedly has translated into significant, sustained increases in primary enrollments, especially among children from poorer income quintiles. Enrollment ratios among the poorest and richest quintiles, in Uganda particularly, are now almost equal.

As underscored above, FPE policies alone are not a panacea to attain universal primary education. In Malawi, despite its being the first Sub-Saharan African country to institute FPE, direct costs of education remain a significant barrier for very poor families. There is almost an 18 percent gap in school attendance between students from the lowest and highest family income quintiles. Moreover, Malawi's relatively low per capita income and high debt ratio present significant challenges to funding and sustaining FPE.

Communication and participation strategies using both mass media and traditional vehicles, such as religious leaders, proved essential to build reform buy-in by key constituencies in Kenya,

Lesotho, Malawi, and Uganda. Mobilizing religious leaders played a key role in building social consensus in Egypt as well. Imams were systematically tapped for community awareness campaigns designed to raise parental demand for schooling, especially schooling of girls and particularly in Upper Egypt where traditionally there has been a low female enrollment rate. In Turkey, television and radio networks voluntarily donated airtime to disseminate information on the new eight-year compulsory education program and to encourage enrollment, especially of girls who were significantly absent from schools in selected areas of the country.

Fostering Institutional Innovations

Most countries that shared their experiences for the global learning process experimented with new institutional structures and statutory mechanisms. Some transformed their education paradigm, moving the system from a traditional, heavily centralized administration to one in which local communities and parents too play major roles. Prime examples include El Salvador's community education associations—ACEs—and the parent-teacher associations and village education committees established in Madhya Pradesh, India.[36] Such entities and statutes provide heretofore largely ignored parents and local leaders with a new voice in their schools—a voice they are unlikely to relinquish easily.

In Bangladesh the opening of the education system to alternative providers, particularly NGOs, not only accelerated increased enrollments but, importantly, also fostered experimentation with such innovations as provision of food or cash grants to families whose children regularly attended school. Female stipend programs offered by the Bangladesh Rural Advancement Committee (the country's largest NGO) rapidly expanded secondary enrollments, particularly of girls from poor families. The well-documented experience led to mainstreaming of stipend programs nationwide.

Among the more effective institutional innovations were those implemented to effect greater public sector accountability for education. Madhya Pradesh's People's Education Act of 2002 provided greater transparency and strengthened education administration accountability to the *panchayat,* via such instruments as District Annual Academic Reports.[37]

In China, a new monitoring and inspection system closely monitored and regulated local government progress toward expanded quality schooling for all children. Special bank accounts, transparent procurement processes, and training of local staff were introduced, with special emphasis on development of a strong cadre for the program's management information system. The resulting more timely and reliable local data flows supported the new national education database and network of information sharing and, in turn, enabled better resource distribution and use.

After analysis revealed substantial leakage of education funds, Uganda decided to post local school budgets at the community level, thus allowing local monitoring of resource use. This disclosure policy signified the government's firm commitment to significantly enhance transparency and accountability for public education funds. It also helped catalyze a strong international movement toward the institution of public expenditure tracking surveys.[38]

Many institutional innovations built on positive achievements of initial, relatively small-scale pilot activities. Egypt drew extensively on four pilot activities to significantly augment the supply of "second-chance" schools, most of which are simple one-room classrooms that offer schooling opportunities for older children and youth who either never enrolled or dropped out. Between 1999 and 2003 alone, some 1,600 girls and 800 boys enrolled.

Less effective over the short to medium term have been several countries' efforts to effect major changes in existing organizational cultures and attitudes at all levels, from central ministries to local districts and schools—reforms that were viewed as crucial to the process of scaling up. As highlighted in the cases studied, this component of an education sector's transformative process can be inherently slow. Thus, after instituting free primary education policies, Lesotho and Uganda decided (at least for the short term) largely to bypass traditional institutions that were seemingly intractable to change—notably including their own education ministries—to accelerate implementation of key aspects of their reforms. Lesotho selected its autonomous Institute of Management to train innovative new cadres of paraprofessional teachers, viewed as crucial to respond to the explosive enrollments, and a managerial corps to lead the education system revitalization process. Uganda relied extensively on external consultants to respond to immediate and short-term system needs, especially primary education curriculum revisions. And Kenya, Lesotho, Malawi, and Uganda created interim "innovation enclaves" within their ministries of education, somewhat protected from the larger bureaucracies, to help accelerate reform progress. These experiences valuably demonstrated the high potential that existed to accelerate reforms. But they also underscored the need to embed good new practices in existing institutions if reforms were to be sustained.

Continuous Learning and Experimentation

Throughout the country experiences, decisions on the overall design as well as optimum starting points for launching effective reforms were consistently well grounded in solid, local, applied research. Egypt's Education Enhancement Program, for example, drew extensively on national research and donor-funded studies as well as on in-country pilot projects and broader international experience. This composite knowledge led to targeting poor, rural, culturally conservative regions (especially in Upper Egypt) that faced serious cultural constraints to girls' education, including traditions of early marriage and preferences among large families to enroll boys. It also disclosed several previously unknown major supply side barriers to girls' education related to school location and infrastructure conditions, teaching practices, and policies for female school drop-outs. Practical solutions for overcoming these barriers were rapidly launched.

In Turkey, design of the RCCE program was informed and guided by a National Planning Office in-depth analysis of the causes of nonenrollment among the 35 percent of hardest-to-reach students. This research served as a catalyst in testing variants of the regular eight-year primary school and several new schemes to meet the special needs of rural poor children. These include, for example, bussing for those residing in small, scattered communities; and regional free boarding schools or schools with pension housing in areas where bussing distances were too great. Further, Turkey established an earmarked extrabudgetary program (the Social Solidarity Fund) to finance meals for bussed children, and provided selected subsidies such as free meals, textbooks, and uniforms to poor students to reduce direct and indirect opportunity costs of schooling and, hence, raise enrollments. It experimented with numerous variants to traditional teacher recruitment, assignment, and remuneration policies, including teacher hardship pay and housing inducements, as well as alternative service delivery models such as "open basic education" for school drop-outs age 15+ years. Further, it attempted to establish municipal and local government cooperation in new school location decisions.

A 1996 problem-mapping exercise in which *panchayat* leadership, teachers, and literacy activists joined forces for a door-to-door survey in Madhya Pradesh, India, served as the basis for a Village Education Register—a veritable "people's information system" subsequently used to monitor local area progress toward universal primary education. Among the main underlying causes of nonenrollment identified were lack of local schools, family economic constraints, and school-related factors. Social resistance to girls' education was found to be not as widespread as popularly believed. These insights transformed *panchayat*-level education plans and refocused reform efforts. A repeat 1999 survey documented achievements and defined strategic future directions. That this government has now mainstreamed the scheme and concomitantly stopped further establishment of government schools has provided the scheme with crucial legitimacy and status, although the model is still viewed largely as an "alternative" elsewhere in India.

Careful evaluation of the room for maneuver politically and technically also appears crucial to effective reforms. That Egypt already had largely resolved broader education access issues provided it the requisite political base to shift attention predominantly to girls—the most lagging enrollment group—via its Education Enhancement Program. El Salvador's EDUCO experience suggests that innovations may best take seed when they are initiated in subgroups or geographic areas least threatening to traditional institutions and systems, such as under- and unserved rural areas. EDUCO addressed a rural access gap that the formal system had not filled, thereby reducing opposition from teachers' unions and other political groups. When its effectiveness was well documented and acknowledged, EDUCO relatively easily expanded coverage from preschool through grade 3 up to grade 6 and then to grade 9, ultimately becoming the model of choice for rural education.

Applied research in several countries has been instrumental in analyzing reform outcomes, identifying potential unintended consequences, and guiding reform adjustments as needed. Kenyan research revealed that early marriage or pregnancy contributed to high drop-out rates among girls, and indicated that "uninteresting" curricula, examination failure, and repetition of grades reportedly were key drop-out causes for all students—rather than school costs, as had been the case prior to FPE. Disability and illness also played a role in drop-out rates. In Malawi and Uganda, in contrast to Kenya, indirect costs of schooling were found to be a continuing constraint on enrollment and retention among the poorest Malawian and Ugandan children, despite FPE policies. Overall, such findings underscore the crucial role of local research in informing decision making on appropriate demand side interventions to complement expansion of supply toward the goal of universal primary completion and gender parity in enrollments.

Most countries experimented extensively with highly differentiated strategies and innovative models. Systematic monitoring and evaluation of those strategies and innovations reduced both perceived and real risks, and played a critical feedback role, guiding wider integration of the most promising approaches. Ensuring that core programmatic information reached the right people in a timely way transformed line ministries into true learning organizations. China is a striking example, with schools participating in the Nine-Year Compulsory Education Project serving as demonstration sites for other community schools. Moreover, richer areas of the country supported poorer counties, and experienced teachers were sent to support newer, less seasoned ones. This internally driven technical cooperation model serves as a key vehicle for sustainable scaling up of China's education reform process.

Ongoing research coupled with close program monitoring can accelerate identification of and appropriate response to unforeseen negative consequences of new reforms. Data emerging from Kenya, Lesotho, Malawi, and Uganda, for example, suggest that children who are disabled or have other special needs may be among the first victims of overcrowded classrooms when enrollments increase rapidly. The numbers of such drop-outs and whether they reflect predominantly push or pull factors merit urgent research attention. A likely contributing factor is reduced teacher time to meet the needs of more resource-intensive students. Uganda data also revealed that school survival rates declined from almost two out of every three students to only slightly more than one in three students after its rapid expansion of coverage following the institution of FPE policies, with poorest children at highest risk of dropping out.[39]

Ensuring not only the capacity but also the political will of education systems to respond in a timely and appropriate way to monitoring and evaluation system feedback has been an essential corollary to effective reforms. When Turkey's monitoring and evaluation system revealed that its consolidation effort in small village schools had adversely affected girls' enrollment, for example, the government decisively reopened 1,200 such schools in the 2003/04 academic year.

External and Internal Catalysts for Change

International and regional conferences, declarations, and commitments played a pivotal role (and continue to exert influence) in accelerating actions to advance educational development, particularly among the poorest countries. Among the most influential was the EFA Conference, sponsored by the United Nations Educational, Scientific, and Cultural Organization and held in Jomtien, Thailand, in 1990. The conference catalyzed a large wave of education reforms over the ensuing decade. For the governments of Kenya, Lesotho, Malawi, and Uganda, Jomtien discussions served as a prime impetus for eliminating compulsory school fees and thus expanding educational enrollments, particularly by the poorest students.

The Jomtien Conference also strongly influenced education reforms in El Salvador and India, among other countries. As El Salvador emerged from a protracted and devastating civil war, the Jomtien Conference and the Declaration on the International Rights of Children were instrumental in mobilizing international support to rebuild its education system. The United Nations Children's Fund also played a key role in the immediate postconflict period, financing a major sector study that highlighted the strong potential for communities to resume the leadership role in the sector that they had assumed during the civil war. While the study guided design of EDUCO's community-managed schools program, subsequent loans and technical assistance from the World Bank enabled that government to redress fiscal and capacity constraints as necessary to launch the EDUCO initiative.

Notably, the fact that donors began to invest heavily in education following the Jomtien Conference provided an important additional impetus not only to reform efforts by governments but also to programs of international and national NGOs. In Bangladesh, for example, donors encouraged the government to allow expanded NGO activity in the sector, thereby contributing to the more pluralistic system that is now operative. Strong reaffirmation of international commitments to attaining EFA, including the Dakar Framework for Action that evolved from the World Education Forum held in Senegal in 2000 and, more recently, the promulgation of the MDGs and the definition of concrete actions, and joint government and international community responsibilities needed to attain them (as outlined in the Monterrey Consensus), have helped sustain interest and momentum.

Regional and international meetings and the increased use of study tours also have been valued sources of knowledge on promising, innovative approaches to accelerating education reforms (although, importantly, adapted to local contexts). Lesotho, for example, introduced community catering of school meals after viewing private sector outsourcing approaches in Asia.

The international community also has catalyzed introduction of new development frameworks, including Poverty Reduction Strategy statements, medium-term expenditure frameworks that have helped governments justify basic education expenditures. Increasing formulation of sectorwide programs has facilitated greater donor harmonization as well as resource mobilization. And the Heavily Indebted Poor Countries Initiative has enabled many education ministries to secure larger shares of the national budget, as required to promote both basic education access and quality.

In summary, among the most powerful external catalysts of education reforms have been mobilization of broad international commitment to EFA via several major international conferences over the past decade, introduction of new development frameworks that better document the importance of investments in education to attain development and poverty reduction objectives, and increased exposure of countries to accumulated global sector knowledge and experience.

Notwithstanding the effects of such external factors, in the majority of studied countries the most powerful catalysts for increasing educational opportunities have been internal to the country. Generally the key catalytic role has been played by the ministry of education through concerted efforts to gain support and forge new alliances with other core ministries, as well as establish new national partnerships for education, particularly with the private sector (including NGOs and communities) in pursuit of shared visions.

In Kenya, Lesotho, Malawi, and Uganda, the main catalyst for expanding primary education came from within, although mobilization of external support from at least one major donor helped accelerate expansion of each education system (including crash teacher training and classroom construction initiatives). The complementary external support was essential not only to rapidly accommodate the large influx of new students, but also to build public confidence in the ensuing reform process. Similarly, in Bangladesh domestic resources were the primary financing mechanism for initial scaling up efforts, thus helping ensure that allocations were available when critically needed and helping foster a strong sense of local ownership in the reform programs. Only later did external assistance play a key role in this process via the World Bank–supported Female Secondary Education project

The Egyptian government mobilized an extensive array of public-private partnerships for education, including the contracting of 171 NGOs and community development associations to support its reform process. Among the more innovative approaches to partnership is the one introduced in 2000 in Madhya Pradesh, India. Although the central government–led DPEP project served as a strong external catalyst for education reform in the state, the "Fund a School" Program, initiated by that state government, has been instrumental in mobilizing private funding to support public educa-

tion. Using a local Website, this adopt-a-school scheme permits donations to be credited directly to a given school's account. Close to
1,000 individuals and institutions have participated to date.

In Turkey, it was largely the national desire to attain full integration into the European Union that afforded the education sector
needed, wide, cross-sectoral support to launch and sustain its reforms. A key element of that strategy was abolition of the primary
school diploma awarded at the end of grade 5, and its replacement
with a basic education completer's diploma offered only upon completion of grade 8. This led over the past five years to a significant
increase in enrollments in the full compulsory cycle, with average
levels of educational attainment of Turkish youth moving much
closer to those of the Organisation for Economic Co-operation and
Development countries. Two other strong push factors can be identified for expanding educational opportunities in Turkey: (1) secur-
ing an International Monetary Fund agreement to a minimum annual allocation to education of 4.25 percent of GDP, thus increasing
government confidence that the proposed RCCE program would
be sustainable and public expectations would be met, if initiated;
and (2) increasing government concern over then-rampant social
instability and its associated terrorism risk, especially among selected population groups perceiving themselves to be excluded
from society.

Moreover, at its own initiative the ISE established in the 1990s
an exciting new social sector partnership with the ministry of education to accelerate education sector development. Earnings from
the ISE's significant financial donation to the public sector have
supported an expansive construction and renovation program, including purchase of furniture and computer equipment, for eight-
year basic education schools. This initiative is targeted especially to
small, rural areas in the poor east and southeast regions of the
country where there are large gender gaps in enrollment. The innovative, competitively selected school designs also provide, for the
first time, access to schooling for disabled students. This partnership has sparked government campaigns to mobilize other private
sector resources to help enlarge provision of both preschool and
secondary education—new focal points of national reform efforts.
The recent introduction of tax deductions for such donations led to
a reported significant increase in resource commitments from such
internal sources.

Latin America's regional Fe y Alegria network comprises private,
nonprofit, Jesuit-run primary schools serving almost 1 million children in the poorest communities of 15 countries. Its dynamic ap-

proach includes strong community participation. At the initiative of AVINA, one of Latin America's leading foundations, this network is now engaged in the Centro Magis Program in which regional business leaders are bringing best private sector management practices and values into the Fe y Alegria education network. Not only has this led to improvements in its management information and financial management systems; it also has promoted more systematic knowledge sharing across its schools regionwide. This partnership is helping this faith-based institution raise a heretofore absent voice in regional education forums—a potentially significant departure from the tightly circumscribed education policy role typically afforded church-operated school systems in many countries.

Other internal factors also are exerting a strong push for promoting education access and quality in some countries. In Bangladesh, the rapidly changing national economic and social milieu, including rising rates of divorce and desertion and increases in dowry size in the 1980s (especially in poor communities), eroded families' confidence in marriage and its traditional role in providing female economic security. Emergence of new female employment opportunities over that same period, including within the nascent export-oriented garment industry, appear also to have strongly encouraged families not only to enroll their daughters but to have them complete at least primary schooling to secure labor market entry.

Continuing Challenges

Notwithstanding the remarkable experiences shared through the global learning process, four immediate challenges remain for many countries to reach their full human development potential.

Ensuring Absorptive Capacity, Fiscal Space, and Sustainability of Financing

Education reform is an ongoing process. Still substantial population growth momentum in many poor countries will exert considerable pressure on already limited human, physical, and financial resources for facilitating access to high-quality education. Moreover, this process is significantly slowed in countries with a high incidence of HIV/AIDS and thus substantial absenteeism and death of teachers—the veritable heart of education systems. Reaching the MDGs in these settings will require that numerous countries mobilize and effectively use unprecedented levels of domestic and external education financing. Such investments hold strong potential for high returns in the longer term through building a more skilled national human resource base. But they also present some important risks. To reap desired returns, all education investments must be carefully prioritized and targeted, and expenditures must be well managed. This is a serious challenge for many developing countries, given their weak sector planning and budgeting execution capacity as well as their common inexperience in the politics of mobilizing and maintaining internal and external partnerships crucial to sustain reform momentum.

The sheer magnitude of total financing required over a sustained period has led numerous countries to seek "fiscal space" to fill financing gaps through significantly augmented development borrowing or grant financing.[40] Such decisions must be weighed carefully to avoid crowding out other productive sector spending amid many competing investment priorities. Moreover, augmented financial flows must be predictable and sustained over the medium to long term, reducing uncertainty and possible high costs of abandoning initiatives after they have started. The flows must be accompanied by systematic measures to reduce, over time, presently high dependence on external financing. As the Egypt, India, and Turkey experiences demonstrate, private sector partnerships can provide a large infusion of needed resources. Caution must be exercised not to shift the financial burden to local communities, especially the poorest ones with limited fiscal capacity, to preclude further inequities in access to quality education services.

Strengthening Institutional Capacity, Particularly at the Local and Community Levels

Many unknowns remain regarding what constitutes crucial conditions for sustaining education reforms. Limited analysis has been undertaken to date on what is needed for the highly transformational, paradigm-shifting changes undertaken in many country initiatives studied to take root and endure. Key questions include these: How long can relatively nascent institutional structures, on which many of these reforms depend, survive before forces attempt to undermine them and return to traditional models? Is the democratic decentralization process that they represent inherently irreversible? How can the international community best sustain these promising reforms?

More shared education reform responsibility among central governments, local governments, communities, and parents presents both special opportunities to accelerate reforms and some serious challenges. As several country examples highlighted, decentralization can be a powerful vehicle for delivery of education services more responsive to local needs and contexts. But present capacity of local governments and communities to fully and adequately fulfill their envisaged major new roles is exceptionally weak in many countries. Hence, high priority must be assigned to strengthening their ability to implement and monitor education services, and to enhance the overall accountability of the systems.

Intensifying Experimentation, Research, and Sharing of Promising Models

Far more knowledge is needed to help understand how to scale up education reform efforts, particularly concerning what models work best in distinct contexts and, relatedly, what are the crucial enabling conditions for their effective implementation. The global learning process was an important first step toward greater knowledge sharing. But much more systematic capture and exchange of knowledge on promising models and reform processes are needed. Of special urgency is research on costs and the cost effectiveness of alternative interventions. Cost data are strikingly absent from the studies prepared for Shanghai, yet they are crucial to project financing requirements more precisely to achieve universal primary education completion and to mobilize requisite funds. Wider analysis, documentation, and dissemination of local experiences is needed, especially with regard to the increasingly large number of programs and projects designed and operated outside the formal sector and official investment channels.

Careful tracking of selected innovations adopted to rapidly expand access to quality education also is essential. Especially needed are studies on alternatives for closing currently enormous human resource gaps that plague so many reform programs. What are the prospects for sustainable use of alternative personnel cadres, such as paraprofessional or contracted teachers? What can be learned from teacher training models that have recruited people with relatively low initial levels of educational attainment and have trained them largely on the job to teach successive grade levels (like those models operating in selected Sub-Saharan countries)? Are programs that now are heavily dependent on contracted teachers remunerated below civil service salaries sustainable over the longer term? Will political forces try to undermine such alternative, more affordable approaches, regardless of the solid teacher performance being documented in numerous countries?[41] Are there other viable alternatives, especially for the poorest countries?

Achieving and Maintaining Quality Crucial to Sustain Momentum

The country examples reviewed for this global learning process suggest that rapid scaling up of the quality of education is far more challenging than that of the quantity of services delivered or the coverage of the system. Indeed the insight of these reforms in enhancing quality is not systematically addressed. Most information provided in the Shanghai studies reflects various input and output measures, such as changes in enrollments, numbers of new teachers mobilized and schools built, or primary completion rates. Virtually no outcome data were presented, such as student achievement levels, labor market entry, or income. High levels of student (as well as teacher) absenteeism continue to plague many education systems, thereby reducing the potential for learning. Unless education services enable graduates to acquire the knowledge and skills to be fully integrated into their economies and societies, reversal of high enrollment levels, where already attained, remains a real threat. Educational assessment thus must be an integral part of all EFA initiatives so as to monitor learning outcomes and adjust systems as needed to ensure high-quality service provision. In turn, this will necessitate a major capacity-building effort in many countries. Momentum for education reform must extend to expanding opportunities for quality secondary as well as tertiary education, with increasingly higher levels of educational attainment essential for nations to compete successfully in the global knowledge economy.

Notes

1. Evidence from the large body of Asian Development Bank (ADB) evaluation work in the road transport and energy sectors suggests that both road transport and electricity help reduce income poverty, with road transport having a stronger effect.

2. The following cases, classified by focus area, are analyzed in the infrastructure section of this chapter. *Access to water:* A. Rohde, T. Konishi, and S. Janakiram, Albania: Reforming Irrigation and Domestic Water Supply and Sanitation Services to Benefit the Poor; M. Shuchen, T. Yong, and L. Ji-

ayi, China's Rural Water and Sanitation Program—Scaling Up Services for Poor People; J. Lane, Ghana, Lesotho, and South Africa: Regional Expansion of Water Supply in Rural Areas. *Transportation:* H. Levy, Morocco: Rural Roads and Poverty Alleviation; H. Mitsui, Impact Assessment of Large-scale Transport Infrastructure in Northern Vietnam. *Infrastructure strategies and policies:* S. Chaterjee, Asia-Pacific: Infrastructure, Regional Cooperation, and Poverty Reduction—Lessons from the Region; D. Yan and F. Hua, China: Infrastructure, Growth, and Poverty Reduction; S. Vyas, India: Addressing Infrastructure Needs of the Poor—The Tamil Nadu Experience with Public-Private Partnerships; A. Markandya and R. Sharma, Tajikistan: Reducing Poverty through Private Infrastructure Services— The Pamir Private Power Project; T. I. Larsen, H. L. Pham, and M. Rama, Vietnam: The Impact of Infrastructure Development on Rural Poverty Reduction. *Integrated urban:* J. Brakarz and W. E. Aduan, Brazil: Favela-Bairro —Scaled Up Urban Development; T. E. Campbell and S. Marjanovic, The City-to-City Challenge in Ghana, Morocco, Tajikistan, and the United States. In drawing conclusions, readers are reminded that the list of cases is quite broad and their format was dictated by the overall research design.

3. A broader definition of poverty refers to progress made toward the Millennium Development Goals.

4. This was the case in Morocco, with two unanticipated positive effects: a sharp increase in school enrollment, especially for girls, and the freeing of women from the daily chore of collecting firewood for cooking—a result of the introduction of butane, itself made possible by a sharp drop in transport cost and improved accessibility.

5. Unfortunately, there is only one case study that dealt with the relationship between infrastructure investments and urban poverty. A large number of cases would have permitted the development of a typology of the range of urban infrastructure projects and their distributive impact on the poor.

6. There are other examples outside the case studies, such as the International Centre for Integrated Mountain Development of Nepal, which promotes cooperation and development in the mountain regions of six countries in Southeast and Central Asia.

7. However, assessing the impact of a large-scale infrastructure project, such as the Vietnam transport infrastructure project, is more difficult than assessing the impact of more sector-specific or spatially defined interventions.

8. Law on Organization and Functioning of Local Governments, No. 8652, dated July 31, 2000.

9. This as opposed to the functional sense of separating generation, transmission, and distribution.

10. The study was a joint effort of the Asian Development Bank, the Japan Bank for International Cooperation, and the World Bank. A copy of the current report is available at lnweb18.worldbank.org/eap/eap.nsf/0/11 BB5BBB5C35E03D85256EB6004EFF2E?OpenDocument.

11. The Shanghai session on judicial reform provided opportunities for reflection and experience sharing from several national perspectives. This section draws mainly on the Shanghai Conference speeches of Dr. Carlos Esteban Larios Ochaita, justice of the Supreme Court of Guatemala; Hon. Protais Musoni, minister of state for good governance of Rwanda; Hon. Hilario G. Davide, chief justice of the Philippines; and Eduard Nikolaevich Renov, deputy chairman of Supreme Arbitration Court of the Russian Federation. They were asked to test the validity and strength of the implementation factors affecting judicial reform cited in the context of the overall conference framework: (1) commitment and political economy of change, (2) institutional development and capacity building, and (3) external catalysts. Using this framework, they discussed some key dimensions of the varied experiences of judicial reform and modernization in their countries. This section also takes advantage of the key comments of former World Bank president James Wolfensohn and Roberto Dañino, senior vice president and general counsel of the World Bank, at this session.

12. The Shanghai Conference brought together policy makers and development practitioners committed to cross-country and cross-regional learning in at least 12 different areas of development work, among them judicial reform. Of the countries of concern to judicial reform, two are postconflict countries (Guatemala and Rwanda). Guatemala and the Philippines also share a number of economic and sociopolitical challenges, and all four countries are working on strengthening and modernizing democratic institutions, but from different vantage points and bases. Three of the four are situated in the global "south." The Philippines is a developing country whereas Russia continues its transition to market-driven economics. All four come from differing legal traditions, levels of development, cultural and traditional backgrounds, and geopolitical regions. They have different track records in judicial reform in terms of how long they have been in this process and what they have accomplished.

13. The quote is from a speech by Roberto Dañino at the Shanghai Conference. He continued, "First, institutions. There must be strong, reliable, and independent institutions, staffed by trained professionals, to effectively support the administration of justice through the transparent application of the law. Second, the legal system. It is essential to have a modern legal structure which is transparent and reflective of social conditions to ensure that justice sector institutions can fulfill their mandate in an efficient and effective way. Third, enforcement. Institutions must have the capacity to effectively implement the legal structure. Fourth, societal com-

mitment. Institutions, law, and enforcement are sustainable over time only with the commitment and active participation of society. The public's understanding of the benefits of a well-functioning legal system is an essential component. For this reason, it is crucial to have a regular and consistent dialogue between all actors involved: government, legislators, the judiciary, political parties, and civil society."

14. Ibid. The earlier Bank-supported stand-alone judicial reform projects were typically geared toward modernizing legislation and developing new codes and the capacity of the courts. Court capacity building has been concentrated on improving efficiency by eliminating backlogs and reducing delays through automation and new organizational structures and working methods. Usually these activities also have been strong on assessments and research, including knowledge sharing to leverage experiences across the region and elsewhere. New approaches to research and development also have been introduced in recent years; they have focused on the uses and users of the court systems. Improving services to facilitate broader access to dispute resolution mechanisms has also been a major component of programs in the sector, targeted on the poorest and socially excluded groups. In the last few years, there have been mixed results in this area, but generally some worthy benefits in improving attention to gender equity and related issues and to indigenous populations and other minority groups.

15. See World Bank (2005), especially pages 86–89 and 246, and Kaufmann, Kraay, and Mastruzzi (2005).

16. The mobile court visits the detention centers and social service centers to address the needs of juveniles, help promote crime prevention, and protect the rights of young people. Many youths have been released who were unjustifiably detained because of inefficiencies in the system. Given that the Philippines has several thousand islands, the option of mobile courts on boats is being considered as a next step.

17. These were the reflections of James Wolfensohn after hearing the speeches.

18. For a good discussion of the benefits of access to financial services at the household level, see Honohan (2004).

19. The following cases were consulted for this section: Bangladesh: Growth, Achievements, and Lessons in Micro-finance; Bangladesh: Scaling Up a Program for the Poorest—BRAC's IGVGD Program; Kazakhstan: Commercial Banks Entering Micro and Small Business Finance—The Kazakhstan Small Business Program; Kenya: Scaling Up Microcredit—The K-Rep Story; Mexico: Integrating the Poor into the Mainstream Financial System: The BANSEFI and SAGARPA Programs; and Mongolia's Agricultural Bank. Unless otherwise noted, statistics and quoted portions of this chapter are taken from the relevant country stories.

20. The following cases are analyzed in this chapter: C. Mesa-Lago, Achievement and Deterioration of Universal Access to Social Services, Cuba; A. Andersson-Singh, An Outreach Intervention among Injecting Drug Users and Their Sexual Partners in Manipur, India; A. Mehryar, Primary Health Care and the Rural Poor in the Islamic Republic of Iran; M. Sharma, Nepal's National Tuberculosis Control Program; J. Rwomushana, Uganda: Conquering "Slim": Uganda's War on HIV/AIDS; and C. Novinskey, West Africa: Defeating Riverblindness—Success in Scaling Up and Lessons Learned. The authors also relied on a working paper for data from Thailand: Ross-Larson et al. 2004. Unless otherwise noted, statistics and quoted portions of this chapter are taken from the relevant case studies and working paper.

21. A framework that ensures that policy makers and service providers are accountable to the communities they serve was discussed in World Bank (2004c).

22. There are three types of decentralization: political, administrative, and fiscal; and four main forms of decentralization: devolution, delegation, deconcentration, and divestment. For a detailed discussion of decentralization, the reader is referred to the World Bank Website (www1.worldbank.o rg/publicsector/decentralization/decent.doc) and to Work (2002).

23. The Joint Learning Initiative Report (2004) discussed the shortage of health workers in detail. According to this report, Africa has only 0.8 health workers per 1,000 people compared with 2.3 in Asia, 2.6 in Latin America, and the global average of 4.2. Innovative institutional arrangements are therefore imperative to scaling up health responses in Africa.

24. Monitoring can be defined as "the periodic oversight of a process, or the implementation of an activity, which seeks to establish the extent to which input deliveries, work schedules, other required actions and targeted outputs are proceeding according to plan, so that timely action can be taken to correct the deficiencies" (WHO 2003).

25. The linkages between education, development, and growth are highlighted, for example, in World Bank (1991), which underscored the importance of investing in people, and in Hanushek and Kimko (2000). For an in-depth analysis of the importance of investing in women's human capital, see Schultz (1995). On linkages between gender and development, refer to World Bank (2001), which concluded that societies that discriminate by gender tend to experience less rapid economic growth and poverty reduction than do those that treat females and males more equitably. For an overview of women's education barriers, benefits, and policies, see King and Hill (1993).

26. Girls' education, in particular, has positive effects on fertility and maternal health by contributing to later marriage, (higher) age at first birth, and fewer and better-spaced children. Girls' education also con-

tributes to the welfare of children, with better-educated mothers assigning high priority to educating their children and ensuring their access to adequate nutrition and timely health care.

27. The multidonor-supported Education for All Fast Track Initiative, in which the World Bank participates, holds promise of accelerating progress in lagging countries through its mobilization of substantial financial resources as well as technical assistance. For a full analysis of MDG prospects, see chapter 2 of World Bank (2004a).

28. This section relies on the following cases prepared for the Shanghai Conference: F. Iqbal and N. Riad, Arab Republic of Egypt: Increasing Girls' School Enrollment; N. Hossain, Access to Education for the Poor and Girls: Educational Achievements in Bangladesh; Z. Tiedao, Z. Minxia, Z. Xueqin, Z. Xi, and W. Yan, Universalizing Nine-Year Compulsory Education for Poverty Reduction in Rural China; D. Meza, J. L. Guzman, and L. de Varela, EDUCO: A Community-Managed Education Program in Rural Areas of El Salvador (1991–2003); V. Ramachandran, India: A Community-Government Partnership That Gets Millions into School in Madhya Pradesh; R. Avenstrup, with X. Liang and S. Nellemann, Kenya, Lesotho, Malawi, and Uganda: Universal Primary Education and Poverty Reduction; Latin America: Fe y Alegría—A Jesuit Education Movement Supported by AVINA; I. Dulger, Turkey: Rapid Coverage for Compulsory Education—The 1997 Basic Education Program. Unless otherwise noted, statistics and quoted portions of this chapter are taken from the relevant country stories.

29. An overview of the DPEP Program is provided in Pandey (2000). A short synthesis of the phased education sector development strategy that India pursued over its post-independence period is provided in Wu, Kaul, and Sankar (2005).

30. Maintaining a long-term, widely shared vision of and commitment to quality education for all, and actively pursuing this objective over several decades, across numerous governments of strikingly diverse political orientations, have been identified as prime factors underlying Chile's achievement of one of the highest levels of educational attainment in that region. For details, see Perry and Leipziger (1999).

31. ISE's role is further discussed in the section on external and internal catalysts for change.

32. The community-led rural school movement has registered most impressive gains, particularly given its concentration on rural students—those at the highest risk of nonentry, late entry, repetition, and dropping out. Over the relatively short 1991–2003 period, EDUCO hired 7,000 new rural teachers and enrolled 362,000 rural students, with EDUCO schools now representing 40 percent of all rural students enrolled in preschool and basic education. The net enrollment rate in rural areas increased from 76 percent to 82 percent over the 1992–2000 period, while

that in urban areas remained stagnant. EDUCO also has reduced late entry to first grade.

33. As the India case study states, "historical experience . . . [shows] that centralized models of delivery delayed the spread of primary education even where resources were identified."

34. According to National Family Health Survey data, 80 percent of boys and 74 percent of girls attended school in 1998/99 compared with only 61 percent and 47 percent, respectively, in 1992/93. Female literacy increased by 21 percent over the 1991–2001 period. And leveling of the gross enrollment ratio across scheduled castes, scheduled tribes, and other social groups also reportedly was attained. Investments included recruitment and training of some 32,000 new teachers, supported by Block and Cluster Resource Centers financed by DPEP, and construction of 26,571 new schools. Some 9 out of every 10 primary-school-age children in Madhya Pradesh now enroll, whereas the number of those out of school declined to 748,000 in the 2002/03 academic year, representing one quarter of the 1996 level.

35. Among the most important lessons learned to date from cross-country research on user fees is the need, before such fees are abolished or reduced, to ensure their replacement with revenues of equivalent effectiveness and levels, wherever such fees contribute significantly to funding for school access and/or quality. Outlays for school fees and related educational expenses represent a significant proportion of household expenditures in many countries, and may present a significant obstacle to student enrollment and retention in school, especially among the poorest families. To date, no systematic analysis has been undertaken of the effects of user fees on access and completion or of the relative effects of alternative approaches that may be adopted to help poor families meet such costs when eliminating fees is not feasible (approaches such as graduated fee structures, targeted subsidies, or scholarships). A review of the user fee issue, including a summary of challenges and opportunities presented by abolishing user fees, is provided in Kattan and Burnett (2004), an update of which study presently is under way.

36. Madhya Pradesh's program also institutionalized women's literacy groups for the express purpose of enhancing women's capacity to participate in school governance. As a corollary, the state government mandated that at least one third of local government positions be held by women.

37. This act operationalized 1992 national constitutional amendments devolving responsibility for primary education to village *panchayats,* whereas the district reports built on DPEP experience with district report cards. India's central government played a crucial role in building state capacity for guiding such reforms.

38. Challenges and promising approaches to strengthen public accountability for social service delivery and to track public education expenditures are provided in World Bank (2004c) and Reinikka and Smith (2004), respectively.

39. Survival rates are the percentages of a given cohort of children enrolled in first grade who are expected to reach each successive grade.

40. For a short overview of the fiscal space debate, see Heller (2005).

41. Extensive research on contracted teachers is being spearheaded by the World Bank in Sub-Saharan Africa, with financial support from Ireland AID and technical assistance from the University of Quebec, Canada. This approach is discussed in World Bank (2004a).

Bibliography

Beck, Thorsten, Ashi Demirguc-Kunt, and Ross Levine. 2004. "Finance, Inequality and Poverty: Cross-Country Evidence." Policy Research Working Paper 3338, World Bank, Washington, DC.

Beegle, Kathleen, Rajeev Dchejia, and Roberta Gatti. 2003. "Child Labor, Income Shocks, and Access to Credit." Policy Research Working Paper 3075, World Bank, Washington, DC.

Caskey, John P., Clemente Ruiz Durán, and Tova Maria Solo. 2004. "The Unbanked in Mexico and the United States." Brussels: World Bank Savings Institution.

Davide, Hilario G. 2004. "Philippines: The Role of the Judiciary in Scaling Up Poverty Reduction." Paper prepared for the Shanghai Conference, May 25–27, 2004.

Gottret, Pablo, and George Schieber. 2004. "Increasing Investments in Health Outcomes for the Poor." Geneva: World Health Organization.

Hanushek, Eric A., and Dennis D. Kimko. 2000. "Schooling, Labor Force Quality and the Growth of Nations." *American Economic Review* 90 (5): 1184–208.

Heller, Peter. 2005. "Back to Basics—Fiscal Space: What It Is and How to Get It." *Finance and Development* 42 (2): 32–33.

Honohan, Patrick. 2004. "Financial Sector Policy and the Poor: Selected Findings and Issues." Working Paper 43, World Bank, Washington, DC.

Joint Learning Initiative. 2004. *Human Resources for Health: Overcoming the Crisis.* Cambridge: Harvard University Press.

Kattan, Raja Bentaouet, and Nicholas Burnett. 2004. "User Fees in Primary Education." Education for All Working Paper 30108, Education Sector, Human Development Network, World Bank, Washington, DC.

Kauffman, Daniel, Aart Kraay, and Massimo Mastruzzi. 2005. "Governance Matters IV: Governance Indicators for 1996–2004." Policy Research Working Paper 3630, World Bank, Washington, DC.

King, Elizabeth M., and M. Anne Hill, eds. 1993. *Women's Education in Developing Countries: Barriers, Benefits, and Policies.* Baltimore: Johns Hopkins University Press.

Littlefield, Elizabeth, Jonathan Morduch, and Syed Hashemi. 2004. "Is Microfinance an Effective Strategy to Reach the Millennium Development Goals?" Focus Note 24, Consultative Group to Assist the Poor, Washington, DC.

May, Ernesto. 2005. "Growth, Investment Climate, and Quality of Judicial Institutions: Perspective from Latin America." Paper presented at PREM Week, World Bank, Washington, DC, April 19–20, 2005.

Musoni, Protais. 2004. "Rwanda: Security and Justice—Routes to Reconciliation." Paper prepared for the Shanghai Conference, May 25–27, 2004.

OECD (Organisation for Economic Co-operation and Development). 2005. Official Sector Technical Co-operation Expenditure and Personnel. Available at www.oecd.org/dataoecd.

Pandey, Raghaw S. 2000. *Going to Scale with Education Reform: India's District Primary Education Program, 1995–99.* Country Studies, Education Reform and Management Series, vol. 1, no. 4. Washington, DC: World Bank.

Perry, Guillermo E., and Daniel M. Leipziger, eds. 1999. *Chile: Recent Policy Lessons and Emerging Challenges.* Washington, DC: World Bank.

Reinikka, Ritva S., and Nathanael Smith. 2004. *Public Expenditure Tracking Surveys and Education.* Paris: International Institute for Educational Planning.

Ross-Larson, B., F. Saadah., E. McCrocklin, and E. Wiley. 2004. "Thailand: Addressing HIV/AIDS—Proven Solutions and New Problems." Working Paper 30786, World Bank, Washington, DC.

Schultz, T. Paul, ed. 1995. *Investments in Women's Human Capital.* Chicago: University of Chicago Press.

Wanis-St. John, Anthony. 2004. "A Culture of Justice: Toward a New Judiciary in Guatemala." Paper prepared for the Shanghai Conference, May 25–27, 2004.

WHO (World Health Organization). 2003. *Water Supply and Sanitation Sector Monitoring.* Geneva.

Work, R. 2002. "Overview of Decentralization Worldwide: A Stepping Stone to Improved Governance and Human Development." Paper presented at the Second International Conference on Decentralization and Federalism: The Future of Decentralizing States. Manila, Philippines, July 25–27, 2002.

World Bank. 2005. *World Development Report 2005: A Better Investment Climate for Everyone.* Washington, DC.

————. 2004a. *Global Monitoring Report 2004. Policies and Action for Achieving the Millennium Development Goals and Related Outcomes.* Washington, DC.

————. 2004b. *Rising to the Challenges: The Millennium Development Goals for Health.* Washington, DC.

————. 2004c. *World Development Report 2004: Making Services Work for the Poor People.* Washington, DC.

————. 2003. *World Development Indicators.* Available at www.world bank/data.

————. 2001. "Engendering Development through Gender Equality in Rights, Resources and Voices." Policy Research Report 21776, World Bank, Washington, DC.

————. 1991. *World Development Report 1991: The Challenge of Development.* New York: Oxford University Press.

Wu, Kin Bing, Venita Kaul, and Deepa Sankar. 2005. "The Quiet Revolution." *Finance and Development* 42 (2): 29–31.

5

Lessons on Community-driven Development Programs

Mohini Malhotra

This chapter extracts lessons from the portfolio of 13 community-driven development (CDD) and social fund programs that were featured at the Shanghai Conference in 2004.[1] The chapter is organized in four sections: an introduction to the CDD and social fund portfolio, general observations on CDD programs and scale, the "how" of scaling up, and questions for future research.[2]

The CDD and Social Fund Portfolio

The reviewed programs all have unique origins and different starting dates; they are being implemented in different countries with different economic, political, social, and cultural contexts; they each express distinct objectives; and they have achieved vastly different degrees of scale. The portfolio of programs is anchored by several renowned CDD programs—the Pakistan National Rural Support Programmes (NRSPs) dating back to 1982, the Brazilian CDD portfolio in the northeastern states in operation since 1985, and the Kecamatan Development Project (KDP) started in 1998 in Indonesia. It also includes relatively nascent experiences in Eastern Europe.

Despite these unique contexts, however, these programs all share common design principles and approaches that give them a shared "brand logo." All of these initiatives seek to increase and improve livelihoods for the poor and poorest populations in one or more of three ways: (1) higher incomes; (2) access to services such as water supply, health, education, and roads, among other things; and (3) increased personal empowerment and ability to influence outcomes that matter for their lives. The programs typically place grant funds and the planning and decision-making process for how to use these funds directly in the hands of poor communities. Although communities are free to invest in whatever area they deem a priority, the grants are typically invested in basic infrastructure and social services—roads, water systems, health clinics, schools, grain mills, and day care centers, among others. Communities cofinance these investments in some specified proportion, and are responsible for operations and maintenance of the investments.

But as proponents of this model would argue, perhaps the most compelling feature of CDD programs is the democratic process by which the programs work. Communities exercise full control over choice and decisions on use of resources granted them, and decisions are made in transparent and participatory forums, as evidenced in the KDP program (box 5.1).

Box 5.1 Anatomy of a CDD Program—How KDP Works in Indonesia

The Indonesian administrative system consists of provinces, districts, subdistricts (kecamatan, pronounced "ketchamatan"), and villages. There are anywhere between 20 and 50 villages in a kecamatan. On average a Javanese kecamatan will have about 50,000 to 75,000 people in it, whereas a kecamatan in the sparsely populated eastern islands can have as few as 10,000 to 12,000 inhabitants.

The basic architecture of the Kecamatan Development Project is deceptively simple. It consists of a system to give block grants directly to kecamatan councils, which they can use to fund development plans prepared through a long participatory planning process of four to six months. The funds, which range from $60,000 to $110,000 per kecamatan, can be used for almost any kind of public good that villagers believe to be a development priority, or for village revolving funds.

The kecamatan councils are formally composed of the elected heads of the village planning group and chaired by the subdistrict head. For many years the councils were inert, meeting at most once a year, but under KDP they have been revived. Additional nonvoting members are elected by popular acclaim. All project proponents are also invited to join the meetings, so the final gathering for the competition among proposals can be very large.

Each village can submit up to two proposals to the kecamatan council. This always leads to more proposals than there are funds, so the villagers must negotiate among themselves which proposals are the most worthy. KDP rules require that any village group submitting a proposal must send a delegation of at least two women and one man to the kecamatan decision meeting where villagers present and decide on which proposals will be funded.

Once the kecamatan forum agrees on which proposals merit funding, nobody farther up the system can modify them. Funds are released from the provincial branch of the national treasury directly to a bank account held in the name of all of the villages, bypassing provincial and district government.

Planning is helped by a tiered system of facilitators. In each KDP village, the villagers elect a man and a woman to represent the village within the project. Their main job is to introduce the project to all of the informal as well as the formal institutions within the village, which in effect means that they spend large amounts of time in the hamlets rather than the village proper. The next level up is the kecamatan, where the project places a social and a technical facilitator. The social facilitator explains the project's rules, monitors participation, and trains the village facilitators; the technical facilitator helps the villagers assess the quality of their infrastructure and trains them in maintenance. District engineers supervise the quality of physical works; and at the province level, a management unit conducts training, supervises progress in the field, and acts on complaints received from villages.

Sources: KDP case study; Guggenheim forthcoming.

Although this chapter groups CDD and social funds under one tent, given their emphasis on a community-led approach to service delivery, the distinction between the two is that the CDD model aims to push decision making over the choice of investments down to the affected communities themselves, and defines the process of decision making as a local responsibility, whereas the social funds receive proposals from community groups but retain decision-making power over which to fund. As these programs mature and evolve, these distinctions become more blurry—many social funds devolve decision making to local communities or local governments, while retaining control over the disbursement of resources.

Findings on Scaling Up CDD
and Social Funds

Five broad observations can be made on scaling up CDD and social fund programs, as illustrated by the programs' experiences.

CDD and Social Fund Programs
Can Be Scaled Up along Many Dimensions

The Rural Poverty Reduction Program in northeast Brazil has supported 55,000 small-scale investments affecting 7.5 million people in 1,500 of the 1,650 municipalities of the northeastern states. Geographic coverage has broadened to include beneficiaries in all 10 states in the northeast. Most significantly, northeast state and local governments are now allocating and transferring funds under other state and federal programs for the rural poor, and integrating programs across sectors using the same principles and institutional mechanisms, such as the community municipal councils established and refined under the CDD program. Every World Bank dollar invested in the program is leveraged tenfold. Municipal councils are evolving their roles by participating in local government deliberations on broader municipal poverty planning and budgets, including integrating activities across sectors and deciding the allocation of federal and state funds available locally. The new generation of CDD projects in the state of Maranhao explicitly aims to use the municipal councils as the institutional linchpin for planning poverty reduction programs (box 5.2).

The social fund programs in Malawi, Yemen, and Zambia have reached nationwide coverage since their launches in the 1990s, and the Yemen fund is reaching a third of the 20 million people in the 20 governorates of the country. And whereas almost all of the programs in the sample started by providing limited infrastructure, power supply, and irrigation, in their second or third phases all are expanding horizontally to include social and economic development projects. Yet, given the timid extent of decentralization in each of these three countries, very little scale has been accomplished in terms of vertical integration into local government administrative structures.

In the KDP context, a large number of people and villages are receiving services. KDP has expanded from a small pilot operation in 25 villages in 1997 to more than 28,000 villages, reaching 35 million people in 30 of Indonesia's 34 provinces. It is expanding horizontally by widening its platform of infrastructure and revolving funds to include health, education, and natural resource man-

---

Box 5.2 The Institutional Architecture for the Brazil CDD Program

Community associations are at the core for project implementation from start to finish, including maintenance, and are assisted by technical specialists with whom they contract.

Municipal councils are project creations with communities and local government represented in an 80/20 mix. Councils allocate resources in open, well-publicized meetings, and assume greater responsibility for supervision, financial management, and technical assistance. There are also variations of further decentralization through councils where the council manages an annual budget allocated by the state technical units.

State technical units are quasi-autonomous bodies, affiliated with the State Secretariat of Planning, that coordinate and plan the projects and focus on oversight and promotion. Most are stable and committed, and have developed extensive technical and administrative expertise.

State governments have assumed responsibility for counterpart funding and have taken on the loans from the World Bank directly.

Source: Brazil case study.

---

agement; it is having an "ink-blot" effect where villagers are demanding that other non-KDP government monies be allocated along KDP's core principles; and it is expanding vertically through the administrative structures of government to the district level. KDP and its urban twin, the Urban Poverty Project (UPP), now form a main pillar of the government of Indonesia's national poverty strategy.

CDD and Social Fund Programs Can Operate and Expand in Unstable and Conflict Settings

KDP began in 1998 as a reaction and a response to the economic, financial, and political crises in Indonesia. The combination of the crumbling of the New Order regime and the search of the World Bank for credibility in Indonesia gave birth to one of the largest and perhaps most touted CDD programs in the world.

The CDD programs and social funds in Afghanistan, Bosnia, Cambodia, and Tajikistan, as well as one in East Timor, illustrate the demand for such programs and the speed with which they take off to kick-start the reconstruction of destroyed infrastructure, generate employment, and infuse stability in postconflict countries. In Tajikistan, the program reached 600,000 people within the first five years, more than twice the number originally planned, in a country with a total population of 6 million.

CDDs Can Provide a Viable Alternative to Public Sector Services

Across the CDD and social fund programs in the sample, costs of infrastructure were typically lower by 25 to 50 percent than the public sector alternatives. The quality of the infrastructure was at least the same or superior to the alternatives, where assessed (Indonesia and Yemen, among others).[3] A 25 percent rate of return on a $1 billion portfolio for KDP leads to cost savings not unnoticed by local government—an important factor in gaining them as allies. Lower costs, combined with community contributions discussed below, make CDD programs a financially attractive proposition to municipal and state governments.

The limitations of CDD and social funds must be recognized, however. They are not a solution for larger infrastructure that requires sophisticated technical standards and higher-order network planning, such as urban sanitation. Nor have most found a good solution to dealing with investments that require recurrent expenses—such as teacher salaries—unless they are well integrated with district or provincial budgets and planning.

Most Funds Have Homegrown Roots, But Cross-Border Learning Has Enriched Design and Implementation Arrangements

Programs have learned from each other, helped each other evolve more rapidly, and adapted operational manuals and lessons to their own contexts. Brazil's CDD programs were inspired by a trip to Mexico made by Brazilian federal and state authorities in 1993 to learn from the Solidaridad social fund program with CDD components. Brazil's programs are now being re-exported to inform new CDD investments in Mexico. The Brazil CDD is being adapted to Argentina, Bolivia, Ghana, Guatemala, six states in India, Malawi, Nepal, Panama, and Sri Lanka. The Yemen social fund, although learning much from the older Egypt Social Fund, is now a source of knowledge and inspiration to the younger Moroccan fund and other social funds in the Middle East. KDP spin-offs are being implemented in Afghanistan, Laos, the Philippines, and East Timor, among others.

During the global learning process, Brazil and KDP discovered that all of their procedures and operational manuals had been translated into Kyrgyz for use by the new Kyrgyz CDD program.

The Optimal Relationship with Government Is Still Unclear

The decision whether to cohabit in parallel with government or seek to integrate vertically into formal government channels has not been reached and is country contextual. Many CDD and social funds realize that the future sustainability of the stream of benefit and processes they have introduced and implemented depends on these very processes becoming part of the bloodstream of how governments work with their citizens. Although one would think that the longer-running programs would provide the best insights into this vertical integration process, this is in fact the most country-contextual aspect of CDD.

The younger Kalahi program in the Philippines, started in 2003, has made significant inroads into working with local government because of the more advanced stage of decentralization in the Philippines, compared with Indonesia, for example, which was just launching its massive decentralization program while KDP was being launched. Kalahi uses an intensive integration approach with local government at entry—the Kalahi cycle is synchronized with local government planning and budgeting cycles so community plans are better integrated with official village and municipal plans, and each Kalahi municipality details a two-year plan for how it will institutionalize Kalahi processes. This has resulted in local legislation adopting these processes as a planning and resource allocation tool.

Now in its third phase, KDP is making significant inroads to scale up vertically to the district level, one level up from the subdistrict level where it cut its teeth. Already beginning its fourth year of life, KDP had launched a matching grants program for districts to add kecamatans or subdistricts by contributing 80 percent of the block grant to the subdistrict from the district's budget. More than one third of all districts participated in the launch year.

The Nuts and Bolts of Getting to Scale

How the various programs achieved their scale is now examined through the lens of the hypotheses put forth by the Shanghai Conference conceptual framework. This analysis is very critical because some studies have shown that, if not done right, it is quite difficult to have CDD programs achieve scale (see World Bank 2005b).

Commitment and Political Economy for Change

None of these programs could have been born without support from the political leadership in their respective countries. This support manifested itself in, for example, financing the programs and transferring lessons learned to national policy and programs for poverty reduction. At a minimum, political leaders grant the funds autonomous status and leave them mostly free of political interference.

Brazil's CDD experimentation began when Brazil returned to democratic government in 1985. Subsequent constitutional changes in 1988 paved the way for testing and expanding decentralized participatory mechanisms for development; for shifting power and fiscal resources to states and localities; and for providing the political, legal, and financial foundations for sustaining CDD initiatives. Positive effects of CDD programs, their cost savings, and disenchantment with previous models of failed rural development support led to CDD principles underpinning the national poverty reduction strategy. At the state level, the state technical units in Brazil have been overseeing CDD program implementation since 1996 and have built expertise, continuity, and commitment to the approach along the way.

In Indonesia, the Asian financial crisis and brewing political disenchantment with the New Order regime gave KDP a window of opportunity to be a solution for the government in search of urgent responses to its population. From the government's perspective, KDP built large amounts of infrastructure in hard-to-reach places, disbursed funds faster than any other World Bank project, and required next to no prefinancing from the national treasury. In addition, KDP was largely a design refinement on a long record of government investment in bottom-up poverty alleviation initiatives. For the World Bank, it provided a way to engage in poverty and governance reform at a time when its lending portfolio shrank by 75 percent, and when it needed to shore up its own image tarnished by association with the New Order government.

And in Pakistan, the NRSP gained support at the highest levels of government based on the achievements of the pilot endeavor in five remote districts in northern Pakistan. The government endowed the program and raised funds for its further expansion, while leaving it political space and autonomy. Similar to Brazil, the Pakistan programs are established with state funds.

Innovations in Scaling Up

The nuts-and-bolts project designs of CDD and social fund programs, once innovations, are by now a template for future planning of similar programs:

- The disbursement system involves direct transfers of funds to the project-created municipal councils in Brazil, for example, bypassing the provincial and district levels of government, or through the government system from treasury to village accounts at the kecamatan level in Indonesia.
- Disbursements are made quickly through a modular system in which each subdistrict operates independently of other subdistricts so the system does not get hung up because of laggards.
- Nonmonetary community contributions are accepted.
- Strong sanctions are enforced for misuse of funds.
- Capacity building of a network of trained facilitators occurs; these facilitators provide services to communities on participatory decision making, getting tenders and engineering, and they provide technical advice. (KDP has built a network of 45,000 private sector contractors.)
- Emphasis is on standardization of simple procedures, forms (typically one page long), and processes, leading to wide-scale branding and franchise-ability.

The rules of the game are transparent. Clear and understood budgets, processes, and procedures lead to increased accountability to clients, and in turn empower them to demand what is their due—a principle re-enacted many times in the programs. An explicit goal of CDD and social fund programs is to build transparent systems of governance to reduce corruption. Budgets are given directly to communities to invest in projects of their choice. Billboards in each KDP village publicize the investment being undertaken, including contracting arrangements and budget amounts; suppliers are required to present their quotations in public meetings rather than through sealed bids; independent nongovernmental organizations (NGOs) are contracted in each province to monitor implementation; and the Indonesian government has a legally binding contract to give the media a blanket, unedited license to report on corruption. Some 850 articles have been published to date, about a third dealing with corruption. These principles, albeit with varying mechanisms, repeat themselves across the many CDD and social fund programs.

Cost sharing is a requirement of all programs to verify that the services are truly demanded by the people for whom they are intended. Whereas the floor on these contributions for most programs was 10 percent, invariably higher contributions were reported.

In the young Bosnian initiative, communities in many cases contributed up to 80 percent of project costs (total project costs averaged $50,000). In Indonesia, there is a wide range of contributions, but on average about 17 percent of costs are contributed by communities. Villagers and local governments in the Philippines contribute about 40 percent of the cost. And in Tajikistan, one of the 20 poorest countries in the world, communities are contributing 10 to 50 percent of project costs (total project costs average $30,000).

Investment in building capacity helped institutionalize the process and expand programs. KDP invested in building the capacity of 45,000 private contractors—facilitators, engineers, technicians—to scale up. The Yemen fund invests in building the capacity of a nascent civil society to develop partners and to facilitate service delivery. The Yemen fund also invests in government line ministries to transfer its experience and lessons to make the government more responsive to its citizens.

These programs typically operate through special-purpose vehicles outside of sectoral line ministries, or through project-created mechanisms at the local level that become the channel for coordinated service delivery. How do multisectoral programs ensure that there will be teachers in the schools that have been built, and medical staff to operate the health clinics? In the Philippines Kalahi CDD program, this horizontal integration is addressed through the municipal interagency committee, an interdepartmental coordination mechanism tried and tested in the predecessor CDD program. In each Kalahi community, this committee is chaired by the mayor, and is made up of heads of local government departments, national agency representatives, staff of NGOs, and local donor representatives. Similarly in Brazil, the municipal councils created in the CDD program are increasingly playing a greater role in planning and allocating resources from the state across various sectors for poverty reduction.

In Yemen, when the health and education ministries failed to deliver sufficient female health workers and teachers to staff the clinics and schools being built by the social fund and communities, the Yemen social fund simply changed course. It stopped building new clinics and schools, and started training health workers and teachers to staff the social infrastructure already in place. This issue of institutional sustainability is perhaps the single most challenging one for CDD and social fund programs, or for any type of program that requires multisectoral coordination and execution.

Decentralized management structures require innovative solutions. As KDP expanded its coverage, most management functions were pushed from the center to regional management units. The Pakistan NRSPs use an interesting model by replication rather than by expansion of a single entity. The 10 rural support programs are separate entities that stay small and locally contextual, but link up through a core network team. And in countries like Tajikistan and Yemen, with inhospitable geographic terrain, decentralization is a necessity to reach poor, dispersed communities, so each program works out of decentralized offices (eight and six offices, respectively).

Communicating lessons on what works is important to the vertical and horizontal scaling up of such programs. The Malawi social fund communicates to communities via radio plays and television dramas. Messages are broadcast explaining the principles of accountability and transparency, and offering instruction on specific technical issues such as procurement and contracting.

Well-managed organizations with committed staff are critical to getting to scale. The social fund in Yemen is a case study in good management practices. Among the many practices are merit-based recruitment, performance-based contracts, and a strong focus on results.

Learning and Experimentation

Brazil had a long trajectory of experimentation, beginning in 1985, with 10 World Bank projects with CDD components, which then became the only components in a reformulation of rural development programs in 1993. KDP built on 10 years of experimentation by the Indonesian government and the World Bank in bottom-up planning approaches, and was able to pull together the various strands into a comprehensive program and scale it up through the same administrators and institutional channels. The Pakistan NRSP was built on the basis of an initial six-year pilot project in five poor districts. Kalahi, too, was seeded in fertile ground and built on a history of participatory approaches executed by the Department of Social Welfare and Development, its current executing agency.

Underpinning the social fund decisions to go to scale is a process of learning by doing and active monitoring through well-designed management information systems. Many of the initiatives stressed the importance of having a sound system in place, particularly to track many small, geographically dispersed disbursements. This investment pays off. Having data on results motivated the state of Bahia to channel additional funds to the CDD program. Engaging local university researchers to take on the monitoring and data analysis function was an innovative way to defray the cost of such a system in Brazil.

External Catalysts

Funds are important for programs to get to scale. To illustrate, KDP and Yemen have mobilized, respectively, approximately $700 million and $650 million from the World Bank to date. The NRSPs in Pakistan have collectively mobilized more than $100 million in external donor support.

Simplified donor procedures and on-site presence have also facilitated program expansion. Simplifying the World Bank's procedures was fundamental in Brazil and Indonesia. Funds were transferred directly through the government system from national treasury to village accounts, counterpart funds could include nonmonetary contributions, and a modular system of disbursement enabled the system to move and not get slowed down by laggard units. An additional key factor in the case of Brazil, KDP, and Yemen has been the on-site presence of a core project team of World Bank staff that provides policy and implementation continuity and timely support.

Sustainability, Impact, and Research Questions Going Forward

At the subproject or community project level, the limited but emerging evidence from the older initiatives points to sustainability beyond their initial achievements. In KDP, more than 80 percent of participating villages have established operation and maintenance committees, and reviews of investments made under the predecessor project found 85 percent of village roads maintained in good condition.

In terms of adoption of the CDD and social fund processes and principles, the Kalahi project in the Philippines is planning to declare victory after three years because of its more established decentralized structures. In Brazil and Indonesia, the design fundamentals have been incorporated into national poverty strategies.

When are projects sustainable? And should programs cohabitate or integrate? At what point are CDD and social fund processes part of the bloodstream of governments dealing with their citizens, as opposed to remaining project motivated? And, correspondingly, how long should external financiers like the World Bank plan to stay involved to see these initiatives through to maturity? The NRSP case argues for patience and perseverance. It took 10 to 12 years to foster community organizations that included 80 percent of all households in each of the initial six districts, the percentage considered to be the critical mass necessary for the process of social mobilization to take root, for the positive effects to become evident and measurable, and to influence national policies and programs in Pakistan. What is the longer-term vision of social funds and CDD initiatives—to become a permanent part of the institutional landscape or a transitional entity with the objective of transferring and integrating their know-how into existing line ministries?[4] (That is a seeming paradox because many ministries do not show a proclivity to take on such functions in many parts of the world, which is why these special vehicles were created in the first place.) The tension is reflected in the fact that social funds that perform well, and at times may be the only development agency functioning well, as in Yemen, attract more and more donor funds, reinforcing their own sustainability and permanence while line ministries wither.

What institutional framework allows for multisectoral integration? Are special-purpose institutions with powerful support that gives them the mandate to coordinate horizontally the only realistic way to go? How can CDD and social fund initiatives get better horizontal coordination at the local level?

If these programs are to be made permanent, they would ideally be institutionalized through *existing* sectoral agencies. That, however, is precisely where tensions of turf and coordination arise, and why many programs never take off from the insulated pilot phase.

Should projects improve conditions where people are or move people to better locales? This issue was particularly debated during the global learning process field visits to Brazil, Yemen, and the poorest counties in southwest China. Should the focus be on improving livelihoods to widely dispersed small rural communities living on unforgiving arid land in unsustainable areas, where provision of basic services is expensive and difficult? Or should people be encouraged to migrate to areas where services are cheaper to provide and where there are more sustainable options?

What do we know about the impact of CDD and social funds? Most of the initiatives are able to point to concrete outputs—kilometers of feeder roads constructed, schools and health clinics built, and water cisterns installed, for example, generated by their own monitoring systems. In a few cases, these outputs were linked to intermediary outcomes measured by their own evaluations. These investments led to increased school enrollments, health care services, clean drinking water, expanded financial services, and reduced travel time to markets and services.

The Brazil case study[5] cites evaluations done jointly by the World Bank and the United Nations Food and Agriculture Organization in 1994, 1995, and 2000. Communities predominantly chose to invest in rural water supply and electrification. The Malawi and Zambian social funds have, together, constructed or rehabilitated nearly 9,000 classrooms, 3,500 teachers' houses, more than 450 health centers and maternity wards, 5,000 water points, 16,000 latrines, nearly 11,000 kilometers of roads, and more than 1,000 bridges since their start in the 1990s.

KDP has built 19,000 kilometers of roads, 3,500 bridges, 5,200 irrigation systems, 2,800 clean water supply units, 1,300 sanitation units, 475 schools, and 140 village posts. Other achievements cited in the case study included time savings in travel, short-term employment for 2.8 million villagers through labor-intensive infrastructure works, access to financial services, empowerment through participation in decision making, and strengthened government accountability.

A 2003 Implementation Completion Report rated KDP as achieving its three objectives—raising rural incomes, strengthening kecamatan and village government and community institutions, and improving public infrastructure through labor-intensive methods. It also noted that the project has increased the role of civil society monitoring by fostering partnerships with the media and with NGOs. In addition to the achievements listed above, it credited KDP with expanding the provision of legal advocacy services and education in selected KDP villages (World Bank 2003b).

An impact evaluation conducted in 2003 of the Yemen social fund showed higher school enrollments, especially of girls. By 1999, three years after inception, girls' enrollment rates in assisted communities were 20 percent higher than in the comparison group, up from 41 to 48 percent. Data from 2003 show the proportion of girls enrolled increased from 42 percent in 1999 to 56 percent in 2003, and overall enrollment rates went up from 60 to 68 percent. The social fund's expenditures in education were 20 percent of total education investments in the country.

CDD programs are built on a very simple premise of giving people choice and control over resources that are intended to benefit them. This principle is increasingly becoming code for how to do "smart development." By incorporating principles of participation, transparency, and accountability, they reduce the scope for corruption compared with top-down projects. The challenge is to see how long external involvement is necessary for the processes to take root and become the norm.

Notes

1. The following CDD and social fund case studies are discussed in this chapter: A. Masefield, Afghanistan: The Role of the National Solidarity Program and National Emergency Employment Program in National Reconstruction; A. Roumani, Brazil: Community-driven Development in Rural Communities of the Northeast; H. Andersen, Cambodia's Seila Program: A Decentralized Approach to Rural Development and Poverty Reduction; W. Guobao, Q. Yang, and C. Huang, Southwest Poverty Reduction Project: A Multisectoral Approach; M. Naqvi, F. Kirlic, and S. Dukic, The Community Development Project in Bosnia Herzegovina: Citizen-driven Decision-making; S. Guggenheim, T. Wiranto, Y. Prasta, and S. Wong, Indonesia's Kecamatan Development Program: A Large-scale Use of Community Development to Reduce Poverty; Malawi and Zambia: Using Social Funds to Expand Infrastructure; S. F. Rasmussen, M. M. Piracha, R. Bajwa, A. Malik, and A. Mansoor, Pakistan: Scaling Up Rural Support Programs; J. Tanaka, The Pakiv European Roma Fund Initiative: A Civic Approach to Combating Socio-economic Exclusion among Roma (Gypsies) in Central and Eastern Europe; Philippines: The Kalahi-CIDSS Project; The South Asia Program for Poverty Alleviation; J. Penrose and O. Vasilenko, The National Social Investment Fund of Tajikistan; W. Struben, The Yemen Social Fund for Development. Unless otherwise noted, all statistics and quoted material are taken from the relevant case studies.

2. Beginning in 2003, the World Bank's Operations Evaluation Department (OED) evaluated community-based and community-driven development (CBD/CDD) projects (World Bank 2003a). OED selected a sample of 84 projects for intensive review. In addition to a desk review of project documents, OED also undertook a review of country assistance strategy documents, poverty reduction strategy papers, and formal and informal economic sector work. Two of the cases discussed in this chapter were part of that evaluation: KDP and Brazil's CDD. Of those two, only KDP was rigorously evaluated in the Shanghai process, and the methodology for that evaluation was not the same as the methodology used by the OED in its multiproject evaluation. OED's findings with regard to Brazil vary greatly from the findings in this chapter, and the Brazil study analyzed here did not include a robust evaluation. In an effort to harmonize these disparities, we will note the findings of the OED study where they differ from the conclusions in this chapter.

3. These findings are not in keeping with the findings of the OED evaluation, which notes that CDD projects are more expensive than non-CDD projects to prepare and supervise. Furthermore, the borrower incurs substantial cost in putting a participatory approach in place. Although CDD projects have helped lower the cost to governments for service delivery infrastructure, the communities now bear an increased part of the cost of that infrastructure. Additionally, the OED evaluation found that it has been difficult to maintain a high-quality flow of services from infrastructure constructed under CDD.

4. OED evaluation found clear evidence that infrastructure and activities have been difficult to sustain beyond the projects:

- Community development projects have been most effective where they have supported indigenously matured efforts.
- Community development projects have helped rehabilitate infrastructure and increase employment following conflicts, but when complementary service delivery components such as teachers or health care workers are lacking, the effects of the projects are reduced.
- The infrastructure and services supported have been difficult to sustain beyond the World Bank's presence.
- Community development projects, especially CDDs, pose a continuing challenge for safeguard and fiduciary compliance.

5. OED believes it is not clear that benefits of this endeavor cited in the case study can be attributed to the World Bank projects.

Bibliography

Guggenheim, Scott. Forthcoming. "Crises and Contradictions: Understanding the Origins of a Community Development Project in Indonesia." In *The Search for Empowerment: Social Capital as Idea and Practice at the World Bank,* ed. M. Woolcock, A. Bebbington, S. Guggenheim, and E. Olson. Bloomfield, CT: Kumarian Press.

Malhotra, Mohini. 2005a. "Community-Driven Development Evaluation: Study Components." Operations Evaluation Department. Available at www.world bank.org/oed/cdd/study_components.html.

———. 2005b. "The Effectiveness of World Bank Support for Community Development: An OED Evaluation." Operations Evaluation Department, Washington, DC.

———. 2004. "Lessons: Scaling Up Successful Efforts to Reduce Poverty." Available at www.reducingpoverty.org.

World Bank. 2003a. "Community-driven Development: A Study Methodology." Operations Evaluation Department. Available at www.worldbank.org/oed/cdd/docs/discussion_paper.pdf.

————. 2003b. "Indonesia: Kecamatan Development Fund Project." Implementation Completion Report 26163, Operations Evaluation Department, World Bank, Washington, DC.

6

Learning and Scaling Up through Evaluation

Ariel Fiszbein and Coralie Gevers

An important aspect of the Shanghai Conference dialogue was establishing the tenet that achieving the Millennium Development Goals (MDGs, see p. xi) will depend not only on increasing resources but also on renewed commitment to adapt and accelerate implementation of approaches conducive to poverty reduction. But how is an approach identified as successful? Rigorous impact evaluations of programs will bring the development community, and policy makers from developing countries in particular, a long way in gaining assurance that the programs they are financing, implementing, and considering for scaling up are indeed having an impact.

Very often, there is a temptation to draw conclusions on "success" from partial or incomplete information. In the search for solutions to pressing development challenges (such as the ones summarized by the MDGs), there is always a risk of jumping to conclusions by extrapolating from the *appearance* of success. This is a temptation to be resisted—and keeping an "inquisitive eye on the evaluation ball" is a good antidote to such a temptation. This, in essence, is the message so dramatically expressed by the late Italian author, Primo Levi (1998, p. 24):

> Since it is difficult to distinguish the good from the bad prophet, we must be suspicious of all prophets: it is better to avoid revealed truths, even if we feel exalted by their simplici-

ty and splendor, even if we find them comfortable because they come at no cost. It is better to be content with more modest and less inspiring truths that are laboriously conquered, step by step, with no shortcuts, by studying, discussion and reasoning, and that can be verified and demonstrated.

Following Levi's lead, this chapter emphasizes that the value of knowledge exchanges (real and virtual), such as the ones that took place in Shanghai, is deeply enhanced when based on robust evaluations of the final impact of these development initiatives. The chapter reviews the use of such evaluations among the Shanghai case studies and discusses key challenges to expanding the use of these types of evaluations as a learning tool and as a necessary step to increase development impact.

Impact Evaluation: A Powerful Instrument within a Spectrum of Evaluation Approaches

A range of evaluation approaches exist and are used in practice. Monitoring progress in the implementation of programs and evaluating whether intended objectives (such as connecting x households to a water system, or building y kilometers of dirt road for a cost of z dollars) are being met is a necessary component in a results-oriented approach to development. By the same token, the systematic documentation of changes in specific outcomes (such as infant mortality or income poverty) is a fundamental input for decision making by policy makers and development agencies.

Such information, though necessary to ensure that a program was implemented properly, may not be sufficient to judge if the program was indeed successful in achieving its objective. Take the example of an education project that aims at increasing primary school enrollment by providing free meals at schools, and assume that, after two years of implementation, the project manager and government authorities observe the increase in primary school enrollment that they had hoped for. As a result they declare the project a success and decide to implement it at the national level. However, in spite of apparent success suggested by the simple comparison of the enrollment rates before and after the project, there is no guarantee that the project was the critical factor that led to the improvement in school enrollment. It may well be that the economy was growing fast during this period, enabling poor families to send their children to school. If so, the expansion of the project to national scale may be a misguided decision and a waste of public resources.

Similarly, one could also imagine a case in which, after two years of implementation of a similar project, the authorities and project manager observe no improvement in school attendance levels and decide to end the project. This could also be a misguided decision: It is possible that, at the same time, the economy was in recession and, if not for the project, parents might have pulled their children out of school.

These two basic examples show that the simple observation of outcomes for participants before and after a project is not a sufficient basis for policy makers to decide the effectiveness of a program and whether to expand it or scale it down.

Alternatively, one could decide to compare outcomes between a group of people who benefited from a project and a group of people who did not participate in that project. This could be misleading as well. The group of participants may have personal characteristics that increase (or decrease) the likelihood of success of the program—for example, they can be more (or less) motivated or more (or less) capable than the group that does not participate in the project. If so, the impact assessed for the group of participants could not be generalized to the whole population. The argument is, then, that policy makers must rely on more rigorous evaluations to decide if a project is the determining factor in explaining the change in outcomes.

To be able to establish such causal links between a project and the observed outcomes, evaluators and researchers have developed and keep developing methods that are commonly grouped under the term *impact evaluation*. Their goal is to assess the specific outcomes attributable to a particular intervention (such as the increase in student learning resulting from a change in teacher profiles, or the higher incomes among microentrepreneurs resulting from improved access to credit). They do so by using a counterfactual that represents the hypothetical state the beneficiaries would have experienced without the intervention. The methodological challenge is to identify a proper counterfactual. Box 6.1 gives a brief explanation of these methods.[1]

Particularly when used strategically to test the effectiveness of specific approaches to addressing key development challenges, impact evaluations constitute the preferred approach to assessing results. Such information is critical not only for the policy makers di-

---

Box 6.1 Impact Evaluation Methods

There are two basic approaches to constructing the counterfactual. Experimental designs (also known as randomized² control designs) construct the counterfactual through the random selection, within a population, of the beneficiaries of the program to assess. This group then constitutes the "treatment group," whereas those not selected for program participation constitute the "control group." Given appropriate sample sizes, the process of random selection ensures equivalence between treatment and control groups in both observable and unobservable characteristics and thus avoids problems of selection bias. The impact of the program is determined by the difference between the mean outcomes of the treatment and control groups. Although considered to be the optimal approach for assessing a program's impact, randomized experiments can be difficult to implement for a variety of reasons, including political reluctance and cost concerns.

The other approach, quasi-experimental designs (also called non-experimental designs), relies on statistical models or design features of a program (that sometimes generate "natural," unplanned experiments) to construct a counterfactual. Sophisticated econometric techniques are used to build a comparison group with initial characteristics as similar as possible to those of the treatment group. The quasi-experimental designs include approaches such as regression discontinuity design, propensity score matching, and instrumental variables. Quasi-experimental methods are much more common than randomized control designs, in part because they can draw on existing data sources to assess a program and can sometimes be used after the program has begun.

For more details on impact evaluation methods, see Baker (2000), Ravallion (forthcoming), or Rossi (2003).

---

rectly in charge of the program evaluated, but also for all others who may be considering a "replication" (or adaptation) of the program in their own country and context.

Historically, impact evaluations of programs in the health and education areas have been the most common in the development field. For example, a recent review of the impact evaluations of projects financed by the World Bank showed that two thirds of these evaluations were concentrated in the human development sector.² The reason for this concentration stems at least in part from the methodological difficulties evaluators face in identifying appropriate counterfactuals for some types of interventions. But researchers are pushing the frontiers of evaluation and developing creative ways to address issues of selection or endogeneity for projects previously deemed impossible to evaluate, such as microfinance, road infrastructure, or even women's empowerment programs.

In the past, such evaluations were constrained by the lack of data and by the technical challenges of developing a counterfactual. Over the past few years, however, some significant improvements in both these areas have made impact evaluations easier to implement on a systematic basis. Microeconomic data—gathered through household surveys or demographic and health surveys—are available for more developing countries and on a more regular basis; and a range of evaluation techniques have been developed to construct the counterfactual—from randomized techniques to quasi-experimental ones (Ravallion forthcoming). As a result, a growing number of impact evaluation studies of development interventions are being produced by government agencies, researchers, and international development agencies. The importance of impact evaluation is increasingly recognized in the development field (see, for example, Deaton [2005], Duflo and Kremer [2005], and Rawlings [2005]).

Evaluations and Lessons of the Shanghai Cases

The Shanghai conference was an exceptional effort at a global review of the evidence on antipoverty programs. Though the descriptions of the case collected through the global learning process often offer little detail on the evaluation approach that may have been used to assess each experience, most of the underlying evaluations were based on rough comparisons of outcomes before and after. Based on the earlier discussion in this chapter of the value of impact evaluation in demonstrating causality between a program and its impact, a search of the evaluation literature was undertaken for each Shanghai case to see which had been the object of an impact evaluation.

Of the 106 case examples reviewed, 16 have been or currently are the object of a rigorous impact evaluation. Many other cases benefited from various combinations of qualitative and quantitative evaluations (see the annex). For example, a few cases provided data on the quality of a development program at targeting poor families; some compared levels of outcomes for program beneficiaries before and after the project. However, only 16 cases can be confidently qualified as "impact evaluations" for which there was

(or is) a serious attempt at comparing the outcomes for the beneficiaries to an adequate counterfactual.

Following the classification adopted in the collection of Shanghai case summaries, the experiences evaluated are presented in
table 6.1.

Table 6.1 demonstrates that the methodologies of impact evaluation can be adapted to a variety of interventions—from one that
delegated school management to associations of parents, like El
Salvador's EDUCO program, to one that provided formal land titling to poor families, like Peru's land titling program.

The evaluation of the Oportunidades program (previously
named PROGRESA) in Mexico provides a powerful example of
the value of this type of evaluation. This program, which started
with a pilot project in 1995, aims to improve the educational,
health, and nutritional status of poor families, and to encourage
the responsibility and active participation of the families in education. At the request of the Mexican authorities, an evaluation component was built into the design of the program from the outset.
The evaluation was undertaken by an independent group, the International Food Policy Research Institute.

The evaluation quickly shed light on the positive impact of the
program: All health indicators among children improved, school
enrollment increased, the gap between girls' and boys' enrollment
narrowed, and total years of schooling increased significantly.
These results convinced Mexican authorities not only to maintain
the program, despite political pressures to change it, but also to
scale it up. The program originally focused on rural areas and benefited 300,000 poor families; today it reaches 5 million poor families all across Mexico.

But the effects of the impact evaluation of the Oportunidades
program were felt beyond Mexico's borders. It sparked interest in
other countries (for example, in Colombia), which initiated similar
programs of conditional cash transfers. In this sense, one can say
that the impact evaluation of one program supported the expansion of the program in its own country but also a horizontal scale
up across countries of an effective approach to reducing poverty.

Table 6.1 also highlights the potential for undertaking comparisons of impact evaluations of similar interventions—also called
meta-evaluations.[3] As will be further developed in the next section,
these meta-evaluations bring a wealth of knowledge to the development community and should therefore become the object of a
concerted effort by that community. They give information to policy makers on what works and what does not—or under what cir-

Table 6.1 Case Studies with Impact Evaluations

Theme	Experience	Method	Status
Microfinance	Brazil: Struggling with the Growth-versus-Best Practice Tradeoff—The CrediAmigo Program of Banco do Nordeste	Experimental	Starting
Education	El Salvador's EDUCO: A Community-managed Education Program in Rural Areas	Instrumental variable	Complete
Health	Philippines: Early Childhood Development Programs—Offsetting the Disadvantages of Poverty	Propensity score matching	Complete
Transportation	Vietnam: Large-scale Transport Infrastructure in Northern Vietnam	Propensity score matching	Complete
Community-driven development/social funds	Indonesia's Kecamatan Development Program: A Large-scale Use of Community Development to Reduce Poverty	Propensity score matching	Complete
	Indonesia's Urban Poverty Project II (an extension of the Kecamatan Development Program)	Regression discontinuity design	Ongoing
	Zambia: Using Social Funds to Expand Infrastructure	Propensity score matching	Complete
	Philippines: The Kalahi-CIDSS Project	Cluster analysis	Ongoing
	The South Asia Program for Poverty Alleviation	To be determined	Starting

Continued

197

Table 6.1 Continued

Theme	Experience	Method	Status
Community-driven development/social funds, *continued*	Yemen's Social Fund for Development	Comparison without counterfactual	Complete
Securing access to land	Peru's Urban Land Titling Program	Propensity score matching and instrumental variable	Complete
	India: Online Land Titling System	Single difference	Complete
	Philippines: Agrarian Reform Infrastructure Support Project	Single difference	Complete
Targeted programs	Brazil's Bolsa Família Program	To be determined	Starting
	China's Southwest Poverty Reduction Project: A Multisectoral Approach	Propensity score matching	Complete
	Mexico's Oportunidades Program	Experimental	Complete

Note: A "complete" status designation does not mean that the project has been completed. Rather, it indicates that at least one evaluation of the project has been published. The annex to this chapter presents a more comprehensive overview of the evaluations for each experience, including details on the evaluation methods, a description of the main findings, and complete references.

cumstances. They also help set benchmarks. Thanks to the evaluations of past projects, a policy maker will know what range of effects he or she may expect when implementing such programs.

Impact Evaluations as a Tool for
Learning and Policy Making—Looking Forward

The Shanghai learning process provides us with a clear sense of the potential of continuing to build on a process of systematic learning from robust evaluations. A forward-looking vision of a global learning effort on effective development interventions could create a good basis for increasing poverty reduction efforts across the developing world. The challenges that need to be met in order to implement that vision are discussed next, and current World Bank efforts to help address those challenges are reviewed.

Challenges of Evaluation as a
Global Learning Tool

As has been recognized before, evaluations (all types of evaluation, but particularly those that focus on establishing causality and thus are more relevant for people not directly involved with the program being evaluated) constitute public goods—often international public goods. Indeed, impact evaluations generate knowledge on what sorts of programs create substantial results. Such information is critical not only for the policy makers directly in charge of the program evaluated but also for all others who may be considering a replication (or adaptation) of the program in their own country and context. Thus, impact evaluations could have tremendous impact in terms of development if adequately provided. But, typically, evaluation studies are nonrival in consumption: The consumption by those who paid for the evaluation is not reduced when others consume the studies as well. They are also, often, nonexcludable: It is (increasingly) hard to avoid the results of such studies reaching other consumers.[4] The nonexcludability and the nonrivalry of evaluation studies make them an international public good that is likely to be undersupplied by the market.

In fact, key actors in the "evaluation game" face an unfavorable cost-benefit equation. Most developing countries have weak capacity (weak statistical systems, relatively little expertise in impact evaluation, and weak links between government line agencies and research institutions that could support them technically) and little incentive to develop it. They will pay all the costs (such as the direct costs of undertaking the evaluation and possible reputational costs—depending on the results of the evaluation—for politicians, implementing agencies, program financiers) and derive a small portion of the benefits (both domestically, because other policy makers cannot be excluded from benefiting from the lessons of the evaluations, and internationally, because other countries will benefit as well).[5]

Furthermore, the public good dimension is complicated by the fact that the "treatments" contemplated (such as improving the quality of education provided in schools) are very complex, because it is not just about the content of the treatment but also about the means by which the treatment is delivered. Context (political, institutional, and cultural) is very influential. Thus, more experiments may be needed to capture heterogeneous context and design variability. These are strong arguments for international-scale evaluation.

The need for international-scale evaluation is worth emphasizing. When comparable interventions are evaluated across countries and regions, the impact evaluation results serve three purposes in addition to the obvious one of providing feedback regarding the individual program. First, the results of the comparisons provide the empirical basis for determining robust performance goals at both project and country levels (for example, what reduction in mortality rates can be expected on average—or for some specific age group—from a particular type of child health program?). These evaluations may help in setting performance benchmarks for similar interventions in a variety of contexts. Second, they can help assess the relative effectiveness of alternative designs of development programs in different country contexts and settings (for example, the effectiveness of conditional cash transfer programs in rural versus urban settings, or with centralized versus decentralized management). Finally, these comparisons of impact evaluations can support the cost-effectiveness analysis of different interventions.[6]

Although not common yet in the development field, more meta-evaluations are slowly emerging. For example, the experiences of several social funds were analyzed as part of the Shanghai consultations. These experiences, and a few others, are the basis for a recent study (Rawlings, Sherburne-Benz, and Van Domelen 2004). Although close to $10 billion in foreign and domestic financing had been allocated to social funds and much had been written about their institutional role, little was known of the real impact of these funds on poverty, health, and education. The meta-evaluation is based on the assessment of six social funds and it combines different types of evaluation methods to assess targeting and sustainability, with some random and nonrandomized evaluation methods to assess impact.[7]

The impact evaluations in the initiatives studied—which involved designing the evaluations and collecting survey data from 21,000 households and 1,200 schools, health centers, and water and sanitation projects—cost less than 1 percent of program resources, on average. By comparing results across the six case studies, the report provided rigorous evidence of the positive impact of these social funds and indicated ways to strengthen their long-term development effects.

Meta-evaluations should soon be possible in other areas. For example, in the area of targeted programs, the evaluations of the experiences in Brazil, China, and Mexico are not the only examples. Several other evaluations are currently being developed around similar conditional cash transfer programs in Bangladesh, Burkina Faso, Cambodia, Chile, Colombia, Ecuador, Jamaica, Nicaragua, and Turkey.

Overcoming the Public Good Dimension

The challenge, as with other public goods (particularly international ones), is how to set up a system to promote or enable an adequate supply. How to address the public good dimension? Lately there has been increased discussion in the development community on these challenges and alternative ways to coordinate efforts. It is still unclear what the specific options are and no consensus has emerged so far, but the ongoing discussions suggest the need to combine actions in a number of areas.

First, common sense suggests there is a strong need for subsidies to reduce the costs of evaluations for developing countries. It appears that the key to reducing costs is subsidizing the production of baseline and follow-up surveys—the most expensive (and risky) part of evaluations. Of course, this needs to be done as part of methodologically sound evaluation designs.

Second, in the medium term, the above-mentioned subsidies can be more cost effective and sustainable to the extent that they are linked to statistical and evaluation capacity building. As an example, the costs of good evaluations are much lower in countries with a well-established system of national household surveys than in those without such a system.

Third, coordination on what gets evaluated is needed to maximize learning from evaluations. Quite often, there are no systematic comparisons of results from individual program evaluations. This is partly caused by the fact that unless the design of individual evaluations is somehow coordinated, the comparability of results may be compromised. More generally, the lack of planning of such meta-analyses may often imply that opportunities for comparative assessments, which could provide valuable lessons beyond the countries where the evaluations take place, may go unnoticed or remain unused. As a consequence, the returns from evaluations, while still high, are much lower than their potential would indicate.

In other words, fully exploiting the benefits from evaluations requires both a strategic approach to the identification of priority candidates for evaluation and a coordinated approach to planning their implementation. There are at least two aspects of this coordination challenge: that between aid agencies (multilateral and bilateral) and that between donor and recipient country priorities.[8]

Although addressing this particular challenge is not a simple endeavor, a necessary condition is to find the means by which to enable strong participation by governments and experts from developing countries, both in the selection of themes for evaluation and in the implementation of the actual evaluations. In other words, it is critical to ensure that the evaluation community in the developing world can be an active participant in this new trend of increased attention to and importance of impact evaluation as a learning tool.

A Scenario for Shanghai II

To pursue the journey begun in the Shanghai global learning process, consider the following scenario: Policy makers and development practitioners from around the world are meeting in 2010 for the "Second Shanghai Conference on Reducing Poverty on a Global Scale." What would that conference be expected to look like?

Shanghai II might involve more than a dozen sessions, each focused on key specific development challenges, such as reducing infant mortality rates, improving student learning outcomes, raising productivity and earnings of poor farmers and microentrepreneurs, reducing vulnerability of poor households to shocks, and so forth. In each of the sessions, practitioners from developing countries around the world would be presenting and comparing tried and tested (impact-evaluated) approaches to addressing those development challenges and discussing their relative cost effectiveness and conditions for adaptability to different contexts. In their discussions they would be referring to evaluation studies, many of which could have been authored or coauthored by specialists from developing countries.

What would it take to make that vision a reality? Essentially, three things must happen to enable this vision for Shanghai II. First, it would be necessary to ensure that impact evaluations of alternative approaches to addressing key development challenges be conducted across countries and regions. For example, given the natural presumption that teachers (their capacities and behaviors) are important factors in achieving better learning outcomes, it is critical that alternative ways of organizing schools and hiring and rewarding teachers be tried, and their impact on learning outcomes be evaluated.

But the results of independent evaluations would not suffice. Thus, the second thing that must happen is that the results of those evaluations need to be compared through meta-analyses. Once again using the example of improvements in learning outcomes, one would seek to test and evaluate, for example, flexible teacher contracting mechanisms in a variety of country contexts to determine how robust the results are and, assuming results are positive, get estimates of the magnitude of the expected effects. Furthermore, in many cases it may be possible to contrast the results with those of alternative approaches to achieving the same outcomes. In this example, the results from evaluations of flexible teacher contracting schemes could be compared with those that measure the impact of school-based management schemes on learning outcomes. With meta-analyses of these types, participants in Shanghai II would be in a stronger position than those in Shanghai I to discuss how best to approach specific development challenges—such as those summarized in the MDGs.

A third challenge would also have to be met for this vision to materialize. Participants from the developing world would need to feel ownership not only of the interventions being discussed but also of their evaluations. Such ownership is at the core of the "spirit of Shanghai."

This is a tall order. Using Shanghai I as a baseline and taking as a reference the analysis in the first part of this chapter, Shanghai II would demand significant efforts in undertaking individual program impact evaluations and their comparative assessments. For example, if we were to start with the same case studies that were part of the Shanghai I learning process, we estimate that methodological advances would now make possible the evaluation of 40 of them (in addition to the 16 cases presented in this chapter)—assuming that funding and evaluation capacity would be available in the countries. Ensuring ownership by representatives from developing countries would require much more involvement in those evaluations by both governments and researchers from the developing regions of the world than has been observed so far.

Expansion of Donor Involvement in Impact Evaluation

Meeting these challenges would require action and effort by all the development partners. In spite of the many efforts to expand the role of the World Bank in promoting and supporting impact evaluations, partial stocktaking exercises suggest a small proportion of World Bank projects have impact evaluation components—and even fewer have actually carried forward those components in a technically sound fashion.[9]

Seeking to contribute to the materialization of the described vision of a global learning effort on effective development programs and to address many of the mentioned bottlenecks, the World Bank has established, under the leadership of its chief economist, the Development Impact Evaluation (DIME) initiative to better coordinate and expand its efforts in the area of impact evaluation.

DIME is seeking to increase the number of World Bank–financed projects with impact evaluation components, particularly in strategic areas, and themes for which there is high demand from its client governments (such as conditional cash transfers, various approaches to improving delivery of education services, and slum upgrading programs). The Bank is also setting up the bases for a process of comparative analysis of results from such evaluations that will provide critical inputs both to results-based management efforts and to evidence-based policy advice offered to World Bank clients. Such a focused approach will enable the systematic comparison of the effectiveness of specific interventions in different settings (countries, regions, and so forth) and alternative designs, and thus provide a unique opportunity to demonstrate the learning power of impact evaluation efforts both in identifying "what works" and "what does not work," and in obtaining robust measures of performance to be expected from successful programs.

Meeting the challenge, though, will require concerted efforts to move further in this direction, such as increased technical and financial support to developing countries to build their own statistical and evaluation capacity, and consistent and persistent commitment by donors and the international development community to support the evaluation of the programs they finance as well as coordinating efforts at distilling the lessons from those evaluations—while ensuring a strong participation by governments and researchers from developing countries. The path to knowledge described by Primo Levi above is not an easy one. But it certainly is the right one.

Annex:
A Comprehensive Overview of the Evaluations

Note: The focus of this chapter is rigorous impact evaluation, generally with the use of a counterfactual. It is important to note, however, that many of the programs included here have been evaluated in other ways as well, including qualitative evaluations, targeting analyses, social cost-benefit analyses, inventories of tangible outcomes, and so forth. For the brevity and focus of this annex, these other types of evaluation have not been summarized here.

Country: Brazil
Program: The CrediAmigo Program of Banco do Nordeste, funded by the World Bank
Program Summary: This program began in 1997 as an autonomous unit within Banco do Nordeste with the objective of improving microenterprises' access to sustainable, formal financial services throughout the northeast region of Brazil. It offers loans to established microentrepreneurs for the financing of their working capital and fixed asset needs. The program uses the solidarity group technique of extending loans with an average duration of three months to small groups of three to five borrowers. It scaled up considerably from 1997 to 2000, quickly becoming the largest microfinance institution in Brazil, and tripled in size from 2000 to 2004. The government will soon relax the eligibility requirements, but has not publicly announced the details of the change.
Evaluation Summary: A sample of applicants ineligible by the old requirements will be surveyed and randomly assigned into two groups: ineligible and eligible (according to the new, relaxed requirements). Several outcome indicators will be used to measure impacts, including those indicators related to business expansion, household income change, women's empowerment, social capital development, and the targeting of credit services. Effects will be considered on the basis of the "intent to treat" (that is,

the difference between assigned eligible and ineligible groups), as well as treatment of those treated (taking into consideration the actual disbursement of CrediAmigo loans). This difference-in-difference method, using a randomized control group, will not only evaluate the effects of this program, but also offer a true data analysis against which nonexperimental specifications can be compared and assessed.

Main Findings: To be released in the summer of 2006

Evaluators: Emmanuel Skoufias, Susana Sanchez, Pedro Olinto (World Bank), and Dean Karlan (Princeton University), in collaboration with CrediAmigo of Banco do Nordeste, in Fortaleza, Brazil

Status: Scheduled to begin in the summer of 2005

Source: Skoufias, E., S. Sanchez, P. Olinto, and D. Karlan. 2004. "Research Proposal: An Evaluation of the Impact of CrediAmigo and the Expansion of Access to Financial Services in Brazil." Photocopy. World Bank, Washington, DC.

Country: El Salvador

Program: EDUCO (Educación con Participación de la Comunidad; Education with Community Participation)

Program Summary: EDUCO aims to decentralize education by strengthening the direct involvement and participation of parents and community groups. Economically disadvantaged communities (as measured by severe malnutrition and lack of access to social services) are targeted as priorities for the introduction of EDUCO programs. These communities take the initiative to organize their own schools, administered and financially supported by an association of households. The EDUCO schools are managed autonomously by an elected Community Education Association drawn from the parents of the students and contracted by the Ministry of Education to deliver a given curriculum to an agreed number of students. The association is responsible for contracting with and removing teachers based on their performance, and for equipping and maintaining the schools.

Evaluation Summary: The evaluators estimated school production functions to compare student achievement on standardized tests and school attendance of rural students in EDUCO schools versus those in traditional schools. Cross-sectional survey data included 311 schools (EDUCO and others) in approximately half of the country's municipalities. The evaluators controlled for student characteristics and selection bias, using an exogenously determined formula for targeting EDUCO schools as an instrumental variable.

Main Findings: The evaluators found that the rapid expansion of rural schools through EDUCO has not adversely affected student achievement, and has diminished student absences caused by teacher absences, which may have longer-term effects on achievement.

Evaluators: Emmanuel Jimenez (World Bank) and Yasuyuki Sawadab (Stanford University). Data were collected by the Salvadoran Ministry of Education with the assistance of the World Bank and the U.S. Agency for International Development.

Status: Complete

Source: Jimenez, E., and Y. Sawadab. 1998. "Do Community-managed Schools Work? An Evaluation of El Salvador's EDUCO Program." Working Paper 8, Series on Impact Evaluation of Education Reforms, World Bank, Washington, DC.

Country: Philippines

Program: Early Childhood Development (ECD) Program; funded by the Government of the Philippines, the Asian Development Bank, and the World Bank

Program Summary: The goals of this ongoing program are to provide services that ensure the survival and promote the physical and mental development of children, and to establish an effective partnership between national and local government units. The program promotes psychosocial development and nutrition of young children through the use of immunization, management of child illness, micronutrient malnutrition control, and parent-effectiveness seminars. Preselected municipalities in two regions received grants to invest in service-provider packages, and they received implementation support as well.

Evaluation Summary: The researchers evaluated the program using panel data collected over three years in two treatment regions that received the ECD program and a control region that did not receive the intervention. Two questions were researched: what was the general impact on children in treatment areas (the "intent to treat") and what was the impact more specifically on children who receive the treatment (the "treatment on the treated")? Because there were initial differences between the control group and both the intent-to-treat and the treated groups, data measured at the municipality, barangay, household, and child levels are used for nearest-neighbor matching to create the counterfactuals. A difference-in-difference between the baseline and later surveys for treatment groups and their counterfactuals is used to estimate the impact of the offer of the program as well as the impact of implementation.

Main Findings: The results based on the matched intent-to-treat comparison indicate that there has been a significant improvement in weight-for-height Z scores among children age 5 and above in the third survey round (age 3 and above at baseline). They also offer evidence of substantial increases in cognitive, social, and motor development scores for children age 3 and below who reside in ECD program areas, relative to those who do not reside in such areas. Finally, in program areas compared with nonprogram areas, there is evidence of an important decline in the proportion of children below age 4 who have worms. The results based on the matched treatment-on-the-treated comparison show no significant effects of the program on the subsample receiving treatment.

Evaluators: Jere Behrman (University of Pennsylvania), Paulita Duazo, Socorro Gultiano (University of San Carlos, Philippines), Sharon Ghuman (University of Michigan), Elizabeth King (World Bank), and Lina Laigo (Government of the Philippines Council for the Welfare of the Child), in cooperation with the ECD Study Team in the Office of Population Studies, University of San Carlos, Philippines

Status: Complete

Sources Behrman, J., P. Duazo, S. Ghuman, S. Gultiano, E. King, and N. Lee. 2005. "Evaluating the Early Childhood Development Program in the Philippines." Paper presented at the Annual Meeting of the Population Association of America, Philadelphia, March 31–April 2, 2005.

Behrman, J., S. Gultiano, E. King, and L. Laigo. 2004. "A Better Start in Life: The Early Childhood Development Program in the Philippines." Photocopy. World Bank, Washington, DC.

Ghuman, S., J. Behrman, J. Borja, S. Gultiano, and E. King. 2003. "Family Background, Service Providers, and Early Childhood Development in the Philippines: Proxies and Interactions." Paper presented at the Population Association of America Annual Meeting, May 2003.

Powerpoint presentation by authors at the World Bank, Washington, DC, on April 5, 2005. Available at http://web.world bank.org/WBSITE/EXTERNAL/NEWS/0,,contentMDK:2048 3008~menuPK:34482~pagePK:34370~piPK:34425~theSitePK: 4607,00.html.

Program Website: http://proxy.dswd.gov.ph/ecd/index.html.

Country: Vietnam

Program: Infrastructure Development: The Vietnam Rural Transport Project I

Program Summary: The program was a large-scale rural roads rehabilitation project that aimed to link community centers (communes) with markets and thereby to reduce poverty. The project was implemented through the central government's Ministry of Transport, which was responsible for deciding which provinces would participate in the project. The project involved poor provinces and it aimed to rehabilitate roads selected on the basis of rehabilitation cost and density of the community served. Both paved and earth roads were to be rehabilitated; no new roads were to be built.

Evaluation Summary: The study analysis involved propensity score matching to construct a control group of communes, using treatment support matching, common support matching, and nearest-neighbor matching. The panel data set includes baseline as well as postproject data for both treatment and control areas in 6 of the 18 provinces, chosen for geographical representativeness. A difference-in-difference estimator was used for commune-level effects. Household stratified survey data were taken randomly from the sampled communes to represent income thirds of the commune and were used to determine whether impacts vary across households with different incomes.

Main Findings: The evaluators determined that the project reached more poor households than it would have reached if it had been equally distributed across rural communes. In general, the project resulted in an improvement in the quality of roads and a switch in rehabilitation focus from earth roads to paved roads. The project increased the availability of freight services and decreased the time required to reach certain services. It also led to an increased likelihood of other government infrastructure projects in the commune. The effects varied significantly across income groups of households, with the strongest effects for the poorest households.

Evaluators: Dominique Van de Walle and Dorothyjean Cratty (World Bank), relying on the Survey of Impacts of Rural Roads in Viet Nam and the 1997/98 Viet Nam Living Standards Survey

Status: Complete

Source: Van De Walle, D., and D. Cratty. 2002. "Impact Evaluation of a Rural Rehabilitation Project." Photocopy. World Bank, Washington, DC.

Country: Indonesia

Program: Kecamatan Development Program (KDP1)

Program Summary: The project's objectives were to raise rural incomes, strengthen kecamatan and village government and community institutions, and build public infrastructure through labor-intensive methods. The four components consisted of block grants to kecamatans; technical assistance for implementation, including national management consultants, province management consultants, and the Kabupaten Engineers; monitoring; and policy studies.

Evaluation Summary: This study uses real consumption expenditure to assess the welfare effects of the program. The three phases of KDP1 are evaluated individually, using a combination of National Socio-economic Survey and PODES (village census) data. Because the data (gathered in 1998, 2001, 2002, and 2003) are a series of cross-sectional data sets rather than panel data, propensity score matching was performed twice for each phase: once for ex ante matching and once for ex post matching. Nearest-neighbor matches were used to compute the mean effect of the treatment on the treated. A bootstrap method was used to estimate reliable standard errors. Separate from the matching analysis, the study also estimated the effects of three other factors on the rate of return: community participation, amount of swadaya money gathered by the community, and quality of project facilitators. The study included a targeting analysis as well.

Main Findings: The matching method found a sizable positive impact of the program on consumption expenditures, with greater impacts for kecamatans with a longer participation in KDP. This result was robust in purging the effect of different disbursement amounts by computing the annual rate of return for each kecamatan in each cycle. The proxies for participation were meeting attendance and decision activity at meetings, and these were correlated with higher impacts. Greater amounts of swadaya money correlated positively as well, after purging for endogeneity by using increases in swadaya and increases in return within projects rather than comparisons across projects. The quality of the facilitator was not measured by the grade received (which could be endogenous), but by promotion status; however the effect was not significant.

Evaluators: Vivi Alatas, with Scott Guggenheim and Susan Wong (World Bank), using data from the National Socio-economic Survey and the PODES census of villages, courtesy of the Indonesian Central Bureau of Statistics

Status: Complete

Source: Alatas, V. 2005. "An Evaluation of Kecamatan Development Project." Draft.

Country: Indonesia

Program: Urban Poverty Project II (UPP2), the second generation of the Kecamatan Development Program, adapted to the urban context

Program Summary: The project consists largely of two main components. The first component provides community development and local government capacity building, including the formation of an elected community organization (BKM) at the local municipal level and the creation of a participatory, three-year community development plan. The second component provides grants to these new organizations. Subprojects will cover a range of poverty alleviation activities with an open menu. There is also a smaller third component that finances a poverty alleviation partnership grant to encourage links between local governments and the BKMs, organized in forums. A total of 15 provinces will be covered, and it is expected that approximately 3,150 local municipalities will participate. The project will work in all districts, with urban subdistricts selected using a simple poverty targeting method. All wards/villages within the selected subdistricts will participate.

Evaluation Summary: Beginning with a baseline, three rounds of survey data will be collected in both treatment and control communities. The evaluators will use a regression discontinuity design to identify differences between treatment and control communities. Quantitative data will be analyzed using difference-in-difference methods. Qualitative data will be used alongside the quantitative data to adapt the evaluation to the local context and to study issues particular to the Indonesian context. The qualitative aspect will also be used to generate specific hypotheses to be tested for generalizability with the quantitative data.

Main Findings: To be released in late 2008

Evaluators: Menno Pradhan, Vijayendra Rao, Vivi Alatas (World Bank), Victoria Beard (University of California-Irvine), Indah Setyawati (GTZ/Siskes), and Andi Achdian (Institute of Political Economy Study), with the participation of the Government of Indonesia and of the ASEM (Asia-Europe Meeting)

Status: Proposed evaluation is being considered for funding.

Source: Pradhan, M., V. Rao, and V. Alatas. 2005. "A Mixed Method Evaluation of Community-Driven Development in Urban Indonesia." Request to the World Bank Research Program for a Research Support Budget Grant. Draft.

Country: Zambia

Program: Zambia Social Recovery Program (or ZAMSIF: Zambia Social Investment Fund)

Program Summary: The Zambia Social Recovery Program spread resources fairly equally across regions, relying on self-targeting to reach poorer areas. The choice of subproject types that the social fund could support was posited to extend automatically to relatively less-affluent communities. The social fund focused on the education and health sectors, as well as on basic economic infrastructure, such as rural roads, bridges and marketplaces, water and sanitation systems, and irrigation projects.

Evaluation Summary: Two evaluation designs were used to measure the effects on the education and health sectors. A pipeline comparison used, as a control group, communities that had been approved for the social fund but had not yet received it. To correct for selection based on observable heterogeneities, propensity score matching was used.

Main Findings: *Schooling:* Positive effects were found on school attendance, significant only in urban areas. Age-appropriate attendance improved and share of education in household expenditures increased. *Health:* Evidence suggests that the fund had no effect on actual sickness, but did increase awareness of health issues. Reporting of illness was significantly higher in the treatment group; the incidence of diarrhea and the likelihood of seeking treatment (when not conditioned on reporting illness) did not differ significantly between the groups. Additionally, the treatment group was significantly less likely to seek hospital care and more likely to seek care at a health center. Also, the effect on vaccinations was positive and significant.

Evaluators: Robert S. Chase (Johns Hopkins University, School of Advanced International Studies) and Lynne Sherburne-Benz (World Bank), in cooperation with the staffs of the social fund and the Zambian Central Statistics Office on survey and sample design, data collection, and institutional insights

Status: Complete

Source: Chase, R. S., and L. Sherburne-Benz. 2001. "Household Effects of African Community Initiatives: Evaluating the Impact of the Zambia Social Fund." Photocopy. Available at http://www 1.worldbank.org/prem/poverty/ie/details_evaluation.cfm?id=63.

Country: Philippines

Program: The Kalahi-CIDSS Program (Kapitbisig Laban Sa Kahirapan–Comprehensive and Integrated Delivery of Social Services), a project of the Department of Social Welfare and Development of the Philippines

Program Summary: The Kalahi-CIDSS seeks the empowerment of local communities through increased participation in local governance and involvement in the design, implementation, and management of poverty reduction projects. The three components are provision of community grants, implementation support to strengthen formal and informal local institutions, and monitoring and evaluation. Using a competitive process, villagers select projects from an open menu and prioritize them for funding. The Kalahi provides services such as roads, clean drinking water, schools, health facilities, day care centers, and electricity. Villagers and their local governments contribute approximately 40 percent of the cost. Projects appear to save both time and money in providing basic services to poor people, as well as providing villagers with structured opportunities for accessing information, expressing their opinions, and influencing local governance.

Evaluation Summary: The targeting of the program to the poorest quartile of municipalities within included provinces makes propensity score matching impossible. Instead, the evaluators will use cluster analysis to match participating municipalities with similar ones to be taken as a comparison group. Currently a survey is under way for which respondents were selected using multistage, stratified random sampling. This baseline survey, along with the planned midterm and follow-up surveys, will provide the panel data for treatment and control groups needed for the impact evaluation.

Main Findings: To be released in late 2008 or early 2009

Evaluators: Robert Chase and Camilla Holmemo (World Bank), in cooperation with the Department of Social Welfare and Development of the Philippines. The baseline survey was conducted by the Asia-Pacific Policy Center.

Status: Ongoing

Source: World Bank. 2005. "CDD and Social Capital Impact: Designing a Baseline Survey in the Philippines." Washington, DC.

Country: South Asia Region

Program: South Asia Poverty Alleviation Program (SAPAP), as scaled up in the District Poverty Initiatives Project (DPIP) in India

Program Summary: The SAPAP was a multicountry effort to address poverty through social mobilization, building organizations of poor people so that they could formulate and manage action programs to meet their needs. The program ran from 1996 to 2003, but since that time it has been scaled up as a variety of different projects throughout the region. In India, the DPIP has been implemented in three states: Andhra Pradesh, Madhya Pradesh, and Rajasthan. The projects were prepared in the 1990s and were approved in 2000. Each project is unique, but all share a primary objective of empowering poor people economically, politically, and socially. Each project also shares the basic notions that people are the best judges of how their lives and livelihoods can be improved, and that resources should flow directly to people to finance activities of their own choosing rather than filtering through line ministries.

Evaluation Summary: A joint assessment of the three DPIPs is currently under way. Each of these projects has baseline data in project and nonproject villages. All three will also have some midterm survey. Except for Andhra Pradesh, however, the midterm surveys were not structured and implemented to allow anything to be said at this stage about project impact using the baseline and midterm household data. The Madhya Pradesh midterm evaluation is scheduled for fall 2005. The Andhra Pradesh midterm assessment is currently under way. Details regarding the methodology are not yet available.

Main Findings: Not yet available

Evaluators: Lant Pritchett, Klaus Deininger, and Salimah Samji (World Bank)

Status: Ongoing

Source: Draft version of "DPIP Joint Interim Assessment: Understanding Project Differences," and correspondence with Salimah Samji, June 2005.

Country: Yemen

Program: Social Fund for Development (SFD)

Program Summary: The SFD's approach to poverty reduction relies on three principal components: community development projects for small-scale, labor-intensive infrastructure works (water supply, sanitation, and feeder roads) and delivery of basic social services (education and health); microenterprise development through technical assistance, training, and access to credit; and capacity building to assist nongovernmental organizations, local communities, and the private sector in identifying, implementing, and operating SFD projects. When financing public works in connection

with the community development program, the SFD first mobi-
lizes communities to prioritize investments and to make contributions to investments and recurrent costs. The SFD's autonomy
from the government bureaucracy has given it considerable flexibility in disbursement and operational procedures.

Evaluation Summary: This evaluation comprised many different focuses and methods. A 1999 National Poverty Survey was available
to use as baseline data for intervention communities. Ex post data
for the intervention group were taken from a survey in 2002 that
also served as a new baseline for pipeline communities. For some
topics, only qualitative evaluation was used. For quantitative evaluations, the focus was a before-after comparison, but data from
the 1999 baseline were not always available. Therefore, for some
topics, 2002 ex post data were compared to the 2002 new baseline
for the pipeline group. For other topics, a mixture of the before-
after comparison and the ex post pipeline comparison was used.
For household development indicators, 1999 ex ante and 2002 ex
post data for intervention communities were compared. Because
of budget constraints, a counterfactual group was not created. Instead, multivariate regression analysis was used to control for possible heterogeneities between the two groups.

Main Findings: The results from the evaluation concerning house-
hold-level development indicators show a significant increase in
gross school enrollment rate for girls and a decrease in children
falling behind in school; an increase in the proportion of ill or
injured individuals receiving health care; no significant effect on
the timeliness or coverage of immunization, the uptake of antenatal care, or the incidence of diarrhea; an increase in the proportion of households getting water from an in-dwelling tap and
a decrease in use of cisterns, tanks without pumps, well water,
and dam water; and a decrease in time and distance required to
fetch water from outside the dwelling. Further results will be
available following an ex post survey for the 2002 baseline communities, which is scheduled for late 2005.

Evaluators: Ian Walker; with the assistance of Vincent David, Fidel
Ordoñez, and Freddy Velásquez (ESA Consultores), commissioned by the World Bank, with help from the Yemeni field work
team on data collection, entry, and processing

Status: Complete

Sources ESA Consultores International. 2003. "Yemen Social Fund
for Development, 2003 Impact Evaluation Study: Final Report."

Tegucigalpa, Honduras. Available at http://www.esa.hn/i_publi
caciones.asp.
Comments by e-mail from Ian Walker, June 8, 2005.

Country: Peru
Program: Urban Land Titling Program: COFOPRI (Committee for
the Formalization of Private Property)
Program Summary: In 1991 a property titling project was instituted in the city of Lima with the goal of converting informal property ownership into registered, titled ownership. In 1996, under
the auspices of the public agency COFOPRI, the Peruvian government established a national property registry to formalize the
remaining properties in Lima and extend the program to seven
other cities. Titles were issued at an extremely low cost to title
claimants who could verify residency predating 1995 on eligible
public properties. The program was expected to raise residential
investment by increasing tenure security.
Evaluation Summary: A cross-sectional survey in 2000 was stratified
on city, with cluster units of 10 households randomly sampled at
the neighborhood level. Five separate impact evaluations have
used these data to evaluate the program's impact on credit supply,
fertility, household labor supply, time use, and residential investment. The evaluations used varied combinations of the following
methods: difference-in-difference, intent-to-treat analysis, propensity score matching (kernal, random-draw, nearest-neighbor, and
stratified matching procedures), instrumental variables, and regression analysis controlling for observable household and neighborhood characteristics and/or employing city fixed effects.
Main Findings: *Time use:* Program households are less likely to keep
a person at home to guard the property, have more household labor force hours, have greater out-of-home employment, have
lower child labor, and spend more leisure time outside of the
home. *Labor supply:* Program households supplied more labor
hours per week, with the effect increasing for newer titled residents and for households with fewer workers; have more months
per year of employment; have more working-age members employed; and have lower levels of child labor (in small families).
Fertility: The program had negative and significant effects on
birth rates; the effect was magnified in households with female
property owners. *Credit supply:* The program resulted in a large
and significant reduction in the rejection rate of loan applications;
the effect is concentrated among households that were asked by

the bank to provide a property title; there was a negative and significant effect on interest rates for loans. *Residential investment:* The program had a large and significant positive effect on housing investment, renovations, housing additions, and out-of-pocket investment.

Evaluators: Erica Field (Harvard University), in collaboration with Maximo Torero (IFPRI [International Food Policy Research Institute]) on the credit supply evaluation

Status: Complete

Sources Field, E. Forthcoming. "Property Rights and Investment in Urban Slums." *Journal of the European Economic Association, Papers and Proceedings.*

————. 2003. "Entitled to Work: Urban Tenure Security and Labor Supply in Peru." Working Paper 220, Princeton University Research Program in Development Studies, Princeton, NJ.

————. 2003. "Fertility Responses to Urban Land Titling Programs: The Roles of Ownership Security and the Distribution of Household Assets." Photocopy. Harvard University, Cambridge, MA.

————. 2003. "Property Rights, Community Public Goods and Household Time Allocation in Urban Squatter Communities." *William and Mary Law Review* 45 (3): 837–87.

Field, E, and M. Torero. 2003. "Do Property Titles Increase Credit Access among the Urban Poor? Evidence from a Nationwide Titling Program." Photocopy. Harvard University, Cambridge, MA.

Country: Brazil

Program: Bolsa Família Program

Program Summary: In 2003 the Social Policy Council of Brazil launched the Bolsa Família Program, seeking to integrate several federal programs, including Bolsa Escola, Bolsa Alimentação, Cartão Alimentação, and Auxílio-Gás. Combining these cash transfer programs and coordinating them with other social programs was expected to eliminate the inefficiencies and administrative duplication resulting from the separate management of the individual programs. The reform created a single, improved conditional cash transfer program intended to immediately reduce poverty through direct monetary transfers to poor families, and to reduce future poverty by providing incentives for investments in human capital. The program has three important focal points: the family unit, decentralization, and a Unified Registry of Social

Programs. A distinguishing feature of the program is institutional coordination—within government, between levels of government, and between government and society.

Evaluation Summary: Rigorous quantitative evaluations for the short term and medium term are in the planning stages. Details of the methodology are not yet available.

Main Findings: Not yet available

Evaluators: Kathy Lindert, Pedro Olinto (World Bank), with local researchers from the Brazilian Ministry of Social Development

Status: Planning stage

Source: E-mail correspondence from evaluators, June 2005.

Country: China

Program: Southwest Poverty Reduction Project

Program Summary: The Southwest Poverty Reduction Project aimed to reduce poverty by augmenting the private and (local) public capital stock of farm households in poor areas. The program comprised a range of income-generating activities, off-farm employment, local social services, and rural infrastructure initiatives.

Evaluation Summary: A baseline survey was followed by annual surveys for four years. A difference-in-difference estimation used nontreated villages within treatment counties as a control group. Initial heterogeneity between the two groups (and its potential to influence the assignment of the treatment) prompted the use of the propensity score matching method (both outer-support matching and caliper-bound matching were used).

Main Findings: The evaluators found a positive and significant effect on income, a positive and significant effect on savings, and a negative effect on poverty (significant when unmatched difference-in-difference and outer-support matching methods were used).

Evaluators: Martin Ravallion and Shaohua Chen (World Bank), in cooperation with the Chinese National Bureau of Statistics on the design and implementation of survey data collection

Status: Complete

Source: Ravallion, M., and S. Chen. Forthcoming. "Hidden Impact? Household Saving in Response to a Poor-Areas Development Project." *Journal of Public Economics.*

Country: Mexico

Program: Oportunidades (formerly PROGRESA)

Program Summary: This program aims to improve the educational, health, and nutritional status of poor families, particularly children and their mothers. The education component consists of educational grants to offset the opportunity costs of schooling, support for school materials, and strengthening of the supply and quality of education services. The health and nutrition component consists of cash grants for food consumption, basic health care services package, nutrition and health education, improved supply of health services, and nutrition supplements. The transfers of cash and health and nutrition provision are conditioned on children's school enrollment with a minimum attendance rate of 85 percent, as well as compliance by all household members with the required number of visits to health centers and mother attendance at health and nutrition lectures.

Evaluation Summary: Eligible poor communities were randomly assigned to either the treatment or the control group, which had statistically indistinguishable characteristics. A baseline survey before the initiation of benefits, and four follow-up surveys at six-month intervals, provided panel data for the two-year experiment. Nearly a dozen impact evaluations have been conducted for this program that assess the effects on education (enrollment, attendance, test scores, age at matriculation, grade repetition, drop-out and re-entry rates), health (clinic visits, provider type used, nutrition, child height, child illness, adolescent and adult health), consumption, intrafamily time allocation, women's status, and intrahousehold relations. Many of these evaluations employ the difference-in-difference methodology, but econometric analysis is used as well to determine cross-sectional differences in indicators for which baseline data are not available. Impact evaluations were complemented by several targeting analyses.

Main Findings: *Consumption:* Consumption of food increased. Diets were more balanced and of better quality. Nonfood spending increased as well, with more spent on clothing and shoes for children. *Health:* Preventive services increased (that is, monitoring of growth/weight/nutritional status, immunization, check-ups, prenatal care). Incidence of disease in children and number of hospital visits declined for young children. Children had higher growth rates, lower morbidity and risk of anemia, and less stunting and malnutrition. Adults reduced the number of activity-inhibited days due to health and increased their ability to walk without getting tired. Prevalence of birth control increased. *Education:* Enrollment increased and the gender gap narrowed in secondary schools. Continuation rates increased and drop-out rates fell in primary schools. Repetition and failure rates decreased, especially

for girls. Total years of schooling increased significantly. *Labor:*
Work incentives among adults were not affected. Child labor decreased.

Evaluators: Michelle Adato, Jere R. Behrman, David Coady, Benjamin Davis, Sudhanshu Handa, Rebecca Lee Harris, John Hoddinott, Mari-Carmen Huerta, Paul Gertler, Susan W. Parker, Raul
Perez, T. Paul Schultz, Emmanuel Skoufias, Beatriz Straffon, Gra-
ciela Teruel, and Ryan Washburn (IFPRI), upon request of the
Government of Mexico, in coordination with Piyali Sengupta and
Petra Todd (University of Pennsylvania)

Status: Complete

Sources Adato, M. 2000. "Final Report: The Impact of PROGRESA
on Community Social Relationships." Report submitted to PRO-
GRESA. IFPRI, Washington, DC.

Behrman, J., and J. Hoddinott. 2000. "An Evaluation of the Impact of PROGRESA on Pre-school Child Height." Report submitted to PROGRESA. IFPRI, Washington, DC.

Behrman, J. P. Sengupta, and P. Todd. 2001. "Progressing through
PROGRESA: An Impact Assessment of a School Subsidy Experiment." Photocopy. University of Pennsylvania (*concerns matriculation, repetition, drop-out, and re-entry*).

———. 2000. "Final Report: The Impact of PROGRESA on
Achievement Test Scores in the First Year." Report submitted to
PROGRESA. IFPRI, Washington, DC.

Coady, D., and R. L. Harris. 2000. "Final Report: A General Equilibrium Analysis of Welfare Impact of PROGRESA." Report
submitted to PROGRESA. IFPRI, Washington, DC.

Gertler, P. 2000. "Final Report: The Impact of PROGRESA on
Health." Photocopy. IFPRI, Washington, DC.

Handa, S., M.-C. Huerta, R. Perez, and B. Straffon. 2000. "Final
Report: Poverty, Inequality, and 'Spill-over' in Mexico's Educa-
tion, Health and Nutrition Program." Report submitted to
PROGRESA. IFPRI, Washington, DC.

Hoddinott, J., E. Skoufias, and R. Washburn. 2000. "The Impact
of PROGRESA on Consumption: A Final Report." Report submitted to PROGRESA. IFPRI, Washington, DC.

Levy, S., and E. Rodriguez. 2004. "Economic Crisis, Political Transition and Poverty Policy Reform: Mexico's PROGRESA–Oportunidades Program." Photocopy. Mexican Institute of Social In-
surance, Mexico City.

Parker, S., and E. Skoufias. 2000. "The Impact of PROGRESA on
Work, Leisure and Time Allocation." Report submitted to PRO-
GRESA. IFPRI, Washington, DC.

Schultz, T. P. 2000. "Final Report: The Impact of PROGRESA on School Enrollments." Report submitted to PROGRESA. IFPRI, Washington, DC.

Teruel, G., and B. Davis. 2000. "Final Report: An Evaluation of the Impact of PROGRESA Cash Payments on Private Inter-household Transfers." Report submitted to PROGRESA. IFPRI, Washington, DC.

Country: India

Program: Online Land Title System in Karnataka: Bhoomi kiosks

Program Summary: The Department of Revenue of the Government of Karnataka has computerized 20 million records of land ownership of 6.7 million farmers in the state. Previously, upon sale or inheritance of a land parcel, requests to alter land records or secure a copy of the Record of Rights, Tenancy and Cultivation (RTC)—a document needed for obtaining bank loans, giving proof of ownership, and so forth—had to be filed with the village accountant. Providing RTCs used to take 3 to 30 days and updating records took one to two years. The Department of Revenue has set up computerized land record kiosks (Bhoomi centers) in taluk (subdistrict) offices to provide farmers with RTCs. The Bhoomi project was expected to speed up delivery of RTCs without delays, harassment, or bribery.

Evaluation Summary: A report-card system was used, based on the users' assessments of whether the computerized system met their needs, and whether it was responsive, reliable, or corrupt. A survey was carried out with a random, stratified sample of citizens who have used Bhoomi kiosks as well as a control sample of those who have used noncomputerized land records providers. The treatment and control respondents were compared based on educational background, awareness about Bhoomi kiosks, and purpose for seeking an RTC. Benefits assessed included ease of use, assistance required, time required, number of officials met, errors in documents, response to complaints, cost of service, return visits required, bribes required, and staff behavior rating. A single difference comparison was performed, using the noncomputerized group as a proxy counterfactual.

Main Findings: The results show that use of the Bhoomi kiosks reduced the number of visits, the amount of bribe, the number of officials met, and the length of time spent in queues necessary to receive land documents. Bhoomi kiosk users also reported more timely response to complaints and better staff behavior.

Evaluators: Albert Lobo and Suresh Balakrishnan (Public Affairs Centre, Bangalore), in cooperation with ACNielsen ORG-MARG, with funding by the Governance Knowledge Sharing Program of the World Bank

Status: Complete

Source: Lobo, A., and S. Balakrishnan. 2002. "Report Card on Service of Bhoomi Kiosks: An Assessment of Benefits by Users of the Computerized Land Records System in Karnataka." Public Affairs Centre, Bangalore, India.

Country: Philippines

Program: Agrarian Reform Infrastructure Support Project (ARISP)

Program Summary: ARISP was an integrated package of support services designed to provide basic infrastructure, institutional development, and agricultural support nationwide. Started in June 1996 and implemented for a period of six years, the concept of the project was to address the need for basic infrastructure facilities that are essential in increasing productivity and income. Hence, the core component was irrigation, complemented by warehouses and solar driers for post-harvest activities, farm-to-market roads for mobility, and institutional development for sustainability of operations. The project covered 76 Agrarian Reform Communities (ARCs) in 33 provinces nationwide.

Evaluation Summary: The study aimed to assess the effects of ARISP on the agricultural productivity, farm income, and socioeconomic status of the beneficiaries by comparing the ARISP ARCs with non-ARISP communities. An ex post survey conducted in 2001 included three ARISP ARCs selected to represent diversity in regional characteristics, agrarian diversification, and level of project success (as measured by the Department of Agrarian Reform's ALDA, or Level of Development in ARC). For each selected ARISP ARC, a non-ARISP community was selected from the same province as a control. Fifty individuals were sampled from each of the six communities. The survey included information on productivity and net on-farm incomes, as well as qualitative perceptions of change since 1996 (based on recall). A single difference, ex post comparison between the treatment and control communities was conducted to assess impact on productivity and farm income.

Main Findings: The yield effect, measured as the difference between treatment and control communities, was relatively weak, but consistently positive. Marketable surpluses in ARISP ARCs exceeded those in control communities. Cultivation effects could not be compared because differences in cropping ratios between treatment and control communities predated the ARISP program. Average net on-farm income was greater in ARISP communities, compared with controls.

Evaluator: Katsumi Nozawa (Asia University), commissioned by the Government of the Philippines

Status: Complete

Source: Japan Bank for International Cooperation. 2002. "Ex-post Evaluation Report: Philippines Agrarian Reform Infrastructure Support Project." Available at http://www.jbic.go.jp/english/oec/post/2002/pdf/Part2_1-1.pdf.

Notes

1. Interested readers may find a more extensive discussion of these methods in Ravallion (forthcoming).

2. A database of the impact evaluations of projects financed by the World Bank is available on the Internet (http://worldbank.org/impactevaluation).

3. For some views on meta-analysis, see Glass (2000).

4. This may be a controversial point because of the lack of transparency and openness in the handling of information by many government agencies in developing countries. Although recognizing this point, it is also the case that the type of evaluation being discussed here typically involves a large enough group of people—and often researchers outside of government—to make it more difficult for the studies to remain as a pure private good.

5. Several countries in Latin America (for example, Chile, Colombia, and Mexico) have, over the recent past, adopted a more organized approach to evaluating the impact of their development programs: They experiment, assess, and adapt programs before rolling them out at national scale or before renewing the budget allocation. The experience of those countries suggests that evaluations may help build support for a program and reinforce incentives for proper implementation of programs by enhancing accountability. Recognition of these factors can increase the perceived benefits of evaluation.

6. For example, Michael Kremer (2003) reported on the relative cost effectiveness of different instruments in delivering one extra year of schooling in Sub-Saharan Africa: The provision of school uniforms costs $99, whereas a school feeding program costs $36, and a deworming program cost a mere $3.50 for each additional student year of school participation.

7. The six social funds are in Armenia, Bolivia, Honduras, Nicaragua, Peru, and Zambia.

8. Experience suggests that the transaction costs of large-scale coordination can be very high. In that sense, opportunistic bilateral or multilateral alliances (for example, around specific development challenges such as HIV prevention or provision of potable water in slums) may be the best option.

9. The stocktaking exercises also show significant differences in the number of impact evaluations across regions and sectors. For example, a database of impact evaluations of World Bank–supported programs shows 2.5 times more evaluations in the human development sectors than for infrastructure programs. Similarly, there are sharp differences between regions: Two thirds of the identified evaluations came from the Latin American region and close to 20 percent came from Africa.

Bibliography

Baker, J. 2000. *Evaluating the Impact of Development Projects on Poverty: A Handbook for Practitioners.* Series on Directions in Development. Washington, DC: World Bank.

Deaton, A. 2005. "Some Remarks on Randomization, Econometrics and Data." In *Evaluating Development Effectiveness,* ed. G. K. Pitman, O. Feinstein, and G. K. Ingram, vol. 7. Series on Evaluation and Development, World Bank. New Brunswick, NJ: Transaction Publishers.

Duflo, E., and M. Kremer. 2005. "Use of Randomization in the Evaluation of Development Effectiveness." In *Evaluating Development Effectiveness,* ed. G. K. Pitman, O. Feinstein, and G. K. Ingram, vol. 7. Series on Evaluation and Development, World Bank. New Brunswick, NJ: Transaction Publishers.

Glass, Gene V. 2000. "Meta-Analysis at 25." Photocopy. College of Education, Arizona State University, Tempe.

Kremer, Michael. 2003. "Randomized Evaluations of Educational Programs in Developing Countries: Some Lessons." *American Economic Review* 93 (2): 102–06.

Levi, Primo. 1998. "Le Opere," as quoted and translated by Diego Gambetta in "Claro! An Essay on Discursive Machismo." In *Deliberative Democracy,* ed. Jon Elster. Cambridge: Cambridge University Press.

Ravallion, M. Forthcoming. "Evaluating Anti-poverty Programs." In *Handbook of Agricultural Economics,* vol. 4, ed. R. E. Evenson and T. P. Schultz. New York: North-Holland.

Rawlings, L. 2005. "Operational Reflections on Evaluating Development Programs." In *Evaluating Development Effectiveness,* ed. G. K. Pitman, O. Feinstein, and G. K. Ingram, vol. 7. Series on Evaluation and Development, World Bank. New Brunswick, NJ: Transaction Publishers.

Rawlings, L., L. Sherburne-Benz, and J. Van Domelen. 2004. "Evaluating Social Funds: A Cross-Country Analysis of Community Investments." Regional and Sectoral Studies, World Bank, Washington, DC.

Rossi, P. , H. Freeman, and M. Lipsey. 2003. *Evaluation: A Systematic Approach*. 7th ed. Thousand Oaks, CA: Sage Publications.

7

Operational Implications

Ronald Kim and M. Ziad Alahdad

The case studies prepared for the Shanghai Conference are impressive in their scope and variety, and rich in experiential knowledge. Their true value, however, is not contained in any magic recipe for reducing poverty. Instead, they offer some new perspectives, clarifications, affirmation, emphasis, and most importantly, country specificity to our understanding of development effectiveness that has emerged over many decades of effort. These are lessons that developing countries, as well as the World Bank and other donors, have already begun putting into practice and are attempting to mainstream fully into their work.

A review of these cases shows that no single factor can be considered the primary determinant of the achievements of any initiative. Indeed, many of the stories illustrate applications of some of the elements that are now foremost in development thinking, such as country ownership and capacity development. The cases also highlight the single biggest challenge faced by countries and donors alike in their development work: the complexity involved in achieving and sustaining poverty reduction. What can the World Bank and other donor agencies learn from these stories as they attempt to promote greater development effectiveness? How can these experiences be useful in improving the way we operate?

In seeking answers to those questions, this chapter has several objectives: to highlight some of the operational implications from previous chapters, using specific cases[1]; to identify ways in which the development community can incorporate these lessons into its efforts to reduce poverty on a global scale; and to elaborate on how the World Bank is changing its approach from an operational perspective and to examine how well the institution is positioned to accommodate, support, and promote programs, projects, and practices that offer such learning potential. This chapter identifies and examines six overarching dimensions that offer insights into the questions posed above: country ownership; capacity development; knowledge, learning, and innovation; sequencing and timing; managing for results; and alignment and harmonization. These dimensions often overlap, which is not surprising given the overall interwoven nature of so many aspects of development, in general, and within the Shanghai cases more specifically.

Country Ownership

Country ownership is the extent to which poverty reduction and sustainable development build on the needs and priorities of an individual country rather than on those of its external partners. This involves broad support within the country's executive office on priorities and broad support among the country's national institutions (parliament and local governments) and internal partners (civil society and the private sector) (Entwistle and Cavassini 2005). Along similar lines, the International Monetary Fund has defined ownership as "a willing assumption of responsibility to formulate and carry out those policies, based on the understanding that the program is achievable and is in the country's own interest" (Drazen and Isard 2004, pp. 5–6). In other words, donors cannot develop a country; a country must develop itself by envisioning the results it wants to achieve, choosing the path it will follow to achieve them, and coordinating donors' efforts and resources to attain its goals (OECD/DAC 2005). The end outcome is the synergy of a country's wealth of specific knowledge and donors' international best practices and techniques.

Initiatives are clearly more effective when they are consistent with the priorities that the government and its people have already established. In such cases, the government is most ready to be involved in the effort and to provide broad-based support for its implementation. This means that all stakeholders are committed to the initiative's goals and willing to work toward them. Not surprisingly, any systematic effort to address a development challenge must be based squarely on the government's sustained commitment to national programs, and the leadership's efforts to create the supportive structural conditions for program effectiveness.

At the country level, as mentioned in chapter 2 of this book, the case of Tanzania (case 1) since the mid-1990s illustrates this point. Following the economic problems that began in the late 1970s, Tanzania adopted an economic recovery program, under which macroeconomic stability was achieved, a wide range of structural reforms were implemented, and a better investment climate was established. A strong sense of ownership of economic reforms early on was driven by public support for and understanding of the issues. The underlying factors of this support included a consultative and participatory approach, the implementation of homegrown programs designed within the country, sustained commitment from political leaders, and ongoing support from development partners. The overall improvement in economic performance resulted in gradual poverty reduction and better public service delivery. In short, broad ownership for reform made possible positive developmental changes in the country and, equally important, made them effective and sustainable.

As detailed in the health section of chapter 4, Thailand's response (case 2) to a growing HIV/AIDS problem in the early 1990s offers additional insights. When it became clear that the problem was more severe than previously thought, and with a potential crisis looming, the government's response was fast and comprehensive, with strong backing from the prime minister and the king. AIDS policy was coordinated from the prime minister's office and there was abundant high-level support for HIV prevention programs aimed at commercial sex workers and their clients. Public spending on HIV/AIDS prevention and control increased dramatically, which helped support a major public information program emphasizing prevention, behavior change, and condom use.

Country ownership, however, is not limited to the government and, as many of the case studies show, there is an overriding need to include the commitments of a wide range of other stakeholders. This involves deliberate efforts to ensure the inclusive participation of all people—individuals and groups, community residents, local civil servants, and others—who would be affected positively or negatively by an initiative, and to keep them informed and involved as the initiative is designed and implemented. At the Shanghai Conference, Benjamin Mkapa, president of Tanzania, underscored the importance of local ownership to the development agenda by stating, "Ownership must be devolved from developed country and multilateral partners to national governments, and must also be entrusted to the level of communities" (Mkapa 2004, p. 3).

It is not surprising, therefore, that a frequent design feature highlighted in many of the stories was a deliberate effort to ensure the inclusive participation and buy-in of a wide group of people. That feature was often directly linked to a program's credibility and legitimacy as a mechanism for promoting poverty reduction. During its crisis in the late 1990s, Indonesia (case 3) demonstrated that, without popular participation in political decision making, the increasingly difficult choices a government must make may lack the legitimacy needed to ensure their effectiveness.

For donor institutions, the operational implications are wide-ranging. First, accepting that the country is in the driver's seat in a poverty reduction initiative cannot be a merely symbolic or good-will gesture. Reducing poverty on a global scale demands that countries set forth their goals and that all donor efforts be designed in a supporting role. Otherwise, as academic research on aid effectiveness indicates, results will not be sustained.[2] The messages from the donor conferences and forums that took place in Monterrey, Rome, demonstrate, and Paris strongly reiterate that countries must own the goals and objectives of any development process or program (OECD/DAC 2005). When a country has set its priorities in a poverty reduction strategy, development programs should be designed to support those aims. It is good news that over the last decade there has been a gradual but fundamental shift in the donor assistance paradigm: recognition and mainstreaming of country leadership and ownership of the development process. Most donor institutions have been changing their practices in this way. Second, in a supporting role, albeit often critical, donors need to understand their clients better and be more responsive to their needs. This could imply such a simple but far-reaching change as donors having a closer geographic proximity to their clients. Accordingly, decentralization has become a major issue for donor organizations. Third, in countries where ownership is weak, donors have an important role. It is not enough to assess and evaluate the degree of ownership; donors must try to build and strengthen it.

At the time of writing, 43 countries with which the World Bank is involved are implementing their own poverty reduction strategies, and 23 of them have been doing so for more than one year. There is some evidence that the country-led model is working. In 2005 the World Bank's Operations Policy and Country Services Vice Presidency, in an assessment of country ownership of poverty reduction strategies, concluded that "integrating PRS [poverty reduction strategy] decision-making processes into a country's broader decision-making processes and systems is key to developing country ownership of PRSs," and noted the value of participation in policy making and implementation through permanent mechanisms and institutions for continuous consultation with stakeholders (Entwistle and Cavassini 2005, p. 28).

To better understand and serve its clients, the World Bank has also significantly decentralized its staff during the past decade, in recognition of how important it is that staff serving a country actually live in that country. In 1996 only 17 percent of its staff was posted outside Washington, DC. By 2005 that figure had grown to 35 percent, including 73 percent of its country directors and 40–60 percent of professional technical staff (level GE+), depending on the region (World Bank 2005b, pp. 124–25). As a current country director commented recently, "Decentralization has enabled us to build much closer working relationships not only with government counterparts but also with donors, the private sector, and broader civil society" (World Bank 2005b, p. 122). Other ways in which the World Bank's overall approach to development is now more focused on the client can be seen in its use of consultation when developing policies and its work to broaden its disclosure policy.

The benefits of real partnership between countries and donors have been underscored by Trensio Chisale, director of distribution and customer service at Malawi's Electricity Supply Corporation. At the April 2005 Malawi Country Program Review meeting, Chisale summed up the value of the program review in this way: "Last week I would have said the World Bank should continue as it has been. But after this workshop, I see that we can ask questions and argue more with the World Bank, and together we can get a clearer idea of what we want to do" (World Bank internal news, April 20, 2005). Although these words describe how the World Bank and other donors are changing, formidable challenges exist. Will changes that in theory promote country ownership, particularly decentralization, guarantee in practice that the World Bank and other donor staff will listen to country perspectives? To what extent are the World Bank and other donors succeeding in strengthening ownership in countries where it is weak? How does this focus on ownership affect the often catalytic role of donors?

Capacity Development

Intimately linked to ownership is the concept of capacity development, which describes the initiative taken by a country to invest in and build on human capital, and to modify and strengthen institutional practices. Although different development organizations may use slightly different definitions, several forms of *capacity* are broadly recognized, including *individual* capacity (the ability of individuals to gain knowledge and skills that can be expanded when new opportunities arise), *organizational* capacity (people working together in a common cause, which includes building institutional capacity and reforms that are owned and driven by countries themselves), and *societal* capacity (the overall incentive environment as well as the rules and norms and the wider political and cultural environment in which people and organizations operate).[3] Capacity development is therefore the process whereby people, organizations, and society as a whole unleash, strengthen, create, adapt, and maintain capacity—their ability to manage their affairs—over time. It is also as much about skills and systems as it is about incentives and behavior; much more than a technical exercise, capacity development is rooted in the political economy of a country (World Bank 2005c).

The role of capacity development cannot be overstated and the cases indicate that it is a stronger factor in scaling up than is financing. The World Bank's *Global Monitoring Report 2005* called capacity development "the quintessential challenge of development assistance" (World Bank 2005d, p. 203). The overarching importance of capacity is now highlighted by nearly every donor, and there has been a newfound recognition that an effective poverty reduction strategy process and a productive partnership can be built only on a platform of strong public capacity: capacity to formulate policies; capacity to build consensus; capacity to implement reform; and capacity to monitor results, learn lessons, and adapt accordingly. In fact, the World Bank's Africa Capacity Development Operational Task Force stated unequivocally in its most recent progress report, "Capacity development should be a core objective rather than a collateral objective in the fight against poverty, whereas the latter is currently generally the case" (World Bank 2005c, p. 2). These words were echoed by Francis Fukuyama, professor of international political economy at Johns Hopkins University, who noted, "The problem of capacity destruction cannot be fixed unless donors make a clear choice that capacity building is their primary objective, rather than the services that the capacity is meant to provide" (Fukuyama 2004, p. 41).

The cases developed during the Shanghai global learning process strongly confirm that for development initiatives to lead to results, the responsible institutions and levels of government need to have the capacity to support the initiatives effectively and, therefore, to establish an environment for capacity development. The Poland country case (case 4) during the 1990s offers an example of capacity development at many levels. Spurred by the desire to join the European Union (see also chapter 2), Poland implemented macroeconomic reforms that led to its rapid socioeconomic transformation, and focused much attention on strengthening a wide array of economic and political institutions. In fact, much of its growth, engendered by favorable business and investment climates, depended largely on the quality, credibility, and sustainability of its institutions and policies. In turn, the factors that determined growth—eliminating regulatory distortions and sources of rent extraction and corruption, creating free and equal access to business activity, and increasing the efficiency of basic public goods—contributed to improved quality of life, lessened inequity, and mitigated the feeling of alienation among a large segment of society.

The story of Indonesia (case 3) in the late 1990s reveals the opposite scenario, where weak institutions can adversely affect a country's development in general, and during a crisis in particular. The precarious position of Indonesia's financial, legal, and political institutions exacerbated the crisis and undermined its ability to manage growing problems. Temporary institutions set up to deal with the crisis had to operate in a weak institutional environment, so they proved to be only partially effective. One cabinet minister said, emphatically, "If there is one final lesson that the Indonesian experience offers, it is that a country cannot start early enough with the building and nurturing of strong institutions . . . there is no such thing as development first, institutions later; development is the development of institutions."

Many of the examples examined during the global learning process demonstrated that providing support for capacity development through investments in human and institutional capacity—in the form of training loan officers, community health workers, teachers, and so forth—was instrumental in scaling up efforts. The Madrassah Early Childhood Program in Kenya, Tanzania, and Uganda (case 5) exemplifies this approach. Started as a small pilot program in the mid-1980s, the program reflects a dynamic and deliberate effort to build on local institutions; the objective is to combine each community's preferences, best practices, and local values and customs that will have an important effect on a child's performance later in life. It puts parents and community leaders in charge and provides them with knowledge, management skills, and mechanisms for long-term financing. There is a special emphasis on selecting and training local women to serve as teachers, heads of schools, and managers, as well as a continuing willingness to invest in staff development.

A number of key operational implications emerge from the cases considered in this book. Although the role of capacity development is now being reflected in nearly every strategic document prepared by donor institutions and can be seen prominently in the statements from the conferences and forums in Monterrey, Rome, Marrakech, and Paris, donors need to go beyond words. Capacity development must be an important part of any poverty reduction strategy and should be addressed at the individual, organizational, and societal levels if improvements are to be sustainable. Efforts to develop capacity need to reflect an understanding of the constraints in each country, and need to target the most germane levels of government and society, using the most appropriate instruments. Therefore, preparing any initiative must involve a solid assessment of the available capacity and, if needed, activities to enhance or renew the capacity of key leaders and organizations. Such activities must be designed to achieve two critical goals: upgrading the knowledge and skills of the development actors involved, and ensuring that these actors' knowledge and skills are effectively applied in carrying out the development agenda.

Donors must harmonize their support with that of other partners to minimize the pressure placed on limited state capacity. They also must avoid "capacity destruction," that is, undermining country capacity through some of their traditional instruments, such as technical assistance and project implementation units.

Most important, donors also must view capacity development as a long-term process and a major goal of their effort, meaning that they often need to be patient and not pursue shortcuts. Nancy Birdsall, founding president of the Center for Global Development, wrote in a recent paper on donor failings, "If institution building in weak states is at the heart of development, then development assistance has to support the creation and strengthening of institutions—a long-term project that requires patience, along with a willingness to accept risk and the stomach for lack of observable short-run progress" (Birdsall 2004, p. 11). In fact, putting capacity development at the forefront of poverty reduction changes fundamentally how donors operate because "asking what it takes for an aid agency to be better at 'capacity-building' is tantamount to asking what it takes to be a better aid agency, period" (Schacter 2000, p. 2).

The World Bank devotes a significant percentage of its lending and nonlending services to capacity development activities. Between 1995 and 2004, it provided nearly $9 billion in lending and

---

Box 7.1 Building Capacity through the Use of Country Systems

The World Bank is learning from experience and independent evaluation that requiring countries to establish special systems to manage World Bank–financed projects and respond to World Bank requirements does little to build the country's own capacity and can even undermine it. Genuine longer-term development impact requires that the World Bank and other donors work more directly with the institutions and systems that countries already have in place and support efforts to strengthen them. In recent years, the World Bank has begun using country systems in specific fiduciary areas, such as financial management (for example, accounting, financial reporting, auditing) and national competitive bidding in countries where such systems are found to be equivalent to its own. Several pilot programs have been launched, including projects in Mexico and Poland.

$900 million in grants and administrative budgets to support capacity development in Africa alone (World Bank 2005c). At a strategic level, a country's capacity development goals are featured prominently, embedded in the Poverty Reduction Strategy Papers or other development strategy, and highlighted in the Country Assistance Strategy (CAS).

At a more general level, the World Bank is engaged in many activities focused on developing capacity. These activities include strengthening the public sector governance agenda and supporting public administration at all levels; bolstering participatory processes; piloting a program that involves using a country's own systems and institutions (see box 7.1); adopting a partnership approach to economic and sector work; making resources available through the Institutional Development Fund, which earmarks funding specifically for institution building; developing specific global programs on governance, knowledge for development, and trade to build capacity in such broad global areas; and creating tools that measure capacity, such as the Country Policy and Institutional Assessment and various governance indicators. These activities, although modest, are certainly steps in the right direction.

Clearly, however, there is a lot more work that needs to be done in this area by the World Bank and the entire development community. Understanding better how institutions develop in a bottom-up fashion, striking a balance between long-term economic planning and actual implementation of projects and programs—these are just two of the issues requiring further investigation.

Knowledge, Learning, and Innovation

A key message from many of the Shanghai cases is that the process of achieving results is usually not linear—that it invariably involves continuous change and adaptation. The linear qualities of an investment project cycle, with its sequential steps of project identification, preparation, appraisal, implementation, and evaluation, were not well suited to the subtleties and complexities inherent in many of the Shanghai examples, where scaling up entailed an iterative process of learning from mistakes, responding to new challenges and needs, and making changes along the way. Even today, these initiatives can be considered works in progress.

For example, as highlighted in chapters 2 and 3, China's poverty reduction efforts (case 6) have involved a process of constant learning and experimentation, which has been institutionalized throughout the administrative system. Its Leading Group for Poverty Reduction under the State Council conducts its own analysis, collects feedback from central and local government agencies involved in poverty reduction programs, draws lessons, and has the authority to influence nationwide policies and specific programs. In other words, it oversees all poverty reduction programs. As an explicit mechanism for sharing and disseminating knowledge, agencies and top-level officials involved in poverty reduction organize regular events to learn lessons from ongoing activities, benefit from outside expertise, discuss issues of policy implementation, and explore the policy implications of lessons learned. In addition, training programs and field visits are organized regularly for local officials to facilitate policy adjustments. This continuous learning process has been instrumental in altering China's approach to poverty reduction by introducing greater participation by the poor, decentralizing the management of programs and projects to local governments and even villages, and modifying the mode of delivery and management of credit funds.

In a similar way, the Pakistan Rural Support Programs (case 7) took more than 10 years of patient effort at the community level in just one province to generate the degree of financial resources, human capacity, and overall results needed to create a convincing basis for scaling up—the initial pilot was given enough time to develop at the point where examples could be drawn. A key lesson, which was incorporated into programs across the country, was that scaling up through replication, rather than expansion, provides advantages in terms of local ownership and support as well as adaptation to new needs and opportunities.

The Shanghai cases are also rich in examples of how countries have learned from each other in their "efforts" to scale up poverty reduction. With its focus on cash transfers to poor families, Mexico's Oportunidades Program (case 8) proved to be an inspirational model for the Bolsa Família program in Brazil (case 9), which in turn has been borrowed and adapted by Central American countries. Similarly, Vietnam's agricultural reforms (case 10) have their origins in earlier efforts in China. One of the most extensively emulated initiatives is Indonesia's Kecamatan Development Project (KDP) (case 11), itself the culmination of more than 10 years of poverty reduction programs characterized by local-level planning and direct community transfers. KDP's core design is being replicated in East Timor's Community Empowerment Project, Afghanistan's National Solidarity Program, and the Philippines' Kalahi-CIDSS Program. These are all good examples of South-South knowledge and learning exchanges.

Developing countries look to donors for the wide knowledge, expertise, and credibility they can offer in addition to their financial resources. For example, in Brazil's Rural Poverty Reduction Program (case 12), the World Bank served as "neutral broker" in a controversial sector, building on its long-standing relationships at both the federal and state levels, offering global knowledge of other ongoing community-driven development efforts, and providing support for pilot-testing. The World Bank also had the capacity to monitor and evaluate program performance, and to ensure that the lessons of new experiences were captured and applied to the program as it expanded.

It is not surprising that donor procedures can hinder or even obstruct adaptation and learning. If donors require a detailed program plan in advance, that tends to lock the implementer into a particular blueprint and to squelch learning and flexibility. For donors this implies the need to do business in more flexible and nuanced ways, and to adopt a new mindset that understands that initiatives can be extremely unpredictable, supports good processes and learning, and even develops a tolerance for and a willingness to accept failures along the way. Adopting this new mindset is critical for intensifying efforts to alleviate poverty, but it is difficult because it runs counter to much of the development literature, which has largely ignored the underlying processes and systems for institutions to innovate, fail along the way, learn from failure, make adjustments, and expand. Staff should be willing to engage in risk-taking behavior and to make adjustments over time to meet the changing needs of their clients, and organizations that will support them. There is already some evidence of this type of support. Some donors, including the World Bank, have been developing more flexible frameworks that make project restructuring easier, and are applying program-based approaches meant to provide flexibility within government sectoral programs, accompanied by a reassessment of results at different phases of implementation.

Another operational implication for the donor community is of equal importance—donors need to invest in developing knowledge and learning activities and tools for clients, with a special focus on fostering the South-South learning that may have significant long-term payoffs. As countries try to emulate positive approaches to new places, or sustain them over time, they must be able to learn from past experience—from mistakes as well as good decisions—and to adapt an approach that worked in one area to new circumstances. Positive and negative experiences that could benefit many countries and communities, however, are not widely shared. The Shanghai global learning process was one step in addressing this gap, but much more needs to be done. Here again, donors must be willing to change their mindset and invest in activities and tools that may not produce the short-term results they desire.

The number of knowledge-sharing venues and tools for various client and stakeholder groups is growing, as are staff in donor institutions prepared to communicate the lessons gained from diverse experiences. This type of South-South learning between clients is extremely powerful and can offer enormous benefits for clients and donors alike. During the last decade, the World Bank has established a number of global knowledge initiatives (for example, the Global Development Learning Network, the Development Gateway, the Global Development Network, and the Development Marketplace) that enable development practitioners worldwide to share their experiences. Learning activities organized by the World Bank and other donors now are more likely to emphasize the insights clients have to offer each other rather than the traditional approach of top-down, North-South training. Study tours have been especially powerful activities in which practitioners from one country study firsthand how their counterparts in a different country have designed a specific initiative. The World Bank also has promoted many "communities of practice," which provide a venue for sustained learning among targeted groups of practitioners, including municipal staff, parliamentarians, poverty analysis researchers, and water and sanitation specialists. In all of these activities, the World Bank is increasingly demonstrating that, although its global experience is useful to clients, its ability to facilitate learning among its clients may be even more valued by them.

Whereas there has been progress in this area, the World Bank and other donors should not be overly sanguine. They must continue their efforts to facilitate the sharing of experiences across countries and regions. In particular, their operational staff must see themselves also as knowledge brokers, view knowledge sharing as a core part of their work, and strengthen the ability of their clients to acquire and use knowledge—a change that remains incomplete (World Bank 2003).

Sequencing and Timing

The case studies as a whole do not offer a magic solution for how programs should be sequenced or when they should begin and end. The basic economic policy ingredients are consistent across many of the case studies, but the amounts, sequencing, and timing were derived at the local level. Because it is crucial to maintain political support and generate some early benefits from reform, the sequencing and details of reform are country specific. Uganda (case 13) followed an early win with phased and sequenced reforms that mirrored citizen priorities. It first addressed security and border issues, then introduced a more difficult agenda of economic reforms for sustained growth, and finally embarked on ambitious poverty reduction programs.

A number of cases demonstrated the effectiveness of first putting formal institutional processes in place to enable the subsequent implementation of specific activities. The Philippines Early Childhood Development Program (case 14) is a good example. The government institutionalized the program in 2002 when it legislated the Early Child Care and Development Act, establishing the overarching governance structures and actual delivery systems for improving services to young children. The legislation also created the Council for the Welfare of Children as the highest-level government policy-making body concerned with children's issues, and gave it the mandate to formulate and evaluate policy and coordinate the implementation and enforcement of all laws and programs for children. After these actions, pilot efforts began in earnest.

They were aimed at investing in local services for young children, their parents, and such local service providers as child care and education programs, health centers, parent education initiatives, and the like.

When it comes to timing, the findings of some of the case studies suggest a paradox: As mentioned in chapter 2, a crisis is not necessarily bad news. In the aftermath of social, political, or financial crises, governments and people are often open to doing things in a different way. Adversity thus becomes a window of opportunity for reform. This was the situation in Indonesia in the late 1990s (case 3) when external shocks, particularly in commodity prices, stimulated a strengthening of the policy regime. As a result of the second oil bust in the early 1980s, the government devalued the rupiah twice and introduced macroeconomic reforms to diversify exports and strengthen productivity growth. In other words, bad economic times provided Indonesia with the opportunity and push it needed to reform its economy and put good policies in place. Many of the cases demonstrate that donors, too, must be prepared to respond to windows of opportunity that emerge at some point in every country. Such opportunities include both positive events, such as comfortable periods of growth, and negative developments, such as internal or external financial crises.

Another timing and sequencing implication is that staff may need to develop a sort of sixth sense about when it is appropriate to push, and when it is better to proceed at a slower pace that may ultimately be more productive. It is often the case that scaling up an initiative demands the creation of a certain momentum, and this process cannot be rushed. In the example of riverblindness in West Africa (case 15), the sheer long-term nature of the illness has helped establish a sustained commitment on the part of many donors. Having a good sense of timing is not enough, however. Staff also need the organizational flexibility that enables them to take advantage of opportunities.

Managing for Results

At its most fundamental level, the results agenda is about helping countries, as well as donor agency staff, ask themselves, "Are we being effective?" and "How do we know?" Information about results is crucial to both learning and accountability (World Bank 2005b). As discussed in chapter 6, impact evaluation can be a powerful learning tool to improve decision making and guide country-led development efforts toward clearly defined goals. An important finding from the examples examined in chapter 6 was the value of using the results of rigorous evaluation to improve and fine-tune programs and projects during their implementation, as well as to enlighten practitioners worldwide.

At an operational level, a number of the Shanghai cases indicate that monitoring and evaluation, as an integral part of managing for results, can be instrumental in furthering experimentation, learning, innovation, and thus the process of intensifying efforts to reduce poverty. Donors must also focus their attention on building sustainable capacities by providing partner countries with assistance to manage their own results. In concrete terms, this means that partner countries should assess their own gaps and needs in such areas as needs analysis, policy formulation, results-based strategic planning, management information systems, and results-based monitoring and evaluation. Donor agencies must invest directly in building partner countries' public sector capacity to ensure that public sector agencies or departments are able to manage effectively for results.[4]

Donors must keep in mind that achieving "results on the ground" does not simply entail collecting data, tracking deliveries, and monitoring project outcomes. These activities are indispensable but the real focus should be on the lives of poor people: "We need to remember to focus on outcomes that improve individual lives—the results are not in the statistics but in human beings," former World Bank president James Wolfensohn emphasized on many occasions.[5]

Particularly since the Monterrey Conference in 2002, the effort to better manage results—to use information to improve decision making and steer country-led development processes toward clearly defined goals—has emerged at the forefront of the global development community's agenda. It is, however, a broad agenda that needs to be tackled systematically to be effective. A number of ideas are being tested, including an examination of specific types of outputs, with the goal of generating measurable results from project designs that then can be more easily linked to desired development outcomes.

The World Bank's work in managing for results has evolved significantly during the past decade, from an initial strategic vision to specific actions in the areas of partnerships, global consensus, quality assessments, and both lending and nonlending instruments. Although much still needs to be accomplished, especially in the area of providing the impetus and means for monitoring and evaluation to its partner countries, since 2003 the World Bank has moved forward with an implementation action plan focused in two key areas:

1. It is strengthening national institutional capacity to manage for results by providing support to strategic planning for poverty reduction strategies, public sector management, statistical capacity, and monitoring and evaluation. Further efforts have led to the 2004 creation of the Statistical Capacity Building Program, which is aimed at improving countries' capacity to monitor their core development outcomes through a strategic statistical plan that provides timely and reliable data.
2. Since January 2005, the World Bank has been pilot-testing results-based CASs that are explicit about country-level outcomes that the World Bank's products and services will influence, and that contain a results-oriented monitoring and evaluation system.

Alignment and Harmonization

The alignment and harmonization agenda, as established at the Rome and Marrakech meetings and most recently at the Paris forum, is fundamentally tied to country ownership. The idea is that donors would *align* their development assistance with the priorities and results-oriented strategies set out by the partner country. Rather than relying on systems imposed by donors, development assistance should progressively depend on partner countries' own systems in delivering assistance, providing capacity development support to improve these systems, and ensuring harmonization in the meantime as country systems are strengthened. In this area, donors should also implement good practice principles in delivering assistance—streamline and harmonize their policies, procedures, and practices; intensify delegated cooperation; increase the flexibility of country-based staff to manage country programs and projects more effectively; and develop incentives within their organizations to foster recognition by management and staff of the benefits of harmonization (OECD/DAC 2005).

In any sector, building on existing country delivery systems, institutions, and programs can be an important factor in effective implementation. Alignment by using existing delivery systems, rather than, for example, creating parallel project implementation units, strengthens country capacity and furthers country ownership. Where institutions are already in place and operating, and where their staffs are already accustomed to working with local people, projects that incorporate them can be up and running sooner and without the expense of creating a new institution. For example, two of the initiatives studied for Shanghai built on existing education programs: In Turkey, various pilot programs and experiments that were taking place when the Basic Education Program (case 16) was launched promoted a rapid widening of the student base enrolled in the new program; and in Bangladesh (case 17), the government works closely with a plurality of providers—communities, nongovernmental organizations, charities, and private actors—to achieve a universal and uniform primary education system. That approach appears to have been critical in expanding enrollment and reaching out especially to poor children and girls.

Other cases demonstrate how effective donor harmonization facilitates the process of reducing poverty on a global scale. In Uganda (case 13), donors partnering with civil society and the private sector coalesced around the government's framework and vision for growth and poverty reduction, and thereby became effective and unified actors in support of reforms. On a more modest scale, the Caribbean Regional Technical Assistance Centre (CARTAC) (case 18) serves as a mechanism to facilitate a greater degree of donor-recipient coordination around economic reform issues. CARTAC operates as a project of the United Nations Development Programme; the International Monetary Fund is the executing agency; and the center is financed from bilateral and multilateral donors and by annual contributions from participating countries.

Donor institutions must offer their resources in a very collaborative way, following the leadership of the client government. If they impose difficult external requirements, they may hinder the implementation of the projects they finance; and if the donors and the government do not work together, their contribution to a country's development will be diminished. Donors need to streamline their own requirements as much as possible and especially avoid requiring countries to set up special systems to serve the projects. By relying on a country's own institutions and procedures, donors avoid the transaction costs of setting up separate systems and they increase the chances of sustainability. Using a country's systems provides a natural focal point for donor efforts to harmonize their processes.

Some case studies showed how donor systems and requirements can undermine the achievement of project objectives. In China's Southwest Poverty Reduction Project (case 19), World Bank procurement and disbursement procedures were seen as a hindrance to smooth implementation. The use of public bidding with multiple project sites, different construction times, and seasonal differences led to both project delays and increased cost; disbursement against completed works created problems for poor areas with critical finance shortages; and the long procedures for project amendments made it difficult to adapt to market changes. Various stakeholders have suggested that the World Bank learn and apply lessons from these experiences by designing projects in ways that are more flexible, speeding up the process of approving changes, and fostering a culture that allows greater risk taking at both project design and implementation levels. In response, the World Bank has been moving in this direction.

The World Bank has joined other donors in modifying its policies to reduce multiple requirements on borrowers and increase the extent to which all donors are working toward the same goals in a country. This ongoing effort requires donors to work in a coordinated fashion with national leaders to ensure coherent policy direction and comprehensive monitoring of program activity. There are some modest signs of progress, as noted in a 2004 study of incentives for harmonization and alignment for aid agencies, prepared by the Overseas Development Institute (ODI 2005). But, as the report on progress, challenges, and opportunities from the Paris Forum indicated, all donors (including the World Bank) need to continue and deepen their efforts if the objectives of increasing aid effectiveness through greater harmonization and alignment are to be achieved. The Paris Declaration on Aid Effectiveness (March 2005) contains the framework of actions—by both donors and partner countries— that need to be implemented, including efforts inter alia that donors base aid solely on national priorities, carry out more joint diagnostic work, share information systematically, simplify procedures and make them transparent, and strengthen incentives for management and staff to work more closely with partners and other donors (OECD/DAC 2005).

The World Bank is engaged in a number of initiatives with the objectives of increasing the impact and effectiveness of donor assistance, reducing the borrowers' and the World Bank's transaction costs, and realigning the World Bank's policies with borrower needs and the evolving design and programmatic focus of investment lending (see box 7.2). Much of the World Bank's simplification effort has been designed to strengthen harmonization. Streamlining and speeding up its procedures and policies—for example, through simplified documentation—are helping provide staff with greater flexibility to meet borrowers' needs by reducing the bureaucratic burden and transaction costs of dealing with the World Bank. Streamlining the procedures for restructuring projects under implementation will also help enhance the success of operations and facilitate scaling them up.

Looking Ahead

Many of the lessons from the Shanghai stories are intuitively expected, and, in fact, a number are now common knowledge for many donors. The significance of these findings for the World Bank and other donors, however, lies in the somewhat unique opportunity they offer to reflect on how development initiatives are started and scaled up, with some immediate implications for how donors should conduct their business in the future. Just as important, this learning opportunity was facilitated by developing countries that brought their own perspectives and a tremendous amount of country-specific knowledge to the table.

A number of overarching and interlinked themes emerge as donors look ahead and try to organize and process the wealth of knowledge gained through the global learning process. These ideas by no means represent an epiphany, but they surely affirm how development thinking is evolving.

There cannot and should not be a one-size-fits-all project, program, or policy. If nothing else, the cases studied reveal the very unique circumstances of each country, region, village, and municipality. Other evidence also supports this notion. The World Bank's Operations Evaluation Department recently conducted a country program retrospective and, not surprising, found that a country assistance program was much more likely to produce satisfactory outcomes if it was tailored to a country's specific context (World Bank 2004). The *2004 Annual Review of Development Effectiveness* found that the World Bank faces challenges in effectively customizing its poverty reduction strategies to individual countries (World Bank 2005a). Practical experience is showing more and more often that an effective approach to development assistance is one that is blended and fine-tuned to suit the country context and needs rather than one based on the traditional project model. In other words, flexibility is critical.

Patience is not merely useful; it is an absolute requirement. One of the strongest findings from the case studies may be the hardest for donors to put into practice—the idea that development frequently takes time. After all, development often involves changing long-standing behavior or entrenched attitudes, something that can't happen overnight. Many of the initiatives studied here led to positive outcomes because they moved slowly and incrementally

---

**Box 7.2 Greater Flexibility in Support of
Learning and Innovation**

Additional Financing: As part of an overall reform of its operational
policies and procedures governing investment lending, the World
Bank updated its policy on additional financing (previously known as
supplemental financing) in May 2005. As a way to align current policy, embodied in the blueprint project model, with the evolving and
specific needs of each country, additional funding offers as a benefit
the ability to scale up projects more quickly and with significantly
lower processing and transaction costs.

   Eligible Expenditures: In April 2004, the World Bank's executive
directors approved widening the range of expenditures that the World
Bank can support under investment lending. Instead of being subject
to the constraints of policies developed in a far different development
environment, the World Bank is now able to finance the expenditures
that borrowers need to make to achieve their development goals. This
change will enable staff to exercise greater flexibility and offer a
broader range of instruments to help borrowers develop investment
projects (and at lower transaction costs). It is a significant step in the
ongoing process of simplifying and modernizing investment lending.

---

toward their goal, taking small and steady steps instead of attempting overly ambitious reforms in a short period.

   Making programs effective to alleviate poverty demands innovative approaches. Development progress often requires creativity, another clear lesson gained from the Shanghai global learning process.
Each country and each initiative involve different challenges and opportunities. Donor and borrower staff need to have the traditional
instruments and approaches at their disposal, but they also need to
be open to new ideas and must be able to take advantage of opportunities that arise. For example, they need to ask themselves the following questions: Has a recent financial, political, or natural crisis
opened a window of opportunity? How could a new project build
on the expertise of an existing stakeholder group? What kinds of incentives would most improve the effectiveness of the project? Are
there innovative ways to build the enabling environment for capacity
building?

   In response to these questions, donors, including the World
Bank, must ask themselves to what extent they are able to accommodate and actively support this kind of creativity. Creativity invariably entails a certain amount of risk. But if development institu-

tions value the evidence of the initiatives studied here in intensifying their efforts, making greater progress toward the Millennium Development Goals will require them to examine their own operating environments to see whether staff possess the flexibility and have the incentives to take calculated risks and approach the challenges of development with true creativity. In what ways are donors working to create such an environment? How are they changing their business model to respond more fully to the complex and evolving needs of client countries? Are the right incentives in place?

As these initiatives and activities demonstrate, the World Bank and other donor agencies are gradually establishing the kind of enabling environment that can nurture the creativity that staff need if they are to develop and carry out projects that can be scaled up. They must continue this process, using the same principle of continuous assessment that is such an important factor in the initiatives, and using the findings to improve their efforts.

The obstacles are formidable in further reshaping how donors operate. But there are some positive signs—a number of good practices have emerged, as the studied initiatives suggest, and these good practices have evolved through learning from mistakes and, significantly, from listening to and learning from clients. The real challenge will be translating the lessons harvested into general practice and operational policy throughout donor agencies. Such translation would signal donor ability, willingness, and commitment to engage fully in scaling up innovative poverty reduction initiatives to achieve the Millennium Development Goals and beyond. There is little choice. As former World Bank president Wolfensohn has said frequently, "Feeling good about individual projects is not enough; the challenges we face are just too big. We *must* move beyond projects and policies to scale up our endeavors and address the enormous task ahead."

Notes

1. The following cases are addressed and cited by number in this chapter: *Case 1*—A. Muganda, Tanzania's Economic Reforms and Lessons Learned; *case 2*—B. Ross-Larson, F. Saadah, E. McCrocklin, and E. Wiley, Thailand: Addressing HIV/AIDS—Proven Solutions and New Problems; *case 3*—B. Hofman, E. Rodrick-Jones, and K. W. Thee, Indonesia: Poverty Reduction and Economic Challenges; *case 4*—M. Dabrowski, O. Rohozynsky, and I. Sinitsina, Poland and the Russian Federation: A Comparative Study of Growth and Poverty; *case 5*—Kenya, Tanzania, Uganda: The Madrassah Early Childhood Program—Nurturing Innovations and Seeking Sustainabil-

ity in Early Childhood Development; *case 6*—W. Sangui, L. Zhou, and R. Yanshun, China's 8-7 National Poverty Reduction Program; *case 7*—S. F. Rasmussen, M. M. Piracha, R. Bajwa, A. Malik, and A. Mansoor, Pakistan's Scaling Up Rural Support Programs; *case 8*—Mexico's Oportunidades Program; *case 9*—Brazil's Bolsa Família Program; *case 10*—A. Markanday, Scaling Up IFAD's Experience with Decentralized and Participatory Rural Development and Poverty Reduction in Vietnam; *case 11*—S. Guggenheim, T. Wiranto, Y. Prasta, and S. Wong, Indonesia's Kecamatan Development Program—A Large-Scale Use of Community Development to Reduce Poverty; *case 12*—A. Roumani, Brazil: Reducing Rural Poverty by Increasing Access to Land; *case 13*—Uganda: From Conflict to Sustained Growth and Deep Reductions in Poverty; *case 14*—J. R. Behrman, S. Gultiano, E. King, and L. Laigo, Philippines Early Childhood Development Programs—Offsetting the Disadvantages of Poverty; *case 15*—J. B. Bump, B. Benton, A. Sékétéli, B. H. Liese, and C. Novinskey, West Africa: Defeating Riverblindness—Success in Scaling Up and Lessons Learned; *case 16*—I. Dulger, Turkey: Rapid Coverage for Compulsory Education—The 1997 Basic Education Program; *case 17*—N. Hossain, Access to Education for the Poor and Girls: Educational Achievements in Bangladesh; *case 18*—W. Anderson, M. Gilbert, Caribbean: CARTAC and the Eastern Caribbean Economic Management Program; *case 19*—W. Guobao, Q. Yang, and C. Huang, China's Southwest Poverty Reduction Project: A Multisectoral Approach.

2. A number of studies have written about this connection between ownership and sustainability. The Comprehensive Development Framework Secretariat at the World Bank has prepared a number of reports addressing this issue. For more information, go to http://web.worldbank.org/WBSITE/EXTERNAL/PROJECTS/STRATEGIES/CDF/0,,pagePK:60447~theSitePK:140576,00.html.

3. See the World Bank Institute's Capacity Development Resource Center Website, http://web.worldbank.org/WBSITE/EXTERNAL/TOPICS/EXTCDRC/0,,menuPK:64169181~pagePK:64169192~piPK:64169180~theSitePK:489952,00.html.

4. The Managing for Development Results Sourcebook (draft) 2005 is available at www.mfdr.org/Sourcebook.html.

5. This statement is excerpted from a speech made by James Wolfensohn at World Bank Corporate Day, May 16, 2005, in Washington, DC.

References

Birdsall, Nancy. 2004. "Seven Deadly Sins: Reflections on Donor Failings." Working Paper 50, Center for Global Development, Washington, DC.

Drazen, A., and P. Isard. 2004. "Can Public Discussion Enhance Program 'Ownership'?" Working Paper 163, International Monetary Fund, Washington, DC.

Entwistle, Janet, and Filippo Cavassini. 2005. *An Operational Approach to Assessing Country Ownership of Poverty Reduction Strategies.* Washington, DC: World Bank. Available at http://web.worldbank.org/WB SITE/EXTERNAL/PROJECTS/STRATEGIES/CDF/0,,contentMDK:203 85021~pagePK:139301~piPK:139306~theSitePK:260799,00.html.

Fukuyama, Francis. 2004. *State-Building: Governance and World Order in the 21st Century.* Ithaca, NY: Cornell University Press.

Mkapa, Benjamin William. 2004. "Shanghai Conference Roundtable: Talking Points for His Excellency." Available at www.worldbank.org/wbi/re ducingpoverty/docs/confDocs/Mkapa.pdf.

ODI (Overseas Development Institute). 2005. "Incentives for Harmonisation and Alignment in Aid Agencies." Working Paper 248, ODI, London.

OECD/DAC (Organisation for Economic Co-operation and Development/Development Action Committee). 2005. "Managing for Development Results Principles in Action: Sourcebook on Emerging Good Practice." Draft. Available at www.mfdr.org/Sourcebok.html.

Schacter, Mark. 2000. "Capacity Building: A New Way of Doing Business for Development Assistance Organizations." Policy Brief 6, Institute on Governance, Ottawa, Ontario.

Wolfensohn, James. 2004. "Opening Address." Presented at the Shanghai Conference, May 25–27, 2004. Available at www.worldbank.org/wbi/re ducingpoverty/docs/confDocs/JDWShanghaiOpening.pdf.

World Bank. 2005a. *2004 Annual Review of Development Effectiveness: The Bank's Contributions to Poverty Reduction.* Washington, DC.

———. 2005b. "Balancing the Development Agenda: The Transformation of the World Bank under James Wolfensohn, 1995–2005." Washington, DC.

———. 2005c. "Effective States and Engaged Societies: Capacity Development for Growth, Service Delivery, Empowerment, and Security." Progress Report, Operational Task Force on Capacity Development in Africa, Washington, DC. Available at http://siteresources.worldbank.org/INT AFRICA/Resources/progress_report_0405_en.pdf.

———. 2005d. *Global Monitoring Report 2005. Millennium Development Goals: From Consensus to Momentum.* Washington, DC.

———. 2004. "Country Program Retrospective: What Have We Learned from OED's Country Assistance Evaluations?" Presentation to the Operations Evaluation Department Conference on Effectiveness of Policies and Reforms, Washington, DC, October 4, 2004.

———. 2003. "Sharing Knowledge: Innovations and Remaining Challenges." OED Evaluation, Washington, DC. Available at www.worldba nk.org/oed/knowledge_evaluation/.

8

Issues for Future Research

Frannie A. Léautier and
Blanca Moreno-Dodson

This chapter draws on the findings from the case study sample analyzed in the preceding seven chapters and highlights some remaining issues for future research.

The chapter is divided into seven sections. The first three sections suggest areas for future research related to the implementation factors conducive to reducing poverty on a global scale that were considered in the original framework, mainly leadership, innovation, learning, and evaluation. The following three sections discuss unresolved issues and relate specifically to the three initial dimensions of scaling up outlined in chapter 1 and illustrated through the book. Fiscal space and external financing refer to the macroeconomic foundations of scaling up. Sustainability over time involves the intertemporal dimension, and the interdependency between rural and urban areas is a reflection of the obstacles encountered when scaling up geographically. Finally, the last section presents the results of the evaluation of the Shanghai global learning initiative.

As indicated in the introduction to the book, the objective is not to make recommendations or give specific prescriptions, but rather to highlight important topics that the international development community should continue to research.

Effective Leadership

As illustrated by the different country stories, effective leadership can emerge in different forms and contexts. Whether leadership is linked to technocratic support, forceful homegrown politicians, visionary civil society actors, or pragmatic entrepreneurs, starting with clear goals is as important as making the right choices during the implementation process.

Because it would not be feasible to find a counterfactual to assess the effectiveness of leaders in a particular country (imagine the programs of China or Uganda implemented under other types of regimes), all we can do is explore the links between leadership and courses of action, as the evidence of those cases suggests.

At the macroeconomic level, all of the following strategies required effective leadership adapted to the existing circumstances: choosing an appropriate pattern of growth for a particular country, like China and Tunisia did; implementing its strategy according to plans, as in Korea; and being able to recover from dramatic changes, as in Indonesia or Poland. Somehow, in each case, planning "strategically" and being able to balance short-term risks against longer-term objectives was crucial. Without looking to recommend a particular system of development planning, we should investigate further what constitutes "strategic" planning and contributes to effective leadership at the country level.

Key issues for research on the question of leadership include the following: How does it emerge? What can be done to support it? What mechanism can be used to sustain a series of policy changes and implementation arrangements to achieve results? What is the relative importance of political continuity compared with policy continuity?

An Environment for Learning and Innovation

Achieving development results is not a linear process, and results can be obtained when least expected and sometimes after long periods of frustration. For that reason it is important to create an environment that encourages learning and innovation, and enables participants to experiment and capture the lessons of trials, errors, and successes—both theirs and others'.

In our country sample, China explicitly introduced experimentation as part of its overall government programs. Can such an institutional decision be made in other countries? Or are developing countries better prepared to stimulate innovation in more subtle ways, such as promoting competition, decentralizing implementation, and eliciting community participation, as Costa Rica, El Salvador, and Chile did in the social sectors, or Indonesia did in the KDP?

Also meriting further attention are the incentives behind the learning and innovation process. In the infrastructure sector, Morocco introduced a results-based culture and managed to turn around the performance of the rural roads network by setting up tangible objectives in terms of access rather than physical targets, and by planning infrastructure investments in an integrated manner. Although the shift to results-based planning is evident, as is its effect on development, many countries still find political and institutional barriers to switching to this type of results-based culture and to planning for integrated development.

The cases point to a number of ways in which countries can create an environment for learning and innovation. There is the case of Costa Rica, where creating competition among health care providers generated new ideas on how to get better results. Other cases indicate that it is through decentralization, and the increased accountability that it induces, that a climate for learning and innovation can be created. For example, consider China, where the provinces were competing with each other. How does the process of participation and citizen involvement lead to the generation of better ideas (Chile and Brazil cases), compared with allowing ad hoc trials by different agents (HIV/AIDS in Manipur, India) or explicit experimentation as in the case of China?. These are questions that would merit further research.

Knowledge Exchange and Impact Evaluation

As most case studies underscored, sharing experiences and the knowledge they impart is crucial to understanding how to scale up, particularly in grasping what may lead to results and under what circumstances. The Shanghai Conference was an important first step in this direction, but the development community must have far more knowledge capture and exchange about promising models and reform processes. Urgently needed are wider analysis, documentation, and dissemination of local initiatives, especially those designed and operated outside the formal sector and official investment channels. The numbers of such initiatives are growing daily, and include many virtually unheard-of pilot activities and innovations launched by the private sector, civil society and nongovernmental organizations.

Knowledge exchange is an essential complement to the informed preparation and planning of development projects, including efforts to improve governance as a pillar of economic development. But learning can take time and it is often necessary to wait until reforms are quite advanced before fully analyzing what has been learned. For that reason, comparing and disseminating the experience of similar initiatives in different contexts adds tremendous value and can reduce the time needed to learn in a particular country.

Although knowledge exchange can prompt useful midcourse corrections, counterfactual-balanced assessment of the final effects of any initiative on the lives of poor people is vital in choosing an effective course of action. Rigorous impact evaluations, a process of systematic and robust learning from experience, could create the basis for reducing poverty on a global scale.

As chapter 6 indicates, the first step would be to ensure that alternative approaches to addressing key development challenges are tried and evaluated for impact across countries and regions. The results of independent evaluations, however, would not suffice. The next step would be to compare those results through meta-analyses. Furthermore, in many cases it may even be possible to contrast the results with outcomes from alternative approaches to achieving the same ends.

Most developing countries have weak capacity for monitoring and evaluation, and few incentives to develop it. Multilateral and bilateral agencies would have to provide well-coordinated support, helping the client country establish and implement its own priorities. It's also critical to ensure means by which the evaluation community in the developing world can be an active participant in this new trend of increased attention to and importance of impact evaluation as a learning tool.

Fiscal Space and External Financing

By definition, scaling up poverty reduction requires a time horizon that differs from the implementation period of a particular intervention. Developing countries must plan strategically to incorporate goals that will take longer periods of time to materialize, and the international community must be engaged to help sustain promising reforms as needed. For international institutions like the World Bank, the issue is for how long they should expect to offer their engagement and stay involved before seeing these initiatives become totally mature and sustainable.

It is true that reaching the MDGs will require many countries to keep mobilizing unprecedented levels of financing, both domestic and external, but there is a correlative concern. Enhancements are needed in recipient countries' absorption capacities if the potential money filling an expanded "fiscal space" is to be used effectively.

And it is not enough to carefully prioritize, target, and execute all expenditures in order to achieve the desired results. Also necessary is a careful weighing of decisions to avoid crowding out private sector spending. In fact, closer partnerships with the private sector, local communities, and civil society in general should be built to enhance public expenditure effectiveness, and increase expected growth rates and poverty reduction impact.

On the financing side, scaling up will truly require that the augmented financial flows are predictable and sustained over the short to medium term, thereby reducing uncertainty and volatility. At the same time, as progress is being achieved and initiatives become sustainable, systematic measures to reduce high dependence on external financing should be strongly encouraged.

Continuity and Overall Sustainability

We don't yet know what factors are crucial for sustainable poverty reduction impact. What kinds of reforms are needed for the positive changes undertaken in many countries to be sustained and to produce durable results? What type of support is needed for some relatively new institutional structures, on which basis these reforms have been accomplished, to foster greater effectiveness and prevent a turnaround?

For example, in the realm of judicial reform, many developing countries lack the institutional capacity itself, as well as the concrete activities, human and financial resources, infrastructure, and services to create the conditions for adequate rule of law, prosperity, and peace. Longer-term capacity building and strong engagement with external factors are required.

Regarding microfinance, providers have reached only a tiny fraction of the poor population in most countries. The challenge is to scale up access to include those who still lack it today. Pro-poor financial institutions must achieve a scale of operation large enough to generate greater efficiency and profitability. Governments must foster dynamic financial markets, and donors must continue to finance these innovations.

In the area of community-driven development, the issue is whether these communities should be totally integrated into government structures, with all the know-how their members have accumulated, or whether they should continue operating outside those circuits, provided they gradually approach sustainability. Scaling up at its full potential should be geared toward the first option. Many countries, however, may not be ready to move in that direction. The projects will only be efficient if they continue serving their communities as they have done to this point, although they may continue expanding their operations to reach a greater number of areas and beneficiaries.

In general, most cases argue for patience and perseverance. If it took more than a decade for many of the initiatives to foster the observed preliminary achievements, more time will probably be needed until tangible and measurable poverty impact crystallizes, and influences national policies and practices in a more durable manner.

Interdependence between Rural and Urban Areas

Small rural communities in areas where the provision of basic services is expensive and difficult, and where income earning opportunities are limited, are still the places where huge segments of the world's poor people live. Should those communities benefit from additional support and should their livelihoods be improved locally, or should they be encouraged to move to cities or regions where they can have access to a better life?

Obviously neither option will completely eradicate poverty. Facing those questions and the challenge of extensive poverty, countries can act on two fronts. On one hand, they can make rural poverty a high priority and promote rural productivity growth, like China did. On the other hand, they can encourage rapid growth in major urban centers to also stimulate rural areas, while removing barriers for labor mobility and rural-urban migration.

Although rural growth can lift entire villages and regions out of poverty, booming urban centers in rapidly growing economies also offer tremendous job opportunities. Acting on both fronts is not always an option in small, undiversified, and slow-growing economies. In those cases, intensified efforts at the rural level should help reduce income poverty and improve access to social services and social inclusion. At the same time, economic, political, and social exchanges with urbanized and more developed cities and regions should be promoted.

An overall challenge remains to meet rising demands in urban areas, with consequent implications on infrastructure, education, and health investments, without creating wider regional or social disparities. Because demand for infrastructure is derived from population and growth, as well as the interdependence between rural and urban economies, as the magnitude and complexities of the urban-rural interaction challenges multiply, so does the urgency for scaling up across areas and regions.

Evaluating the
Learning Process

When the Shanghai one-year learning effort was designed, it was done with the idea that it could be evaluated, and the lessons learned could be used to design future events. Also, perhaps, the lessons would offer guidance to development practitioners who may want to put in place similar systems. An evaluation was done based on four key activities: (1) an online survey of participants in the Shanghai learning process that engaged respondents from 49 countries; (2) one-on-one interviews with participants in the Shanghai learning process and its organizers (102 interviews in 10 countries); (3) focus group discussions with participants in the learning process and organizers; and (4) a desktop review of materials relevant to the Shanghai experience.[1]

The findings from the evaluation indicated that participants were highly satisfied with the quality and effectiveness of the Shanghai learning process. They were relatively more positively affected by the field trips and the case studies, but had high opinion of the global dialogues and the conference itself. Active and open engagement of practitioners and policy makers is what was seen as the most distinguishing feature of the learning process.

More than 90 percent of the people who participated report having used what they acquired from the Shanghai learning process. Main impacts were seen first at the personal level, followed by the process of learning that Shanghai activities engendered. This is mostly in terms of tools and approaches for reaching poverty reduction at scale.

The process was considered relevant for all country types, whether low-, middle-, or high-income economies. However, middle-income countries, who could learn from high-income countries, from each other, and from low-income countries, found the learning process most effective.

These results show that it is possible to design a learning process that enables practitioners to interact with one another and with policy makers. Through such a process, valuable lessons can be learned and shared. The usefulness of such a process is lasting, and goes beyond a one-time event. The critical aspect is to see what features of this learning process would be relevant for a project or program or for a country seeking to enhance its approach to learning and idea sharing. This is a key subject for future work that the staff of the World Bank Institute will be undertaking,

Note

1. The results of the evaluation will be published in a separate evaluation report, which was undergoing an editorial review when this book was published.

Index